METAPHYSICS AND ABSURDITY

――――――――――――――

H. Gene Blocker

University Press of America,® Inc.
Lanham · Boulder · New York · Toronto · Plymouth, UK

Copyright © 2013 by
University Press of America,® Inc.
4501 Forbes Boulevard
Suite 200
Lanham, Maryland 20706
UPA Acquisitions Department (301) 459-3366

10 Thornbury Road
Plymouth PL6 7PP
United Kingdom

All rights reserved

British Library Cataloging in Publication Information Available

Library of Congress Control Number: 2012951795
ISBN: 978-0-7618-6023-5 (paperback

TABLE OF CONTENTS

PREFACE	v
ACKNOWLEDGMENTS	xxiii
CHAPTER ONE: INTRODUCTION	1
CHAPTER TWO: CAMUS	23
CHAPTER THREE: SARTRE	41
CHAPTER FOUR: IONESCO	77
CHAPTER FIVE: BECKETT	107
AFTERWORD	141
BIBLIOGRAPHY	185

PREFACE

Metaphysics and Absurdity is essentially a reprint of an earlier book, *The Metaphysics of Absurdity*, but it could also be described as an abridged trilogy combining two earlier books of mine, *The Meaning of Meaninglessness*[1] and *The Metaphysics of Absurdity*[2], along with a new book, *Metaphysics and the Middle Way*. The abbreviated version of the first, *The Meaning of Meaninglessness*, appears here as a Foreword, and the shortened new book, *Metaphysics and the Middle Way,* appears as an Afterword to *The Metaphysics of Absurdity,* reprinted here in its entirety.

For many of us outside the profession of academic philosophy the central question of philosophy is—or ought to be—the meaning of life. But, as you can probably guess, the academic philosophers are going to immediately turn this into an *analysis* of the *concept* of "meaning." What do words like "meaning," "meaningfulness," "meaninglessness" mean? Since these are words, we might at first simply check out a good dictionary. But when we talk about *life* being meaningful or meaningless, we're not talking about *words*. So, what *are* we talking about? This is precisely what we will explore in this foreword.

The Meaning of Meaninglessness

We use words like "means" and "meaning" in a variety of ways. Consider the following examples of ordinary English.

1. I mean to help him if I can.
2. It was never meant to be.
3. Keep off the grass. This means you.
4. He meant more than met the ear.
5. He means well.
6. Buzzing means bees and bees mean honey.[3]
7. Money means little to me.
8. Procrastination means putting things off.

Of these eight examples only the last has to do directly with the meaning of words and sentences.

To clarify the issue of meaninglessness we need to reduce this variety by classifying the different uses of the word into a few broad headings. Most recent attempts at classification seem to agree on the following as the main senses of "meaning," only one of which, the last, is the standard dictionary definition of words. The following senses of "meaning" correspond to the examples above:

1. to intend
2. to design something for a specific purpose
3. to intend a remark to have a particular reference
4. to intend to convey an individual thought or feeling by a standard form of speech
5. to be well-intentioned
6. to lead to or be somehow connected or associated with
7. to have a specified degree of importance to someone
8. linguistic meaning, that is, the standard dictionary meaning of a word

What emerges as the dominant idea of "meaning" is that of purpose and intention and the purposeful connections between things.

The modern sense of "meaning" appears to include the following: the sense of being designed (for a certain purpose), linguistic meaning (the intentional use of words and language to communicate), the quasi-intentional association of one thing with another (money "for the sake of" happiness, clouds "in order to" warn of rain, bees "for the sake of" honey), and the purposively described place of X in a system of things (the heart "in order to" pump the blood, the veins "in order to" carry the blood, the eye "for the purpose of" seeing). Dark clouds mean rain and bees mean honey, but not the reverse—rain doesn't mean dark clouds, nor does honey mean bees. Why? Because in terms of human (and Teddy Bear) purposes the relationship works the other way round. Pooh wants honey; that's why he is interested in the bees. The bees mean honey in the sense that they lead him to honey. I am interested in rain for my own purposes: I want my cabbage plants to get wet but not myself as I walk to work. I interpret dark clouds as a forecast of rain and make my plans accordingly.

Physical objects have meaning because of their purposeful place in a human context. I see what looks like a book, and that leads to an unspoken, implicit prediction that if I were to open the object I would find flexible pages with print on them, and when those implicit predictions turn out as anticipated, my initial judgment that what we are looking at is a book is confirmed. There are many causal dispositions of any given object—the book could be used for throwing at a yowling cat on the fence or for propping open a window, but our primary interest in books is for the sake of reading them for the sake of their content (Yellow Pages, or a cook book). So in this case, Pooh is always hungry and he is always hungry for honey—his interest in the buzzing is not academic but pragmatic—the buzzing will lead him to bees and the bees will lead him to honey.

Basically, then, it is people who mean because it is people who intend and plan purposefully. Once a group of people have decided on a standard means to convey their intentions, such as language, the sense of meaning is gradually transferred from people's intention to the words used to convey that intention. Similarly, we speak of what a book says as a way of describing what the author says in the book. Nonetheless in the primary sense it is people who mean just as it is the author who speaks. Because people purposefully intend, they see the world in terms of intentional links, and in a secondary sense the web of purposeful links gives meaning and structure to the world as human beings experience it.

Words have meaning because people assign them meaning. There are two extreme theories about linguistic meaning, and the truth probably lies somewhere in between: the first, that words eternally have meaning; the other, that words can mean whatever I say they mean (as Humpty Dumpty said to Alice in "Through the Looking Glass"). The truth is that once we agree on linguistic conventions, meaning becomes permanently attached to words—well, not permanently, but for long stretches of time—and this creates the illusion that the words themselves intrinsically have meaning. Over time we lose sight of the conventions originally established to govern the use of those words.

When we examine recent empirical investigations into meaning we find much the same intentional, nonlinguistic story. Contemporary anthropological studies, for example, view meaning as the place of an action or remark in a particular social context. According to a number of leading anthropologists like Evans-Pritchard and Levi-Strauss, the meaning of a social form of behavior lies in its "social syntax," that is, in the functional interdependence between it and different forms of behavior within a specified area.

For example, an anthropologist may want to explain the meaning of the following behavior. A group of men are seated in a circle around a container of small stones. One man removes several handfuls, placing them in a separate pile. A second man then takes some of the stones from the second pile and puts them back in the original container. The first man repeats his original action, transferring a smaller amount of stones to the second pile, and so on, until neither man moves any more stones from one pile to the other. What does this mean? To find out the anthropologist tries to locate this behavior within a larger pattern of social interaction. He will note that the men belong to two families and that the second man brought the stones to the house of the first man. He will also observe that following this activity, men from the second man's family brought exactly the same number of goats to the house of the first man as the final number of stones in the second pile, and that shortly thereafter a ceremony took place which the anthropologist already understands as the marriage of the second man to the daughter of the first. Knowing this, the meaning of the original activity becomes clear: the men were bargaining over the "bride price," the meaning of which we have come to understand by seeing its relation to other activities in the broader "social syntax." The meaning of the bride-price itself could be made more intelligible by seeing its place within the broader spectrum of tribal marriage, divorce, family life, and so on.

Meaning, then, in one important sense refers to functional interdependence, the intended place of X in a socially-understood system of things. Knowing the meaning of X in this sense is not necessarily an explicit, conscious understanding as our understanding of linguistic meaning is generally thought to be. An outsider to a given society, such as an anthropologist, understands the meaning of X by seeing explicitly its relation to Y and Z, but a member of that society knows the meaning of X without this explicit understanding. She simply has a sense of being at home in this system, knowing her way around, experiencing no surprises or confusion. Ironically, the system as such becomes apparent to her only if and when it begins to break down or when she views it from an alien perspective. In other words, a native knows the meaning without understanding it as such.

We usually think of meaning as an articulate, expressible thing which words have—in their definition. So, if we insist on thinking of meaning exclusively as dictionary definitions, then we will probably hesitate to say that the interrelatedness of things in a social system constitutes meaning. Instead we may want to say that functional interdependency is what makes meaning possible, or that in terms of which we understand the meaning. But I think our inventory of different senses of meaning indicates pretty clearly that dictionary meaning is only one kind of meaning, and the interrelatedness of things in a system is another. When we say a social system has meaning or has lost meaning, what do we understand that it has or has lost but this interconnectedness of things? Similarly, when we say we understand the meaning of an action in its broader social context, what do we understand but the place of X in its social context in relation to Y and Z?

It is true that we cannot express this sort of meaning in words. We do not say a social system has *a* meaning, which invites the question, "*what* meaning?" We say that it has meaning, that it is meaningful. The question of the translation meaning of words and sentences is simply out of place here. Indeed, as we will see, in the final analysis linguistic meaning must be understood in terms of such nonlinguistic forms of meaning as functional interdependency.

At any rate, it is this sense of contextual meaning we have in mind when we wonder about the meaning of life, or our job, or our relationships with people—we are wondering whether the individual parts of our lives hang together in a purposeful web, or whether there is any overall purpose for our life or human life in general. As Sartre says, we tend to transfer our concept of the human purpose for which we make and do things to the purpose for which we, ourselves, were created.

Even where we no longer accept the existence of God, the idea of a divine plan lingers on in a quasi-intentional or purposive manner as the idea of a fixed and abiding human nature. Despite the contemporary bias in favor of linguistic meaning as the primary sense, both Wittgenstein and Heidegger, who provide the conceptual foundations for most contemporary discussions of meaning, regard nonlinguistic meaning as basic. Meaning for both Heidegger and Wittgenstein is ultimately the place of things in a humanly-interpreted world—the world as a system of relationships seen from a human point of view. For Heidegger, as for Pooh, this involves regarding everything as though it were designed to serve our own needs; a pencil to write with, a chair to sit on, bees to give us honey, and the forest as firewood, timber, potential farmland, recreation, or wilderness. Man is a purposive creature and the world hangs meaningfully together because he projects that sense of purposefulness onto the world. Although the defining of concepts remains the most familiar concept of meaning, philosophers are coming to realize that linguistic meaning, and the possibility of linguistic meaning, can only be understood against such an anthropological background of contextual, nonlinguistic meaning.

What do we mean by the "purposive" meaning of something like trees? We are often told that trees serve an ecological purpose (absorbing carbon dioxide and creating oxygen), and some people believe they have a purpose in God's master plan. What I am suggesting is that trees serve a quasi-purpose as an extension of human purposes (for the sake of shade, beauty, recreation, agriculture (in the case of fruit or nut trees), etc. We often talk about ecological balance in nature—we need trees in order to supply oxygen and to absorb carbon dioxide. If we get rid of all the large predators (wolves, mountain lions), we have too many deer or rabbits—so we need the wolves and mountain lions in order to keep the natural balance.

This kind of talk is expressed in the language of purposes—X "in order to" Y, Y "in order to" Z, etc. We also talk about the organic interrelations of the parts of our own bodies—why do we have a heart? In order to pump the blood. Why do we have blood? In order to carry food and oxygen and carry away wastes. We have eyes for seeing things at a distance; legs to get us to the things we see that we want and away from those we want to avoid—the fox sees the rabbit and runs after it for a tasty lunch; the rabbit sees the fox and runs to its hole in the ground to avoid being lunch. Children often ask why men and women are different—and, hard as this is for most parents, the explanation is generally in terms of the "purpose" of this organ, the biological function of that organ.

We call it quasi-intentional and purposive because, although we don't really believe there are conscious purposes, intentions, or plans involved, we find that the language of purpose and intention is the best we can do as human beings to understand and explain these relationships.

Certainly, it is only the loss of some nonlinguistic meaning that can explain the modern sense of meaninglessness. We can begin to understand the experience of meaninglessness in terms of the loss of meaning in one or more of the nonlinguistic senses already discussed—meaningless, for example, as the lack of purpose or reason (the sense of absurdity), or the loss of a pattern or structure holding things together (the sense of things falling apart, or of our being lost in a maze), the lack of any recognizable shape or form (a sense of strangeness, alienation), the loss of importance, savor, zest (the sense of being dead to life or love), the loss of a sense of the consequences of one's actions (the sense of impotence, hopelessness).

The problem with nonlinguistic meaning is that it is not perceived explicitly and self-consciously as meaning, and this makes it difficult to analyze. The main difficulty with this type of meaning is our inability to *say* what an event, action, or phenomenon means. Because of the environment in which I was brought up, a chair is a "meaningful" item in my experience in a way it would not be for someone who had never seen European furniture. I see it and recognize it as something to sit on, rest in, and so on. But if the chair has meaning, one could ask, what exactly does it mean? Well, nothing—or rather, nothing we consciously or explicitly understand and could put into words. The meaning does not appear *as* meaning; it consists simply in my having an ordered, systematic perceptual experience, in which everything fits together. Let us call this type of meaning being-as, which is a play on the psychologist's term seeing-as, as in Jastro's famous duck-rabbit image which can be seen as a duck or as a rabbit.

The world we know is "concept-laden." In the world as I experience it there are no mere things but only things of a certain kind. To see a thing is therefore to see it as this or that, a pencil or a grasshopper or a tuna fish sandwich. As Aristotle put it, substance is essence. I can't see X without seeing it as a member of a conceptual class or kind; I don't just *know* its classification, I actually *see* it that way. Hence, the tacit familiarity and implicit identity of things to the native speaker. She doesn't realize that she is seeing the world in terms of conceptual categories; things just look like that to her. She would not say, "I see that as a chair," precisely because she does see it that way. The seeing-as is so successful, in other words, it never occurs to her that it could be anything else. Being-as is the mute recognizable identity of things which makes the world a familiar place. On the other hand, being-as is not an utterly sterile notion. We can indicate, though in a roundabout way, what the chair means. We simply have to suggest or imagine an alternative, that is, what it would be like if the chair were *not* recognized as a chair.

We could do this by an imaginative contrast with the Australian aborigine's first experience of a chair (is it a god or a weapon?), or that of a child; we can discuss it in terms of our own behavioral anticipations and expectations (how sad and empty, for example, a room looks without any furniture, or how strange chairs would look hung from the walls like paintings, or neatly arranged in the middle of a superhighway), and so on. In this sense we can, and just did, put into words what the chair means, but not "just like that," as in a dictionary, just as we can, in a sense, say what a work of art means, though not in the sense of an adequate translation identical with and substitutable for the work of art. And the same intentional character of meaning applies to actions, as well as objects.

Imagine this situation. You are walking by a middle school and through the window you see a child raise his hand. What is he doing? Raising his hand. But why? To identify fully what he is doing we need to know why he is doing that. He is probably seeking permission to speak. But he could also be voting in a class election, or trying to catch a rubber ball that is being tossed around the classroom while the teacher is not looking, or maybe he needs to go to the restroom.

How do we know which it is? From the context—that is, we have to know the whole scenario and the institutional rules that govern it. The rule that if you want to speak you should raise your hand to get permission from the teacher, or the rule that you can vote for someone by raising your hand—things like that.

Four Kinds of Meaning

From our analysis of meaning four primary senses of meaning have emerged:

1. linguistic (translation equivalence),
2. being-as (recognizable identity),
3. interrelatedness of things in a pattern (contextual meaning), and
4. intention and purpose.

The importance of this division lies in the relationships it provides among these four types of meaning. Linguistic meaning presupposes and would be impossible without being-as; being-as presupposes the systematic interrelatedness of things; and this presupposes human purpose and intention. Knowing what the word "table" means presupposes the ability to know and identify an object as a table; but this depends on an understanding of the place that thing occupies in a system of socially-intelligible relations (seeing it as something to write on, eat off of, put flowers on, and so on). This type of understanding would be impossible without our ability to assign purposeful or intentional relationships to things (tables designed for the purpose of eating off of, writing on, and so on).

Imagine you are trying to explain to someone of a totally different culture what "chalk" means. You might first point to a piece of chalk, and call it "chalk." But the person will not understand unless he knows what chalk is and what it is for. How can you explain that? You could explain that chalk is used for writing. "Writing, what's that?" the person will wonder. Writing is for the sake of communication; it's like talking. "Then why not just talk?" We write to communicate to a broader audience than those who happen to be within earshot. "But why?" As you can see, this would be tough.

Ultimately the foreigner would have to understand our whole way of life. Now imagine the reverse problem which would confront you trying to figure out the meaning of a Yoruba woman wearing a small lbeji figure round her waist (Nigeria, West Africa). The figure represents her dead twin brother. But why wear it? To keep her brother's spirit from possessing her. Why would it do that? And so on. We can't understand this until we understand the total Yoruba conception of man and the universe. To take a simpler case, imagine your first day at work in a large factory. The layout of the plant is strange, incomprehensible, and you feel uneasy. Six months later, as you learn your way around, everything falls into place, the individual pieces of machinery lose their alien, threatening look and you feel at home working among them.

Four Kinds of Meaninglessness

We are now in a better position to understand meaninglessness as the absence of meaning in these four senses, with the exception of linguistic meaning. Meaninglessness we now see as:

1. the loss of recognizable identity (being-as),
2. the frightening strangeness and repugnant otherness of mere things devoid of meaning,
3. feeling unwanted, not at home in an alien world, estranged and alone, disconnected, uprooted, lost in a maze, in a thoroughly Catch-22 world, and
4. the purposelessness, irrational absurdity and pointless futility of life.

This is a reasonably faithful characterization of our ordinary experience of meaninglessness, and it accords very well with the Absurdist literature we will be discussing in this book.

The Tragic Sense of Absurdity

Wild describes meaninglessness as a "clashing dissonance between being and meaning." Expressed abstractly, the modern experience of meaninglessness is the perception of the clash between meaning as naively identified with reality and meaning as humanly constructed or projected. The awareness of projection or being-as is tragic because it fails to match up to our *a priori* concept of reality.

Projection and being-as bear tragic consequences not of themselves, but because the awareness that meaning is human projection implies the *loss* of objective meaning. Like crying over spilt milk, the rich man who has lost all his money views his poverty more tragically than the man who has never had anything. The modern fictional literature of absurdity approaches the clash of meaning and reality in two ways, as we will see: as the loss of a transcendent source and guarantee of meaning and as the confrontation with a brute matter stripped of meaning—man cut off from God and man cut off from nature.

In Camus the tragic sense of the absurd springs from a comparison of projection with the ideal of a world of objective meanings. To live in a meaningful world, this projection must be blind. The meaning we project on the world must *seem* an objective, inseparable feature of reality, and not something stamped on it by its human admirers.

Projection is what makes a meaningful world possible, and, ironically, this follows from the thesis that meaning is projection. If meaning is projection, then there is as much meaning as there is projection. Since we do project, we have a meaningful world. If meaning is projection, projection can take away from meaning only if projection is understood as displacing the *non*-projective ideal of meaning; only where "meaning is projection" is understood to mean "meaning is *not* a real part of the thing itself." Like the old double-question, "Have you stopped beating your wife?" the affirmation that the world is meaningful and the denial that it is not presuppose the same questionable premise—that the world ought to be meaningful in and of itself. Camus is himself keenly aware of this.

> I said before that the world is absurd, but I was too hasty. This world in itself is not reasonable, that is all that can be said. But what is absurd is the confrontation of this irrationality and the wild longing for clarity whose call echoes in the human heart...[4]

What's the difference between something's being unreasonable and not being reasonable? The maple tree in my front yard is not reasonable, while my neighbor is often very unreasonable. How so? A tree is not the kind of thing we expect to be reasonable, whereas a human being is the kind of entity that can be and that we expect to be (or at least hope to be) reasonable. We cannot say that the world is ugly because there are no objective values. Nor can we condemn the world as wicked on the grounds that goodness is a human convention. Likewise, it does not follow that the world is insane just because it lacks human reason. In ordinary English we distinguish something's being immoral and something's being amoral. Something is immoral if it is wicked, but it is amoral if, like a carrot, it is neither moral nor immoral. To say that something is immoral presupposes that it could and should be moral, an assumption not implied in the claim that it is merely amoral. Similarly, we need to distinguish what is simply not reasonable from what is irrational. The tragic sense of meaninglessness springs from the idea that the world is irrational, meaning that it *ought* to be something which it is *not*.

Transcending the Absurd

As Camus argues, the world is not irrational, it is just not reasonable. A stone is not reasonable, neither is a cabbage, but there is nothing tragic about this since no one thought they *should* be reasonable in the first place. As one leading commentator, Alain Robbe-Grillet, said, "The world is neither meaningful nor absurd. It simply is." Like Camus and Sartre, Ionesco's denunciation of the absurdity of life also seems to presuppose an alternative, the possibility of rising above it in some way.

> If I denounce the absurd, I transcend the absurd by the very fact of my denunciation. For by what right should I declare a thing to be absurd, unless I had before me the image...of something that was not absurd?[5]

If we are irretrievably stuck in the midst of absurdity, as all these writers maintain, how do we transcend it? If this is possible at all, it is only possible from an absolutist point of view. When we are engaged in the mundane events of everyday life, we are not aware of, and so cannot condemn, meaninglessness. But in rare moments such as a death in the family or an important turning point in one's life, or simply during a walk along the beach at night, when we stand back and look down on things from an Olympian height, the same mundane problems may appear pointless and absurd. It is from this "higher" perspective that existentialist writers describe man's absurd existence, but in doing this aren't they also projecting and interpreting the world themselves? Is the absolutist perspective from which the absurdity of the world is condemned any truer or more basic or more genuine than the mundane attitude of everyday existence?

The tragic sense of meaninglessness lies in the failure of the world to live up to our ideal, arising from a sense of what ought to be there but is not. But is this ideal justified? Why should the world live up to our idea of it? Perhaps the onus for meaninglessness falls on this ideal rather than on the world for failing to live up to it. The tragic contrast between man and an alien world of mere things is ascribed by Heidegger to man's "transcendence." The being of man ("existence" or Dasein) is understood by contrasting it with the being of something like a stone. A stone just is; it doesn't know that it exists, nor does it foresee what it might become. It cannot understand itself in terms of an idea, hope, or desire realizable by planning and thoughtful action. In this sense it is stuck in what it is; it cannot rise above this. But man is different; he understands and judges his existence and that of other things. He can experience dissatisfaction with the status quo and imagine preferable alternatives, some of which he can bring into being through his own efforts. Even where he can't bring about change, he knows how things stand and he can imagine what they might be like. In this sense, man transcends his existence, he rises above mere being.

Buddhist Emptiness

The meaninglessness of the world and things in it is simply the recognition that we project human meanings onto things. Thus, there is nothing inherently tragic about the "meaninglessness" of the world or of things in the world. This solution to the tragic sense of meaninglessness was developed, over a thousand years ago, in Indian and Chinese Buddhist philosophy. Far from perceiving the meaninglessness or emptiness of the world as depressingly sad and tragic, Eastern philosophers, and especially Indian and Chinese Buddhist philosophers, regard the recognition of meaninglessness as the key to blissful happiness—indeed, as the solution to our central human problem. Let's look at this in more detail.

The central problem in Buddhist theory is to extricate the basic religious doctrine of salvation from any conceptual, and especially any metaphysical entanglements. And yet the language in which Buddhist ideas were expressed led to such conceptual problems. For example, the Buddhist scriptures said that everything is Buddha and also that one should try to become Buddha. But if everything is Buddha, then each of us already is Buddha, so why should anyone train for 25 years or more to achieve Buddhahood? Also, to take a related example, the state of enlightenment (vidya) was contrasted with a state of ignorance (avidya), yet all dualistic thinking was emphatically rejected. If there is no difference between the two, then, again, why should anyone spend hours of meditation trying to give up one in order to achieve the other?

The texts also said that there were no things existing in the world except the Buddha reality (sometimes referred to as Mind). Did that mean there was only one thing existing, namely the Buddha Mind? If so, what sort of thing is that mind? Is it a gigantic consciousness with no body? Assuming it is mental in nature, is it like the dreaming state or the waking state of our minds? Does it think different thoughts in succession, or does it just stare at one thing only (and what would that one thing be)? These questions are obviously endless, and the debate, though philosophically interesting, is religiously beside the point.

A good example of this attempt to transcend metaphysics can be seen in Nagarjuna (c. 200 A.D.), founder of the Madhyamika school of Buddhism. Nagarjuna taught the doctrine of Emptiness (sunyata): all is empty, there is no real existence anywhere. He didn't mean that reality is literally a void; in fact he expressly rejected the annihilation of anything. "Matter is empty in and of itself," he said; "it doesn't have to be wiped out." What he meant was that reality is beyond linguistic and conceptual predication. We cannot say reality exists, not because it doesn't exist, but because "exist" is a word and words have no absolute fix on reality. Nor can we say it is empty or void, because "empty" and "void" are also human concepts that have only a rough application to reality. Thus Nagarjuna's doctrine of Emptiness is not a metaphysical theory that reality is void, but a linguistic doctrine about the relationship of words to the world.

In China Nagarjuna's Madhymika school of Buddhism combined with traditional Chinese Taoist thought to produce what Chinese called Chan Buddhism, and which we know in the West through its Japanese pronunciation, Zen. The goal of Zen, like that of other Buddhist schools, is to discover the Buddha nature within oneself. It is the Zen methods for achieving this that are different, and particularly its solution to the recurring problem of eradicating metaphysical speculation. The Zen solution, which has so intrigued many Western philosophers, is to use philosophy to overcome philosophy.

This is very much the view of Ludwig Wittgenstein (1889-1950), the founder of the Anglo-American movement of "Analytic (or Linguistic) Philosophy." Wittgenstein said that philosophy is a disease which only better philosophizing can cure. Basically, he said, the cause of the disease is a faulty view of the role of language in relation to the world, and the cure is, accordingly, a more accurate theory of language. The very form of words we use causes what Wittgenstein called "mental cramps," and the only way to relieve these cramps is to analyze the misuse of language which has led to them. The Zen approach is very similar. Wittgenstein said that philosophy is like a ladder which we must use to get ourselves out of the hole philosophy has gotten us into—a ladder we promptly discard once we are out, having no further use for it. Zen, borrowing a line from the earlier Taoists, puts the point more succinctly: "Once the fish is caught, what further need have we of the trap?"

The Zen solution to this "metaphysical disease" is ingenious. Rather than asserting one metaphysical position against others or, as the original Buddha, Siddhartha Gautama, supposedly did, simply refraining from metaphysical discussions, the Zen masters explained away all metaphysical problems as linguistic problems arising out of a primary misunderstanding of the relation of thought to the world. This approach eradicates the problem by going straight to its source. Discussing metaphysics simply encourages it and avoiding it just puts it temporarily to one side. The Zen approach "dissolves" the problem away, as Wittgenstein said in another context, rooting it out completely.

Zen is neither another metaphysics nor a refusal to play metaphysics, but a thorough diagnosis of metaphysical worries of all kinds as linguistic excesses. Consider, for example, the Buddhist assertion that reality is empty, that nothing really exists in the world. Metaphysically understood, this means that the world is void of objects, like empty space, empty in the sense in which a clear sky contains no objects or differentiation. This is hard to swallow. But understood as a statement about language and its relation to the world, the statement begins to make sense. It means that there is nothing in the world corresponding exactly to human concepts and categories of thought; that thoughts are not identical with the objects they denote and the objects denoted are not exhausted by but transcend the words we use to describe them. As the eighth-century Zen master Nan-ch'uan puts it,

> During the period before the world was manifested there were no names. The moment Mind arrives in the world there are names, and so we clutch hold of forms... If there are names, everything is classified in limits and bounds.[6]

This is less a metaphysical assertion about the nature of reality (that it is void) than a statement of the limitations of language. It is a denial not of the existence of things, but of the objectification (or projection) of our concepts onto things. It is less a theory of reality than a theory of language. Huang-po (d. 850) is aware of this when he writes,

> Men are afraid to forget their own minds, fearing to fall through the void with nothing on to which they can cling. They do not know that the void is not really the void but the real realm of things.[7]

Naturally, when you tell someone that his individual mind, with all its particular thoughts, and all physical things which he can see and touch are unreal, he understands these words metaphysically and, like the Existentialists, becomes terrified, as though the truth of the statement would wipe out the whole of existence! Huang-po says that, properly understood, the assertion of emptiness is not a denial that things exist in the world, but an assertion of the emptiness of these things. It is not an attempt to wipe them out, but to point out something about them, namely, that they are in themselves distinct from the meanings we as human beings attach to them, and in this sense, empty.

Human concepts, in other words, are not attached to objects as properties or labels. Huang-po maintains that emptiness is a condition of the world: "Who told you to eliminate anything? Look at the void in front of your eyes. How can you produce it or eliminate it?" If the world is empty, it doesn't make any sense to advise people to empty it, for this implies that it is full and needs emptying. But this is precisely what students of Buddhism were taught, or at least this was the most literal and therefore simplest way for them to understand what their instructors required them to do.

The task Huang-po faced as a Zen master was the problem of textual interpretation in the instruction of young Buddhist monks. The sacred Buddhist texts typically asserted that things were unreal, empty, and void and that all duality was illusory; they then went on to prescribe various techniques for eliminating all discriminating thought—"polishing the mirror" of the mind, as it was called, so that it would reflect everything and retain nothing. Understood in a literal way, as a metaphysical theory of reality, such assertions are nonsense and lead to a state of self-hypnotic tranquility or pretense that all those things wiped out of the mind weren't really there in the first place.

The way to correct this constant source of misunderstanding was to interpret the emptiness of things as the emptiness of objectified concepts, to realize the interpretive nature of thought without changing it. In other words, don't try to change either your thoughts or the world, but just your mistaken theory about those thoughts and how they relate to the world. As the San-lun scholar, Seng-chao (384-414 A.D.) had written earlier,

> When we say that there is neither existence nor nonexistence, does it mean to wipe out all the myriad things, blot out our seeing and hearing, and be in a state without sound, form or substance before we can call it absolute truth? Truly, absolute truth is in accord with things as they are and therefore is opposed to none... Not being existent and not being nonexistent do not mean that there are no things, but that all things are not things in a literal sense. As all things are

not things in a literal sense, what is there in relation to which a thing can be so-called? Therefore the scripture [of Nagarjuna] says, "Matter is empty by virtue of its own nature; it is not empty because it has been destroyed."[8]

In Seng-chao's view there are things and they are empty. In so far as we interpret the world, there will be a diversified collection of objects and multiple distinctions. We are not to deny or destroy this world, but only to recognize that it is an interpretation, or projection, that in themselves there are no conceptual categories exactly corresponding to and exhausting reality, and that concepts are human labels used to package the world into convenient, self-contained units.

Similarly, when Huang-po writes,

> There is no 'self' and no 'other.' There is no 'wrong desire,' no 'anger,' no 'hatred,' no 'love,' no 'victory,' no 'failure.'[9]

We must be careful how we understand him. In one sense the assertion is true; but in another sense it is quite false. Of course, there is hatred, love, and failure in the world. If our understanding of language views words like "hatred," "love," and "failure" as illuminating certain genuine aspects of the world from different human standpoints, then it is obviously true to say that there is hatred, love, and failure. But if we view language as naming inherent properties, literally corresponding with objects, then it would be false to say that hatred, love, and failure exist in the world. Huang-po's assertion that there is no hatred or failure means that hatred and failure are to be viewed not as things in the world but as concepts we use with varying degrees of success to illuminate aspects of the world.

Since religious instruction, like all instruction, must rely on linguistic media, there is a persistent and permanent danger of confusion which much Zen writing is designed to correct. The difficulty is unavoidable insofar as it is built into the very nature of language. To express the fact that men mistake concepts for reality, classical Buddhist texts contrasted ignorance with enlightenment, the emptiness of reality with the fullness of things in the ordinary world of appearances. This view suggests some special state of mind to be achieved, namely Enlightenment, and that this Enlightenment consists in the realization that the world is utterly empty! However, this is the very way of thinking the texts were trying to overcome!

Some of the most puzzling and yet philosophically interesting comments in Zen literature are concerned with eliminating this linguistic source of misunderstanding. As Huang-po says,

> There are no Enlightenment men or ignorant men, and there is no oblivion. Yet though basically everything is without objective existence, you must not come to think in terms of anything nonexistent; and though things are not nonexistent, you must not form a concept of anything existing. For "existence" and "nonexistence" are both empirical concepts no better than illusions.[10]

It is not a question of asserting or denying objects or properties in the world; the question is primarily how we understand the words we do use to describe the objects which we do experience. "Oblivion" and "emptiness" are concepts we use to suggest the interpretive nature of human thought and the open-ended character of things in the world of ordinary experience. These terms are useful devices and properly understood lead to true assertions about reality, but contrary to their intended meaning, they also suggest the false position that there exists a special state of mind in which reality is apprehended as blank oblivion.

There is a similar point of view in the "negative way" (*via negativa*) of many mystic writers. Reality, they say, is not A or B or C or anything else you care to mention. If we understand such expressions as denying these features of reality in the ordinary naive way, we arrive at the preposterous interpretation that reality is a formless void in the light of which our ordinary experience is an utter hoax. But if we view such statements as putting forward one view of language at the expense of another, then they begin to make sense. Reality is not A in the sense that A does not fix or exhaust reality; A is simply a human interpretation which clarifies for us certain facets of reality from a given point of view. As Huang-po puts it, reality

> is not green nor yellow and has neither form nor appearance. It does not belong to the categories of things which exist or do not exist... It is neither long nor short, big nor small, for it transcends all limits, measures, names, traces and comparisons. It is that which you see before you—begin to reason about it and at once you fall into error. It is like the bound-less void which cannot be fathomed or measured.[11]

The point is not that we can't meaningfully and truly make comparisons and draw distinctions, which we obviously can, but that reality "transcends all measures and comparisons." The error is in objectifying concepts, that is, naively projecting our concepts onto the world without knowing we are doing so. At first when Huang-po says that reality does not belong to any of our categories, that it transcends all limits, and so on, we may begin to think of some gigantic, mystical stuff underlying everything, encompassing all. But when he goes on to say that "it is that which you see before you," we are brought back to earth once more. It is not Reality (with a capital R) which transcends our categories, but simply things like the computer you are using right now. "Computer" is an English word which designates a class of things of which this object is a member. But this is a very general description. This thing is not just "a computer," but an individual, existing thing in its own right.

No matter how detailed your description of it is, it never exhausts the simple object in front of you, both in the sense that that description could apply to another computer and in the sense that you could, if you had the time, think of other true things to say about this object.

This is why many religious thinkers prefer to express themselves in terms of non-duality: "It is neither X nor non-X, nor both X and non-X, but we use the term 'X' to call attention to it." As Nagarjuna put it,

> It cannot be called void or not void,
> Or both or neither;
> But in order to point it out,
> It is called "the Void."[12]

This overcomes the metaphysical tendency by literally wearing it out. Every metaphysical possibility is carefully and systematically exhausted. As Huang-po said, "It is like the boundless void." We use the idea of the void, not to deny the multiplicity of things in our experience, but to call attention to the fact that the lines of demarcation between things are lines we have traced from our own point of view for our own purposes.

> So let your symbolic conception be that of a void... Eschew all symbolizing whatever, for by this eschewal, is "symbolized" the Great Void in which is neither unity nor multiplicity—that Void which is not really void, that Symbol which is not a symbol.[13]

Really there is no Great Void and no giving up of symbolizing, but these are two symbols we use to point to the same thing. To encourage us to give up symbolizing in the wrong way we speak of the Great Void, then, when the metaphysical impulse is in danger of converting that symbol into a new metaphysics of Nihilism, we explain the Great Void as a way of getting people to give up symbolizing in the wrong way. But they're all symbols, including the symbol "symbol"!

Back to Square One

In the end we are brought back to our everyday perception of ordinary objects in the normal day-to-day world of our experience. In a sense, there is thus a "return to square one." At first we naively suppose that things are meaningful because meaning seems objectively to attach itself to objects. Later when we discover that this is not the case, that meaning is projection, we tend to skepticism, idealism, and meaninglessness. But this is logically inconsistent, as we have seen. When we complete the argument, we reaffirm that things are meaningful precisely because we project meaning.

So, we're back where we started, but with this important difference in our attitude toward projection. In the first case we project blindly; in the second case, reluctantly, despairingly; in the third case, we accept projection knowingly and with responsibility. Only in this sense is the awareness of projection "authentic." There is no alternative to projection; only differing interpretations of it—the tragic and misleading interpretation that it is a source of meaninglessness and the interpretation we are urging that it is a source of meaning. This view has been beautifully expressed by the Chinese Buddhist philosopher, Ch'ing-yuan.

> Before I had studied Zen for thirty years, I saw mountains as mountains, and waters as waters. When I arrived at a more intimate knowledge, I came to the point where I saw that mountains are not mountains, and waters are not waters. But now that I have got its very substance I am at rest. For it's just that I see mountains once again as mountains, and waters once again as waters.[14]

We begin by supposing that objects are identical with our way of describing them; we naively accept a meaningful world of projected meanings. Later we see that these meanings are projected and this leads to the idealist denial that there are any mountains or waters in reality. However, it does not follow from this that we do not live in a meaningful world of being-as. And so we are led to a final assessment which neither denies nor affirms, but simply takes note of the projective nature of meaning and the being-as character of the world. Naively, mountains are mountains, but this naive view is wrong; mountains are not simply mountains, that is, reality is not exhausted by, but overflows our concept of "mountain," and in this sense mountains are not mountains. But once we get beyond this naive view of meaning, we are free to say once again that in the sense that "mountain" does illuminate a perceptible aspect of the world from a certain point of view, mountains are mountains. In the end we live in a meaningful world of projected meanings knowing they are projections and valuing them as such.

Thought and language can never do more than point to reality; they cannot capture or fix it in the traditional objectivist sense. Once we thoroughly grasp this point we are free to accept and describe a meaningful world of humanly disclosed, projected meanings. Thus, we can reject the tragic sense of meaninglessness by affirming the essentially projecting nature of thought and language.

Notes

1. H. Gene Blocker, *The Meaning of Meaninglessness*, (Martinus Nijhoff, 1974).
2. H. Gene Blocker, *The Metaphysics of Absurdity*, (University Press of America, 1979).
3. A. A. Milne, Ernest H. Shepard, and E.P. Dutton (Firm), *Winnie-the-Pooh*, (New York: E.P. Dutton & Company, 1926).
4. A. Camus, *The Myth of Sisyphus, and Other Essays*, (Vintage, 1955).
5. G. Lerminier, "Dialogue avec Ionesco," *Pensée française*, 1959.
6. In Fung Yulan, *A History of Chinese Philosophy*, vol 2, Derk Bodde, trans. (Princeton University Press, 1952).
7. Huang Po, *The Zen teaching of Huang Po on the transmission of mind : being the teaching of the Zen master Huang Po as recorded by the scholar P'ei Hsiu of the Tang dynasty*, (New York: Grove Press, 1959).
8. Seng Zhao, *The Book of Chao; Three Treatises of Seng Chao*, Walter Liebenthal, ed., Monumenta serica Journal of Oriental Studies of the Catholic Univerrsity of Peking, Monograph XIII (Pekng: Catholic University of Peking, 1948.
9. Nagarjuna, *Nagarjuna, a translation of his Mulamadhyamakakarika with an introductory essay,* Kenneth K. Inada, trans.,1st Indian ed. Bibliotheca Indo-Buddhica series (Delhi, India: Sri Satguru Publications, 1993).
10. Huang Po, *op. cit.*
11. Huang Po, *op. cit.*
12. Nagarjuna, *op. cit.*
13. Huang Po, *op cit.*
14. "The Transmission of the Lamp: Early Masters," Sohaku Ogata, trans.o, *Philosophy East and West*, v. 44, University of Hawaii Press.

ACKNOWLEDGMENTS

This book is the product of love stretching over decades, representing my entire philosophical career, both in teaching and in scholarly writing. There are so many people to thank it's hard to know where to start.

Going back to the beginning and moving forward in time, I'd like to thank Paul Gorner and Bill Hart for exploring with me what was at the time somewhat forbidden territory in Anglo-American philosophical circles—Continental philosophy of phenomenology.

Then my colleagues at Ohio University, especially David Stewart and Stanley Grean, who allowed and sometimes encouraged my explorations into new course development, in particular the then new, experimental course I introduced , Philosophy of Literature, out of which the central part of this book , chapters 1-5, evolved. Probably no one helped me more writing this book than several generations of students who forced me to get off my high horse and make things clear—"can you explain that?" "what does that mean?"

More recently, Joe DeMarco and James Petrik have helped me "stay in the game," Joe by involving me in his Seedpub multi-media philosophy web courses, and James, in stepping in to help David Stewart and I publish our 7th and 8th editions of *Fundamentals of Philosophy*.

Finally, in getting this book into print, Julie Kirsch and Laura Espinoza of University Press of America have provided invaluable assistance in getting an unwieldy manuscript into the proper printing format. Most of all I would like to thank my daughter, Forrest, who has patiently taught the old dog some new electronic tricks.

Excerpt from *The Unnamable*, copyright © 1958 by the Estate of Samuel Beckett. Used by permission of Grove/Atlantic, Inc.

Excerpts by Jean-Paul Sartre, translated by Lloyd Alexander, from *Nausea*, copyright ©1964 by New Directions Publishing Corp. Reprinted by permission of New Directions Publishing Corp.

An abbreviated version of *The Meaning of Meaninglessness*, by Gene Blocker, first published in 1974 by Martinus Nijhoff, here reprinted with kind permission from Springer Science+Business Media B.V., Dordrecht,The Netherlands.

CHAPTER ONE: INTRODUCTION

On several occasions, Ionesco has said of his work,

> Two fundamental states of consciousness are at the root of all my plays..., those of evanescence on the one hand, and heaviness on the other, of emptiness and of an overabundance of presence; of the real transparency of the world, and of its opaqueness; of light and of heavy shadows.[1]

The aim of this book is quite simply to explain that statement, especially the paradox of heaviness and lightness as interpretations of and responses to absurdity.

In Absurdist literature "absurdity" is a technical term referring to the divorce of thought from reality, or, as it is variously expressed, the split of word and object, meaning and reality, consciousness and the world. It is, in short, the perceived distance between man as the source of meaning and intelligence and an independent and thoroughly distinct reality. The problem which these writers set themselves is to describe as faithfully as possible what that object is like when it has become stripped of human meaning. And, as indicated in the passage above, the description most frequently offered is that the object alternates between extreme heaviness and excessive lightness.

Not all absurdist writers emphasize both in such a balanced equation, some, like Sartre and Camus, stressing heaviness, others, such as Beckett, emphasizing lightness. Earlier accounts of absurdity tend toward the heavy side of the equation, later accounts, toward the light side. The heavy characterization also tends to be a statement of the *problem* of absurdity, while lightness is more often an attempt to formulate a *solution*. Still, why these two seemingly contradictory characterizations, and how are they related to one another?

The answer I am going to suggest is admittedly somewhat surprising, *viz.*, that the literary problem of absurdity is basically a metaphysical problem of being, that the lightness/heaviness distinction is the perceived correlate of the metaphysical distinction of being as essence and being as existence, being in the sense of *what* a thing is and being in the sense simply *that* it is; on the one hand, the "is" of predication, as in "A unicorn is a mythical beast" and, on the other hand, the "is" of existence, as in "There *is* no unicorn." As a preliminary definition, we may say that "existence" refers to the object as it is in itself, quite apart from any human interest in it, while "essence" is our interpretation of that object. The central concern of absurdist writers is the metaphysical distancing of word and object, thought and reality, essence and existence.

In ordinary experience the two are naively joined together, or, more accurately, are simply not distinguished. This failure to differentiate the two is what makes for the ordinary experience of a meaningful world, in which my concepts, concerns are projected on to the world, successfully adhering to that world with no sense of separation. The world then appears familiar to me and I read into it and find within it my own projected concerns and conceptual biases. But when, under various circumstances, I see meaning as mine and the world as other than my own, the union dissolves and the two split apart—meaning on one side and an alien world on the other. A meaningful world, in short, is a *synthesis* of essence and existence, while a meaningless or absurd world is the product of their *separation*.

We can now begin to appreciate the heavy characterization of the object without meaning. Shorn of human significance the object becomes an alien, inhuman, brute, recalcitrant, mere thing, indifferent to my will and thus dense, heavy, etc. Metaphysically this corresponds to the idea of being as existence, that is, an independent reality as it is in itself removed from all human contact. Take away the human interpretation or essence from an object and all that is left is bare existence, and that is heavy.

But there is another important conception of being in Western metaphysics and it is this second conception which explains the alternating lightness of the meaningless object. Being is also understood in terms of essence, *what* a thing is, its identifiable kind, or semantic category in which we place the object. Stripped of meaning or essence, objects are just there, brute, bullying, real existence with no admixture of human interpretation. But stripped of meaning these same things are also nothing. *What* are they, that is, what do we *call* them, what meaning do we attach to them? By definition, nothing. Hence, they *are*, in this sense, nothing; they have existence in the metaphysically technical sense of reality without meaning, but they have no being or essence. They are there, but they don't exist for us. Hence, their overt heaviness dissolves into an empty, hollow unreality. What is all-too-real one moment suddenly dissolves into dizzying emptiness. Hence the surrealist tension in absurdist writing between the oppressive heaviness of the super-real and the alternating dreamlike quality of empty phantoms.

Metaphysically, we may say that meaningful objects in the ordinary world of intelligible experience have both essence and existence. That is, we interpret individual existing objects as belonging to definite conceptual categories, and this is what gives the world its meaningful shape. Objects in our world do not exist as bare particulars, but only objects of a definite kind—that is, as a tree, as a chair, or as a person. Being is for us always being-as. This defines the *full* sense of being, including both essence and existence, though a partial sense of being occurs whenever either of this pair is absent. In a weak sense, therefore, there are objects like Tom Sawyer; that have a meaningful essence but no existence. Objects shorn of human meaning, on the other hand, have existence but no essence; that is, they have being in the sense of existence, but they have no being in the sense of essence. In that case there occur the two related experiences of absurdity, the first toward a kind of soulless materialism, full of brute, unthinking, blind matter; the second toward a kind of mystical Void empty of any meaningful content. The first is the presence of existence, the second is the absence of essence. In this sense the two opposed states are surprisingly complimentary and compatible and even require one another. They are indeed like two sides of the same coin.

In arguing a metaphysical interpretation of absurdist fiction, I don't want to suggest that absurdist literature, or any literature, for that matter can be equated with philosophy in any and all respects. Fictional literature and philosophy are clearly distinct forms of writing, the most pronounced difference being the portrayal of concrete individuals in a specific setting in literature as contrasted with the abstract conceptual framework of philosophical writing. What I am urging is a relationship between these two forms of writing.

But what exactly is that relationship? Can a philosophical idea be expressed in a literary form, and if so, how is that possible? It has become fashionable since Croce's identification of expression and intuition to assert the complete inseparability of form and content in literature. Indeed this has become a rallying cry of literary formalists and purists for years. Since what you say always depends on how you say it, it is impossible to express the exact same content in more than one literary form, and certainly it is not possible in two such profoundly different forms of writing as systematic philosophy and fiction. In this sense, clearly, novels and plays are as "untranslatable" as Eliot thought poetry was. But this must not be so narrowly understood as to prevent our identifying in a general way literary themes and subject matter. Otherwise we should be totally unable to express, even in a rough way, what representational art works are about. A sensible middle ground, avoiding this extreme while remaining true to the spirit of those who urge the inseparability of form and content, would be to argue that while the *precise* content cannot be expressed independently of some particular linguistic format, the *general* class into which that particular content falls, along with members of a shared family of related contents, *can* be independently articulated.[2] In this sense a novel, a political speech, a father's advice to his daughter, and a play might all express the same theme, though each in its own way and each with something unique to say within this broad area. In this sense philosophical ideas *can* be expressed in works of fiction.

How then, *are* philosophical concerns expressed in Absurdist literature? If we follow Arthur Danto's definition of philosophy as a concern for the "space" or relation between thought and reality,[3] we see the absurdist interest in the divorce or separation of thought and reality as *fundamentally* philosophical. This is supported by the fact that many of these European writers are extremely concerned with philosophical issues, having read and written widely on philosophical matters. Jorges Borges includes in *A Personal Anthology* a piece of philosophical prose, "A New Refutation of Time," in which he discusses most of the major figures in modern philosophy, including Kant, Hume and Bergson. Camus has written a cogent refutation of both Kierkegaard and Husserl as a way of defining his own position; Ionesco has written similarly comparing his position to that of Heidegger; while Beckett has discussed for many years his preoccupation with 19th century pessimists, such as Schopenhauer and Leopardi, and ancient philosophers, such as St. Augustine and the Stoic, Diogenes the Abdurite. Beckett's first published work was, significantly, a poem about Descartes' meditations on time. And of course Sartre's connection with philosophy is well known, if admittedly special. The point is that these writers, perhaps more than their American counterparts, see their own work in a philosophical light. They regard philosophy as the primary means of stating the broad cultural concerns of the age, and they see themselves as addressing these broadly philosophical issues. Obviously this has as much to do with differences in philosophy east and west of the Atlantic (and the English Channel) as it does with differences in styles of fiction.

Several additional factors are responsible for the pronounced philosophical orientation of this particular group of writers. Since Schopenhauer the idea that systematic philosophy deals with things indirectly through generalities and abstract concepts has been seen by many as a limitation, not an advantage. Thus the idea that art deals with the same issues concretely and directly has come to be seen by many artists and writers since the last century as a better way of doing philosophy. As Ionesco remarks,

> Because the artist apprehends reality directly, he is a true philosopher. And it is from the range, the depth and the sharpness of his truly philosophical vision his greatness springs.[4]

Camus writes in a similar vein,

> People can think only in images. If you want to be a philosopher, write novels.[5]

> A novel is never anything but a philosophy expressed in images. And in a good novel the philosophy has disappeared into the images.[6]

As we will see, it is on precisely this basis that Camus criticizes Sartre's *Nausea* for being too abstract, for a content too divorced from concrete images.

Also, most of these writers see themselves in direct relation to the 20th century philosophical movement known as Phenomenology, in which philosophical themes are often explored by analyzing structures of human experience (for example, in Being and Time Heidegger explores the philosophical question of being by analyzing the structure of free-floating anxiety). As we will see shortly, while themes of existence and nonexistence can be felt and experienced, they cannot be conceptually articulated and linguistically developed. Given the philosophical orientation of phenomenology, it seems only natural therefore to suppose that the best way to write about the divorce of thought and reality would be through the eyes and ears of some concrete fictional character in a novel or play who is actually experiencing that divorce, such as the protagonist in *Murphy* or Roquentin in *Nausea*.

Finally, a careful reading of the nonfiction works of these writers reveals such a profound interest in philosophical theory that one must begin to seriously question the widespread but simplistic notion of artists and writers as emotionally sensitive creatures who prefer to leave the theorizing to the theorists. As we will see, the absurdist writers are knowledgeable philosophically and are capable of making penetrating philosophical points in a logical, as well as a literary format.

Nonetheless, the most important philosophical connection is simply the profoundly philosophical nature of the central theme underlying absurdist writing—the separation of thought and reality.

Nor is this relationship between literature and philosophy an accident or quirk of recent history. Despite the "ancient quarrel between poetry and philosophy" which Plato first observed, the basic problem underlying absurdity, the separation of thought and reality, is an old and perennial problem in Western philosophical thought. It dominates Plato's concern to find a relation between the sensible particulars and the Ideas, Aristotle's insistence that the two coexist in a form-matter synthesis, the old and the modern problem of skepticism, and various problems of dualism, such as the mind-body problem, which we find in Descartes Locke and Kant. Nor is this underlying problem alien to art and theories of art. Romanticism is primarily the attempt to bridge the gulf which developed in the 18th century between a mechanistic conception of reality and human sensibility. This Romantic bridge is based on the idealist belief that human thought is actively creative, and attempts to expand that idea to cover an *artistic* creative thought remaking the world *aesthetically*. Romanticism, likewise, founders on the realist insistence that this is only wishful thinking with no correspondence to an independent reality. Some of the absurdist writers such as Camus and the early Beckett, write directly out of this Romantic point of view. The world is cold and ugly, and so humans have remade that world more in their own image and more to their own liking. The main difference between the Romantic and the Absurdist point of view in this regard is the half-hearted optimism of the Romantic that this creative enterprise of remaking the world is a process of discovering a new truth about the world, as contrasted with the thoroughly pessimistic outlook of his Absurdist counterpart that such an enterprise, however creative, just shows all the more clearly the unbridgeable gap between man and the world. According to Herbert Marcuse, the awareness of the gap between thought and reality defines all art up to, though significantly excluding, our present "one-dimensionality." In its break with traditional art, modern popular culture abandons that "two-dimensional" sense, which is essential to art, of distance between reality and our *interpretations of* reality.

More generally, aesthetic consciousness has traditionally been characterized since the 18th century as requiring a self-reflective "distance" or subjective "detachment" from the objective world. All of which indicates that the problem of the separation of thought and reality is hardly new, either to philosophy or to literature.

The problem of absurdity, then, we want to understand as part of a much broader metaphysical issue over the separation of essential being from existential reality. The world stripped of human meaning is a dense, heavy world of sheer existence, but it is also a world stripped of essential meaning, and in that sense it is empty, evanescent and light. Because of the prevalence of materialist thought in our culture over the past several hundred years, the image of real existence stripped of all human interpretation as something heavy, dense and indifferent to human purpose is a reasonably familiar one. A classic statement of this heavy materialist side of the problem outside the existentialist-absurdist framework is Bertrand Russell's "A Free Man's Worship."

> Brief and powerless is Man's life; on him and all his race the slow, sure doom falls pitiless and dark. Blind to good and evil, reckless of destruction, omnipotent matter rolls on its relentless way; for Man condemned to-day to lose his dearest, to-morrow himself to pass through the gate of darkness, it remains only to cherish, ere yet the blow falls, the lofty thoughts that ennoble his little day;... proudly defiant of the irresistible forces that tolerate, for a moment, his knowledge and his condemnation, to sustain alone, a weary but unyielding Atlas, the world that his own ideals have fashioned despite the trampling march of unconscious power.[7]

What is not generally recognized, certainly not by Russell, is the metaphysical compatibility of materialistic heaviness and mystical lightness. Indeed, as two sides of the same coin, neither can be understood completely without the other.

Because of the prevalence of materialistic thought in recent times, we are far less familiar with the light side of absurdity. At first glance it may seem odd to call the semantic category in which we classify objects a kind or sense of *being*. It may even seem preposterous that what we *call* a thing can alter the object in any way, or, especially, affect its being. Call it what you like, if it is, it is! We don't create objects when we create names for them; neither do objects disappear because we don't have a name for them. Nonetheless, the fact remains that it is impossible for us to *think* of or *describe* an individual object without first determining what *kind* of thing it is. Where there is no word for something, we simply don't notice it, though of course it might exist nonetheless unbeknownst to us. As an illustration of this, consider how much you can remember of your life before you learned to speak. So far as we *know*, objects don't exist without essence.

Essence is therefore an integral part of our notion of being, and indeed until fairly recently, essence was the *dominant* conception of being. In order to understand this aspect of absurdity, then, we need to clarify the notion of being as essence. And the best way to do that is a brief excursion into the history of this remarkable idea.

The story begins somewhat awkwardly and naively with Parmenides. Parmenides simply identifies being with what can be thought, that is, with essence and meaning. This, of course, implies that only those things which are intelligible or rational can be, and this raises an enormous problem. Many things we come across everyday cannot be reduced to a rational, intelligible order. What are we to say about these things which exist but which do not meet Parmenides' criterion of being as that which is intelligible, meaningful and thinkable? Parmenides says these things only seem to be. Even if we perceive something, such as change, and can talk about it, as we can, for example, about things which don't exist, but can't consistently, logically *think* them, then such "things" are not really, but only seem to be. Thus, radically unique individual existence, change, nonbeing which can't be rationally thought have no being but only a seeming. And this seeming has no connection whatever with being. There are simply these two "ways" of talking-the way of being and truth and the way of seeming and ignorance. Since the way of seeming includes all of common sense, everyday perception, and science, Parmenides' position is an extremely unhappy one. Even to speak of a seeming requires some link, however tenuous, with real being. An appearance must be the appearance *of* something which is not itself an appearance but something real. And this has been the basic problem over appearance and reality, existence and essence ever since—to find how to relate the two.

If you identify reality with essential being, as Parmenides does, you must show how real essence is related to the appearance of individual existence. If you identify reality with existential being, as modern materialism does, you must show how this reality is related at least to its mental appearance and verbal expression—hence, the mind-body problem in Descartes and the problem over real and nominal essence in Hobbes and Locke. In either case, the problem is how to relate the two. But unlike modern materialism, Parmenides identified being with essence, equating existence with mere appearance. He left it to his successors, Plato and Aristotle, to establish some relationship between the two.

Plato adopted Parmenides' logical criterion of being, but tried to overcome the gap between being and seeming, essence and existence by relating the two in terms of "similarity," "approximation," and "participation." This grants a limited reality to existence (seeming), but only through its relationship to essence (reality), That is, something was real only because and to the extent that it participated in real, essential being, which Plato called the "Ideas." Like Parmenides, real being was defined in terms of essential thought. The objects of rational thought were real; what you think about when you think correctly about justice, right triangles, piety and the like obey the laws of thought, such as the law of contradiction, and so are by definition real. Their existential exemplifications in the physical, spatio-temporal world break these laws of thought through imperfection and change, and so are not truly real. In so far as we think of such existents in *terms of* their ideal counterparts and in so far as they exist *because* of these ideal counterparts, they have a limited reality, rolling about, as Plato described it, between being and nonbeing. Thus Plato does provide some sort of relation between essence and existence. But, as Plato himself seems to admit in *Parmenides*, it is not a very clear relationship, and, as Aristotle pointed out, is not much of a link to begin with.

If the Ideas, or Essences could exist apart from existing sense particulars, then the entire material world was gratuitous. The particulars required the universals, but the universals did not require the particulars, and indeed, could not, by definition, be in any way touched or affected by the particulars. And if explanations were always about Ideas, then the Ideas were equally gratuitous for explaining the particulars. This left them remote and disconnected, and so the problem of relating the two realms of essence and existence continued. Aristotle tried to develop a more intimate relationship in which the material existent and the ideal essence were synthesized into the particular, existing objects we find in ordinary experience, trees, men, etc. Real being, then, is the synthesis of formal essence and material existence. As Ross says of Aristotle,

> An individual must have both being and character; without matter it could not have being, but without form it could not have character. And being and character are inseparable from one another;... form and matter exist only in union and are separable only in thought.[8]

But although Aristotle put the two together, each remained as unchanged as in Parmenides and Plato and therefore as incompatible. Like oil mixed with water, the essence-existence mix soon separated, first in Aristotle's own philosophical development and then, more so, in those philosophers who followed Aristotle.

Ironically, in trying to locate essence in material existence and make sense particulars the center of reality, Aristotle nonetheless gravitates towards the essentialism of Plato. Why? Because essence is all that can be known, thought or spoken of anything. We remain convinced, instinctively, that there *is* something else, variously called matter, existence, substratum, which thoughts are *about* and essences are *of*, but we can't say or think *what* it is, for as soon as we do, what we say becomes an essence! This is what later became known in the Latin tradition as the essence/existence problem and which comes through the history of philosophy as the Idealism-Realism debate.

In modern logical parlance, existence cannot be an attribute or predicate, nor can it be defined. The difference between a real object and an imaginary one is a big one, of course, but it cannot be conceptually thought or verbally articulated. Whatever you can say about a real person could be said about an imaginary person. It is on this basis that we tell lies and construct stories. Nor can we conceptualize or articulate the difference between a truly described individual and all the other individuals to whom this description also happens to apply. I am, for example, an individual person. But 1 am not the only individual person. "Individual person" is the name for a large class of entities of which I am only one. How can I characterize my individuality? I am a man rather than a woman, thin rather than fat, a father and a son, and so on. Each of these qualifications narrows down who I am. But clearly no matter how many qualifying descriptions I tack on to this list, I am still left with the name of a class of many possible entities, not the unique one which I am. Existence can't be put into words or thoughts, in short, not into essence.

Yet we can't ignore existence either, as Parmenides tried to do. We know there is a real world existing independently of human consciousness, but we can only describe it in human generalities. Since all we know or can say about existence is essence, existence becomes a gratuitous, superfluous notion, and this is what leads eventually to Idealism, the view that the only things we have any knowledge of are the thoughts of thinking subjects, thus agreeing with Plato that being is essence but internalizing Plato's essences and converting them into subjective phenomena. This is Berkeley's position, for example, that since we have no knowledge concerning an underlying material substrate, we ought to ignore it. This puts the Realist in the odd position of Dr. Johnson who reportedly went out and kicked a stone to refute Berkeley, *i.e.*, a stubborn but inarticulate insistence that there *is* a reality out there, but with nothing to say about it. Realists also admit the comprehensible world of meaning, or essence, that is, *understood* reality, as a semantic or psychological reality and so usually end up with the kind of irreconcilable dualism with which it all started in Parmenides, though now existence is real and essence is appearance, the reverse of Parmenides. Locke and Kant, for example, insist on the existence of a reality completely transcending conceptual understanding, accepting at the same time all the difficulties consequent upon such a notion, difficulties which spring in every case from the complete separation of thought (essence) and reality (existence). How, for example, do we know, in the case of Locke, that our ideas are caused by real external beings, and how do we know that our ideas of primary qualities resemble their external causes? Or, in the case of Kant, how do we know that a particular bit of sensible reality has been correctly classified by the concepts of the understanding? As both Kant and Locke acknowledge, there is simply nothing to say about this independent reality except that it *just is*. Beyond that we can only classify it in terms of meaningful essence. Even the *idea* of the being and nonbeing of an entity, beyond the stubborn, gut-level insistence that it just is, is absorbed in essence. To say that X is, is to say that X is an A, where A is a meaningful concept, category or essence, such as "a tree." Similarly, to say X does not exist is to say that X no longer belongs to category A but has begun to be included in category B (it is no longer classifiable as a tree, for example, but now falls under the concept of a log). On the level of articulate thought, then, the being of an entity is tied up with its comprehensible essence, though in the gut-level, irrational sense that is "just is," existence continues to be the ultimate object of thought, transcending any humanly comprehensible essence.

But if there is nothing to say about a totally independent reality or existence, how can there by a *theory* of reality or existence? Strictly speaking, there can't, although there *can* be a voiced concern with problems which have a direct bearing on existence—God's creation of the world out of nothing, the idea of life after death, the unique individuality of the person or human soul, and other post-Greek, *i.e.*, Christian themes. Thus the contemporary resurgence of existence over essence begins, with Kierkegaard, as a religious objection to abstract philosophical thought. Because existence is inarticulate, the revolt against essence is a revolt against philosophy—indeed a revolt against all rational thought. As Gilson says, "the reaction of existence against essence is bound to become a reaction of existence against philosophy."[9] This is also why the best existentialists have been the absurdist writers of fiction who seem to agree that while existence cannot be logically articulated, it can be artistically evoked.

In the modern period, as we have seen, the ancient reality/appearance character of the essence/existence split is reversed. While Plato held that essence was real and material existence was merely an appearance, modern thought on the whole tends to hold that material existence is real (though unknowable) and essence is "all in the mind." An intermediary position was held in the medieval period which claimed that essences were ideas in the mind of God, thus enjoying a relatively independent status from men's minds where they have been firmly lodged since Descartes. Most philosophers after Aristotle can, therefore, be classified as either Realists or Idealists, Realists tend toward a sharp dualism between meaningful being (essence) and existence, which is independent of meaning and human consciousness. There *is* an independent reality (existence) which we interpret to ourselves (as essence), but there is no comprehensible link between the two. Because of the lack of any such meaningful link, Idealists drop the idea of an independent reality and, like Parmenides, equate meaningful essence with being.

This age-old debate between the realists and the idealists, then, comes down to this. Either a thing is conceptually meaningful or it is not. For the idealist this is simply the distinction between being and non- being. If something is conceptually meaningful, then it is something and has being; if it is not conceptually meaningful, then it is nothing and has no being. For the realist, on the other hand, that which is conceptually meaningless includes not only nothing, or nonbeing, but an uninterpreted underlying reality which ultimately transcends human thought, a reality which we try to understand but which we never completely succeed in reducing to terms of human thought. Thus, leaving aside for the moment the ontologically nil category of nonbeing, the realists admit two ontological categories—reality (or existence) and meaningful being (or essence), while the idealists allow only one, meaningful being (or essence). Hence the clash of essence and existence only occurs within realism and does not appear within idealism.

In the chapters to come we will see how Husserl and Heidegger (at least in *Being and Time*) fit into the broadly idealist category, while Sartre, Camus and the other Absurdists fall into the realist camp. In fact, any statement of absurdity as the separation of thought and reality presupposes the duality of thought and an independent reality which we have defined as Realism. For Heidegger and Husserl, on the other hand, there is no such contrast between meaningful being and reality, but only that between meaning, which is being, and non-meaning which is nothing. Hence they understand being exclusively in terms of essence. Either we have an understandable something or we have nothing. There is no sense of an independently existing, transcendent but unknowable reality "out there ," prior to understanding, which we find in Sartre, Camus and Ionesco, with which are contrasted *both* essential, meaningful being and nothing. It is precisely in criticizing Husserl's "idealism" that Sartre and Camus reintroduce the Realist position as a way of defining the gap between thought and existence.

Unfortunately, the *full* sense of being, as a *synthesis* of essence and existence, gets lost in this separation of essence and existence, a separation which is *experienced* as absurdity. The being of an object is the meaning or essence which resides in and *belongs to* that existing object; it cannot be a mere idea in someone's head set off against a totally incomprehensible independent reality. The problem of being is precisely how to relate essence and existence, while the problem of absurdity is just the experience of their separation.

This central dilemma is nowhere more apparent than in Aristotle's *Metaphysics*. On the one hand Aristotle believes that the world is composed of individual entities. These may be supersensible, such as God, the intelligences or sensible, but they are nonetheless individual particulars. But when Aristotle asks in what intelligible sense these things *are*, he is led into the realm of what is statable, thinkable, and thus into meaningful essence, rather than individual existence. Thus the beings Aristotle is interested in are existing individuals, but the *being of* these beings is essential being, just as in Plato.

Metaphysics has always been a puzzling book since it appears to contain two quite different accounts of metaphysics. According to Jaeger and others, there is an earlier view which is basically Platonic.[10] In this sense metaphysics is the science of supersensible entities, such as God and the intelligences which Aristotle thought controlled the planetary movements. On this interpretation, physics would study sensible particulars and metaphysics would study supersensible particulars. This is the view of metaphysics as a kind of theology. But in Book Z Aristotle asks a new and entirely different question, "What is meant by the being of sensible things, what is it to be an individual thing?" This is not, as in the earlier concern, an extension of physics into a supersensible realm, but arises directly out of speculation about ordinary physical objects. As Randall puts it,

> The aim of every science can be stated as the attempt to answer the question, What is it to be a certain kind of thing?... Now generalizing, we can drop off the distinctive kind, and ask merely, What is it to be any kind of thing, any subject matter whatsoever?... [And the answer is] "To be" anything means "to be something which can be stated in discourse." It means to be something of which we can ask the question, "what is it?" *ti esti*? and get the answer, "it is thus and so"—of which we can state "what it is ," its *ti esti*.[11]

To be is therefore to be a thing of an identifiable kind. The central question, therefore, is, What must any entity have in order to be and to be known, that is, what are the criteria for our judging that so and so is and is an object of knowledge? These questions clearly indicate a concern with the question of being (the being of beings) which Heidegger wrongly claims had already been forgotten a generation before Aristotle.[12]

Aristotle's answer in Z is that to be is to be the object of knowledge and discourse, something answering to the question "what is it?" a *what* which it retains through a series of natural changes and a what into which it develops. But, of course, the answer to such a question is always a concept or essence, such as "an oak," or "a man." The question of existence is taken for granted; assuming there *are* oak trees, what is it to be an oak tree, that is, some definite kind of thing; what is the being of such things? Or, to put it still another way, What is responsible for that thing being what it is, namely an oak tree or a man? Thus, the cause of being is essence. As Ross points out, "the general tendency of Z... is to carry Aristotle away from his earlier doctrine that the sensible individual is 'primary substance,' to one which identifies primary substance with pure form (essence) and with that alone."[13] As a realist Aristotle postulates a material world of existence whose being is nevertheless *understood* by us in terms of definable essence.

There is, consequently, a persistent and problematic ambiguity which haunts Aristotle's discussion of being which is never satisfactorily resolved. On the one hand reality consists of concrete, existent individuals; on the other hand, reality is composed of general essences, just as in Plato. If we ask, pointing to Socrates, what is it, we can answer either with the proper noun, Socrates, or with the common noun, a man. The first is individual, the second general. This appears in Z as the ambiguity between substance as the individual (existence) and substance as a knowable and identifiable kind (essence). In *Metaphysics* Aristotle considers the following problem. What is Socrates? What makes him be what he is? Socrates is a man, his essence is human nature. Without this he would not be Socrates, but a tree or an insect. But this human nature is also Callias' essence. If their essential being is the same, what differentiates them? Only their matter, Aristotle proposes, only the fact that the same essential form or essence appears in two different bits of matter. As Aristotle puts it, Callias and Socrates are "different in virtue of their matter..., but the same in form."[14] But this won't explain how we know they are different and can tell them apart, since matter is totally incomprehensible. Throughout Aristotle insists that matter is altogether unthinkable. If it were thinkable, he reasons, it would be an essence and then there would have to be something else nonessential for this essence to inhere in. For a realist there must always be an uninterpreted reality transcending human thought and essential meaning, but whatever a realist chooses to contrast with essence, whether it be existence, matter, sensation, space or time, it will have to be something unknowable, and this will always create problems. Thus we see Aristotle in Z struggling for the first time with the problem we now know as the essence/existence problem. For Aristotle the problem is that his theory implies that we can't know individuals, which we obviously can. As Ross says, "Individuals are indefinable: if they have an essence it is at least indefinable."[15]

More generally, assuming that real being is composed of particular individuals, we can go on to ask what *makes* them individual, what is responsible for their individuality. Thus we can analyze the *individuality of* individuals, in the same sense as Aristotle asks about the *being of* beings. In creating a *science* of being Aristotle was not content merely listing all the existing individuals in the world; he wanted an account of what it is *about* these individuals which qualifies them for this description as existing entities. As Ross notes, "Aristotle is not content to leave it at that...; he strives to find the substantial element in individual substances."[16] "Individual substances" are concrete, particular existing individuals, while "the substantial element *in* individual substances" is being in the sense of general essence. In terms of the logical distinction between meaning as the denotation and meaning as the connotation of a term, we can say that the denotation of "substance" or "a being" is simply all those discrete particular individuals which make up the world, that is, all the dogs, trees, sunflowers, and so on; while the connotation of the term is the theoretical account or definition or essence of what makes a substance a substance, a being a being—a definition, in short, of its substantiality or being. But since this is all we can rationally *understand* about being, the distinction between a being and the being of that being is far from clarified. We can feel the distinction in our bones, but we can't say what it is.

Various candidates are proposed in Z to answer the question of the being of an individual, and most are rejected because they do not provide an account of why this individual is the particular individual it is. The Platonic Idea won't do since it is not individual and cannot exist on its own. Nor is matter sufficiently individual and separate. The most satisfying answer in Z is essence since this does provide an answer to what makes what would otherwise be a heap of undifferentiated matter into a single, unified thing of an identifiable kind. Essence in this sense is obviously more than a conceptual or semantic category ("man," or "horse"); it is also the internal principle which organizes the many parts of a horse, say, into a horse. In fact the main difference between ancient essentialism (Parmenides, Plato and Aristotle) and modern essentialism (Idealism) is that the ancients saw essences as objective realities, while modern essentialists see them subjectively as psychological or semantic categories which exist only "in the mind." If we ask what is responsible for the being of a particular entity, the answer is its essence; that is what makes it what it is. But this does not mean that the object simply is the essence; the essence is still the essence of [the object, and it is to make clear this distinction that Aristotle proposes a second formula, that substance is a synthesis of form (essence) and matter (existence). The object is essence *and* matter, though the essence alone explains *why* it is what it is. All that we can understand, articulate and explain about this individual thing and why it is contained in its definable essence; the ultimate material elements are completely unthinkable and indefinable. Why does Aristotle retain an undefinable, unknowable term in his account of being? Like Locke and Kant much later, it is simply to maintain a realist position that reality transcends conceptual meaning or essence.

In so far as Aristotle stresses essence as the intelligible being of a thing, his account is very much like Plato's view that being is what can be known, understood, defined. In so far as Aristotle insists that this essence cannot exist apart from a material embodiment, he retains a realist posture, though a very unstable one. Like most realist positions, Aristotle's existence/essence, matter/form duality is constantly on the verge of collapsing into an idealist monism of essence, that is, into Platonism, due to the sheer unintelligibility and hence gratuity of material existence. Since existence is gratuitous, and since dualism is not as tidy as monism, the drift has always been since Aristotle toward essentialism in which being is understood as intelligible, meaningful being. There may be something else *of* which this understood being is an understanding, but since it cannot in any way be defined or thought or spoken, it is questionable whether it should be introduced at all. Thus when Sartre asserts that existence precedes essence he is attempting to overturn two thousand years of philosophical thought which has held steadfast to the notion that because of intelligibility, essence precedes existence,

Aristotle has introduced two conceptions of being which have been in competition ever since, being as essence and being as existence. He also insists that these two conceptions of being must be combined, although it is not very clear how. Aristotle was the first philosopher to raise the central question about being and, in my view, he was basically right in his answer to it. At first it seems odd to say that what makes an individual be the individual, it is its definable essence, that is, the meaningful concept under which we classify it. Surely, what we *call* something doesn't make it exist or cease to exist. But however ironic or paradoxical, when examined closely, we see that this is the case. Consider the life story of an oak tree. At some point a flower appears on an oak tree, is fertilized, the ovary then expands, the acorn drops off, sprouts, grows into a sapling, then a tree, which is eventually cut down, and becomes a rafter in a tavern. Notice how many questions relating to the existence and nonexistence of the tree depend on our conceptual categories, that is, on essence. How many existing individuals make up the story, for example? It depends entirely on the system of classification employed. The English "flower," "seed," "sapling," "tree," "log," "rafter" classificatory scheme dictates that there are six objects. But clearly there are other ways of breaking up the continual growth process into as many or as few categories as we like. How many distinct colors are there in the color spectrum? As many as you like. And so with the tree. Imagine a language in which "hunk-of-wood" covered both living and dead wood; that is, including what we designate "tree," "log," and "rafter." In this language the number of objects involved in the above story would only be four: flower, seed, sapling and hunk-of-wood.

Consider now another question, at what point does an object begin to exist within this story, and when does it cease to exist? Again, it clearly depends on what we're talking about, that is, it depends on the category in which we place the item. In the hunk-of-wood language there is no point in the story when the tree ceases to exist and a log begins to exist; in our imaginary language the occasion on which the tree is felled and prepared for milling is simply an episode within the lifespan of a single entity which remains what it is throughout, *viz.*, a hunk-of-wood. And it would remain a hunk-of-wood until something happened to it which removed it from that category and placed it into some other category, for example, when it is ground into pulp and made into newspaper. In short, things can be said to exist or cease to exist, to come into existence or pass out of existence only as objects of a certain kind, or essence. Similarly when we consider what changes are of the radical sort which make the object stop being and which are of the relatively minor sort which merely form an episode *within* its life history, we see that it depends in every case on the category in which we place the object. If the concept in question is "tree," then cutting it down and removing all the branches is a radical change which makes it cease to exist. Of course, "it" does not cease to exist entirely; like the magician's rabbit which simply disappears, it merely ceases to exist after that point a£ a *tree*. "It," or another "it" which takes its place, continues to exist, though this time as a log. The irony is that there is no existence or nonexistence of distinct individual entities without humanly assigned concepts or essences which define the kind of entity in question. There are no distinct individuals without lines to demarcate one from the other, and there are no lines of demarcation without human concepts. Individual existence turns on its general essence; being is being-as. An individual object is neither an existent entity nor a conceptual interpretation of that entity but the synthesis of the two, the interpretation *of* that entity as a thing of a certain kind. You can't have existence without essence. As Roquentin observes in *Nausea*, when words and concepts cease to "attach" themselves to objects, objects cease to exist as discrete particulars and begin to dissolve into one another in a way which Roquentin describes as a kind of "fog." From this point of view we can understand the mystic claims, which have impressed both Ionesco and Beckett, that the world is empty, not in the sense that a new house is empty but in the sense that without human concepts there are no *distinct individual* entities which come into being at some point and later pass out of existence. There is a rainbow, but there are no discrete colors in it.

Apart from mystical notions of the void, there is a long debate in philosophy over the meaning of statements about nonexistent entities. Parmenides felt that since the objects of thought could only be, nonbeing could not be an object of thought. Plato tried to find room for meaningful statements about nonexistent entities by analyzing nonexistence in terms of difference. To say that Theaetetus is not tall is not to say something about a nonexistent giant Theaetetus, but only to say that the category into which Theaetetus falls is a different one from that into which tall persons fall. This is like our tree-log example; to say the tree no longer exists is not to speculate about something called The Void, or Emptiness which suddenly swallowed up the tree, but only that what had been previously classified as "tree" is now classified under a different label, "log." Just as being, in the sense of essence, is defined in terms of the semantic category into which an entity falls, so nonbeing is defined in terms of the semantic category into which it *fails* to fall. This notion of negation has been revived in the present century in the work of Heidegger and Sartre. Heidegger's "Das Nichts nichet nicht" means that nothingness is not an objective power or force or thing in the world, but arises only out of a peculiarly human way of perceiving the world. We expect something, and when that expectation is disappointed, we speak of absence, of something not being there. In Sartre's famous example, we look in at a cafe and see that Peter's not there. There is no Nothing, no Void inside the cafe; indeed there are plenty of people, tables and chairs there. There is only a failed expectation, that is, there is nonexistence only relative to a human concept or essence. We can *feel* existence in our own case and worry over our potential nonexistence on a gut-level; we can even try to evoke this feeling in art or fiction. But we cannot *think* either of them logically. Existence and nonexistence appear as independent entities, that is, only on a rudimentary, instinctive level, as in the situations typically explored in existentialist novels, *e.g.*, a man about to be executed. On the level of articulate thought, both existence and nonexistence are defined in terms of essence. Philosophically, essence precedes existence.

It is only within this ironic tension between essence and existence that the important question of being arises, where both the object and the what of the object are perceived as inseparably related, where existence and essence are distinguished but operate in a mutually dependent way, in the inseparable union of X-understood-as-A. Only on an abstract level of words and concepts do the two appear distinct and separable. So, for example, it seems plausible for Descartes to inquire first *whether* something exists and then *what* that something is, as though we could determine whether something exists before we know what kind of thing to look for. As an experiment, look around the room and determine the number of medium sized bliks in the room. Of course, you can't do it until you know what a blik is. If we define a blik, for example, as any manufactured article with three or more separately made parts, you will then have no difficulty counting the bliks, that is, all the chairs, tables, and so on in the room.

Similarly, Ross and Gilson in their criticisms of Aristotle likewise assume a sharp and clear division between existence and essence, as though we could consider the two issues in isolation from one another. They criticize Aristotle for confusing two quite distinct senses of being. Gilson, for example, writes, "What is true is that essences are and that individuals exist."[17] Therefore, according to Gilson, Aristotle,

> bungled the whole question. The primary mistake of Aristotle, as well as of his followers, was to use the verb "to be" in a single meaning, whereas it actually has two. If it means that a thing is, then individuals alone are, and forms are not; if it means *what* a thing is, then forms alone are and individuals are not.[18]

Chapter One: Introduction

But this sounds a little too neat. It is not clear that there are two distinct senses of being. The two are not separable but mutually dependent sides of the same coin. Aristotle's intuition that being only arises out of the *synthesis* of the two is therefore more fundamentally correct than his critics' charge that he *confuses* the two.

Nonetheless, historically, the synthesis which made the question of being and our experience of the world meaningful became unstuck, and the question of being degenerated either into an unclarified notion of bare existence (Locke and Kant, for example), or, on the other hand, into an idealist identification of being with conceptual categories, or as the most encompassing and therefore most abstract conceptual category. That is, the notion of being degenerates historically either into the idea of existence without essence or into that of essence without existence. Since there is nothing to say about the former, except that it "just is," metaphysical speculation gravitates toward essentialism. Since in the modern period essences are internalized and psychologized into mental ideas and conceptual semantic categories of classification, essentialism drifts further in the modern period into some form of transcendental logic (Kant) or subjective idealism (Berkeley). Metaphysics, in other words, becomes a science of concepts, and a science of reality only where minds and their concepts are said, by idealists, to be the only reality. Absurdity is the *experience* of this degeneration of the question of being.

For Aristotle the question of being is, what is it that makes something be, what is it in virtue of which we say it is, what do we *mean* when we say it is. The answer to which, as we have seen, is the significant identification of an existing entity as a thing of a meaningful, essential kind, a category which reveals that entity to us as a thing which we can know and understand. This is a philosophical articulation of the common sense merging of existence and essence, in which there is no separation of the thing from what we call it. But due to the early Platonic doctrine in *Metaphysics* (metaphysics as theology, the study of immaterial beings), the question of being very early split into two subspecies, metaphysics as theology and metaphysics as being qua being, the *being of* beings, which we find in Z. Throughout later Greek, Roman and Arabic philosophy the central problem of metaphysics was reconciling these two conceptions of metaphysics. Eventually the second notion, being qua being, collapsed into a notion of being as the broadest and thereby the most empty class concept. "Plant" is a broader class than "tree," and "living thing" is still broader, and so "being" is the broadest of all, including *everything* within it. But the more items a concept contains, the less specific is its meaning; thus "being" as the class of everything is as emptied of concrete meaning as "thing," and just as uninteresting. But whether as theology or as the largest class concept, what we *mean* by "being," that is, the question of being, gets lost.

In the modern period the essences which Plato and Aristotle took to be real, non-mental constituents of the world become mental concepts by which human beings classify things in the world in thought and language. Metaphysics now becomes a science of concepts, a "transcendental" logic in Kant, exploring the form of our thought rather than the substance of the world. In the post-Kantians this psychologistic transformation of essences continues. By dropping the notion of the *ding an sich* as gratuitous, and reifying and objectifying the concepts which Kant had studied transcendentally, *as* concepts, essentialism comes to rest finally in idealism. Within the idealist framework, reality *is* thought, so the science of concepts becomes the metaphysics of a mental reality. Although idealists objectify mind as the only reality, essences remain psychologized as the subjective mental states of this mind reality. For Kant the notion of the thing-in-itself, though severely truncated, kept the science of concepts on the thought side of the realist divide of thought and reality, within what Kant called the "transcendental" or "critical" philosophy. By dropping the *ding an sich* as gratuitous, the post-Kantians, Fichte, Schelling, and Hegel objectify logic. In so far as Phenomenologists, like Husserl, reject the notion of a non-phenomenal, transcendent reality, they continue, though perhaps unwittingly, the tradition of idealist metaphysics.

Hegel, for example, reinterprets Kant's notion of Reason as the critique of conceptual paradoxes of Understanding as positively, objectively founding a new science of a dynamic reality. Where Kant saw Reason *exposing* contradictions, Hegel sees Reason as *discovering* contradictions; where Kant saw Reason's job to undo contradictions (antinomies), Hegel sees Reason as discovering objective syntheses which objectively overcome real contradictions. This is a bizarre twist on the ancient tendency to read criteria of thought into reality. Instead of the traditional dictum we saw in Parmenides, "if there are no thought contradictions, there are no real contradictions," Hegel says, "since there are thought contradictions, there must be real contradictions."

But in this intricate, meandering historical Odyssey the question of being gets lost. The question of being, the being *of* beings, presupposes a *synthesis* of essence in existence. But this synthesis, which is clearly reflected in the common sense refusal to differentiate concept and object and which Aristotle sought to rationally defend in *Metaphysics*, is left far behind in the course of metaphysical speculation. Practically from the outset, word and object, thought and reality, essence and existence have become irreconcilably estranged from one another.

Absurdity is the *experience* of these metaphysical problems of splitting word and object, essence and existence, though as we will see in the chapters to come, these metaphysical themes will surface in absurdist literature in a variety of different ways. First, in the characterization of the ordinarily meaningful world of naive experience as the union or cohesion of thought and reality, concept and object. Then, in the description of the loss of meaning as the breakdown of that union and the consequent separation or divorce of two distinct terms—the human and the nonhuman, along with the insistence, especially in Camus, that the problem of absurdity depends on the recognition of an independent, alien reality. For both Sartre and Camus, to experience absurdity one must be a realist; without an independent reality to which thought can fail to correspond there is no disappointment and no problem. Absurdity, therefore, can never appear within the framework of idealism. Then, in Sartre and Ionesco, there is a penetrating description of the experience of a world without humanly assigned meanings, first as a dense, brute, bullying, nonhuman matter proliferating, choking and crowding us out, and then, as a transparent, light, empty world devoid of meaningful human content. And finally, in some of Ionesco's work and most of Beckett's, there is a reappraisal of the light side of absurdity as a positive solution, transcending the two term gap which creates the problem.

Part of the absurdist concern is with the divorce of word and object, language and reality, as a function of the more general thought-object split. Consequently, language is a key concern of these writers. Ordinarily, the conventionality of our own language is transparent to us, a matter of blind Habit, as Beckett calls it. Words successfully attach themselves to objects, and the world is linguistically packaged and hence intelligible. In the experience of absurdity, on the other hand, words will no longer project themselves outward nor attach themselves to objects, and so become opaque entities in their own right. The result is the frustration of a useless language no longer performing its proper function, as in Sartre's *Nausea* and Ionesco's *The Bald Soprano*, but resulting also in a feeling of wonder in the presence of a world suddenly stripped of its familiar film of language and looking brand-new, which is a frequent theme of Ionesco, As we will see, a great deal of absurdist writing is concerned to demonstrate and even to bring about that alienation of language from the world. Since language is the medium of fiction, this is important both in terms of the form and also the content of absurdist writing, the first concern being to expose (make opaque) the ordinary naive attachment of word to object in everyday speech. This results in a powerful dramatic technique of placing ordinary, mundane conversations in bizarre situations that dislocate and distance the language. In *Amedee*, for example, an ordinary middle-class couple are worried what the neighbors will think about a giant corpse which threatens to grow beyond the bounds of their small apartment. Secondly, following this exposure of the opaqueness of language, there is the resulting difficulty in describing the "naked World ," as Sartre calls it, which has been stripped of its familiar garb of identifying labels. And, finally, just as objects without words are alien, so are words without objects. Hence a frequent theme in absurdist literature is the threatening aspect of language once it has been dislodged from its proper function in a worldly habitat, a wild, hostile force completely out of control. In *The Lesson* words not only can but actually do kill!

However dominant these metaphysical themes in absurdist writing, it is important to emphasize that these themes are integrated into related social and psychological themes. In Ionesco, for example, heaviness appears as social conformity (*A Stroll in the Air* and *Jack*) and human brutality (*The Killer*, *Amedee* and *The Lesson*), as well as metaphysical alienation. The relationship between these themes is actually much closer; metaphysical themes are generally expressed in social and psychological terms. As a work of fiction the metaphysical themes are conveyed, not in abstract concepts, which would result in an odd sort of fiction, but in what Eliot called their "objective correlative" of social and psychological reality. As Camus said, the philosophical ideas must be expressed in images. On the level of images, for example, a man rents an apartment and then proceeds to be buried in tons of his own furniture (*The New Tenant*), but this is clearly meant to be understood metaphysically as an analogue for the sense of mechanical proliferation of oppressive matter (dense, heavy existence divorced from essence), a favorite theme of Ionesco (*e.g., The Chairs, Amedee*). In Beckett's *Endgame*, to take another example, a young man named Clov debates leaving his master, Hamm, and their stifling abode for an emptied world outside, which on another level, conveys the possibility of choosing the positive, liberating lightness of absurdity over its suffocating heaviness.

Also, as we will see, these themes are not always presented in their purest or most extreme form. In *Nausea* there is a progressive dissolution of word and object, beginning with the simple failure to identify a single object (the stone, or the tree root) in a context of other, still identifiable objects (the beach, the park), continuing to an awareness that *all* distinctions demarcating objects are dissolving into a kind of fog, and coming to rest finally in an almost Buddhist sense of total emptiness. At first, that is, the object without meaning retains a kind of thingly identity. It is recognized generally, say as a piece of furniture, but not more specifically as a chair. But this is only the thin edge of the wedge. As Kant showed, even the identification of it as an *object* involves the projection and objectification of linguistic concepts on to the world. As these more fundamental concepts become dislodged, the sense of emptiness spreads until it becomes total, as toward the end of Beckett's *Murphy*. There are degrees of absurdity, and the experience and portrayal of absurdity can appear at any point along this continuum.

There are also clearly marked differences in the absurdist treatment of emptiness or lightness. At first lightness is a disturbing sense of being lost, cut loose from a familiar world, and is therefore experienced negatively as a disquieting loss of orientation or direction. Later, however, as in the radiant city in *The Killer, A Stroll in the Air*, the end of *Amedee*, and *Endgame*, this same emptiness is embraced as a solution transcending the dualistic problem of the word-object separation.

Despite these complications, the unraveling of which will occupy the bulk of the following chapters, the thesis I will maintain throughout is that the underlying theme of the works of all these writers is the metaphysical separation of thought and reality, essence and existence.

Notes

1. Eugene Ionesco, "Point of Departure," Leonard C. Pronko, trans., in *Theatre Arts*, June 1958.
2. Gene Blocker, "The Meaning of a Poem," *The British Journal of Aesthetics*, v. 10, 1970.
3. Arthur Danto, "The Transfiguration of the Common-place," *The Journal of Aesthetics and Art Criticism*, v. 33, 1974. p. 141.
4. Ionesco in Martin Esslin, *The Theatre of the Absurd*, (Harmondsworth, England: Penguin Books, 1968), p. 130.
5. Albert Camus, *Notebooks, 1935-42*, Philip Thody, trans. (New York: Alfred A. Knopf, 1969), p. 10.
6. Albert Camus, "On Jean-Paul Sartre's *La Nausee*," from a review in Alger-Republicain, October 20, 1938, in *Lyrical and Critical Essays*, ed. Philip Thody, Ellen Conroy Kennedy, trans. (New York: Alfred A. Knopf, 1969), p. 199.
7. Bertrand Russell, "A Free Man's Worship," from *Mysticism and Logic, reprinted in Selected Papers of Bertrand Russell* (New York: Random House (Modern Library), 1927), pp. 14-15.
8. W.D. Ross, *Aristotle's Metaphysics,* vol. 1 (Oxford Clarendon Press, 1958), p. cxv.
9. Etienne Gilson, *Being and Some Philosophers* (Toronto: Pontifical Institute of Medieval Studies, 1952), p. 142.
10. Werner Jaeger, *Aristotle,* Richard Robinson, trans. (London: Oxford University Press, 1948).
11. John Herman Randall, *Aristotle,* (New York: Columbia University Press, 1960), pp. 110-111.
12. Takatura Ando, *Metaphysics,* (The Hague: Martinus Nijhoff, 1963).
13. Ross, *op. cit.*, p. ci.
14. Aristotle, "Metaphysics, 1034a5," from *The Basic Works of Aristotle*, Richard McKeon, ed. (New York: Random House, 1941).
15. Ross, *op. cit.*, p. xcii-xciii.
16. Ross, op. cit.
17. Gilson, *op. cit.*, p. 50.
18. Gilson, *ibid.*, p. 49.

CHAPTER TWO: CAMUS

For our purposes Camus represents the classic definition of absurdity in its clearest, simplest terms. We will therefore begin with Camus and examine the other Absurdists by way of contrast with Camus, looking not only for similarities and differences, but ways in which Camus' initial concept is subsequently developed, enlarged and refined. As such Camus will assume a position in this book as the most straightforward and least sophisticated account of absurdity. This strategy is somewhat unfortunate in that it does not fairly represent Camus' broad perspective and balanced point of view, and we must make it clear at the outset that and how it does not.

First of all, absurdity for Camus is only the beginning, not the end of wisdom. One begins with absurdity because this is the problem to be solved. Camus is therefore critical of writers like Sartre who, in Camus' view, appear to give absurdity the last word.

> Accepting the absurdity of everything around us is one step, a necessary experience: it should not become a dead end. It arouses a revolt that can become fruitful. An analysis of the idea of revolt could help us to discover ideas capable of restoring a relative meaning to existence, although a meaning that would always be in danger.[1]

And in the Notebooks he writes, "One must not cut oneself off from the world...My whole effort...must be to make contact again...with nature first of all."[2]

Secondly, even in the beginning recognition of the problem, absurdity cannot be properly analyzed in purely negative terms. Absurdity for Camus is always a *tragic* response, and, as he argues in "On the Future of Tragedy," tragedy is born of the irreconcilable opposition between an unacceptable reality *and* an unlimited hope. It can exist, therefore, only within a tension of both positive and negative elements of experience.

> People have thus been able to write that tragedy swings between the two poles of extreme nihilism and unlimited hope. For me, nothing is more true.[3]

As he makes more explicit in *The Myth of Sisyphus*, the tragedy of absurdity depends equally on both factors, both the human expectation and the world's refusal to meet that expectation. Without the former there clearly could be no *failure* or *refusal* of the world to honor human demands upon it and thus no problem or tragedy. Thus the tragedy of absurdity ironically requires a sense of the great and elevating side of life to balance its grim opposite. Moreover, if that positive sense of life is not to be dismissed as a completely groundless, irrational dream, it must have some basis in reality.

In his early critique of Sartre's *Nausea* Camus not only argues, as mentioned earlier, a lack of balance between the philosophical content and the imagist form of the novel ("a lack of balance between the ideas in the work and the images that express them"[4]). He also condemns Sartre's lack of balance, essential to tragedy, between the wretchedness and the beauty of life. Without this balance, he argues, there simply is no tragedy. Sartre's failure in *Nausea*, Camus charges, is "the failure...to believe that life is tragic because it is wretched. Life can be magnificent and overwhelming—that is its whole tragedy."[5]

And finally, there are indications, here and there, in Camus' writing, which we will examine more closely toward the end of this chapter, of a *solution* to the problem of absurdity, not just the heroic acceptance of a problematic situation which we find in *The Myth of Sisyphus*, but an attempt to overcome that problem through an intense love of natural beauty.

Nonetheless, it remains true despite all this that the most lucid and explicit statement of absurdity in its grimmest outlines is contained in Camus' *The Myth of Sisyphus*, which we will consider the basic conception of absurdity.

The problem Camus addresses in *The Myth of Sisyphus* is quite simply whether there is any alternative to the absurdity of life besides suicide.

> There is but one truly serious philosophical problem, and that is suicide... The subject of this essay is precisely this relationship between the absurd and suicide, the exact degree to which suicide is a solution to the absurd... Does the Absurd dictate death?[6]

For Camus absurdity is essentially the divorce of meaningful human thought from reality. The first awareness of absurdity, accordingly, is a sense of the strangeness and wonder of objects ordinarily wrapped in the familiarity of our own conceptual garb. Everything we had attributed to the world we now see as springing from ourselves.

When we consider exactly what it is which we project on to the world, which in the experience of absurdity the world is perceived to be missing, we find in the absurdist literature two closely related answers, reason and meaning, and, corresponding to this, two related notions of absurdity—either a world without reason or things without meaningful identities. That is, what we supposed was part of the world but in the experience of absurdity suddenly discover to be part of ourselves, are the reasons we offer in explaining things in the world and the concepts by which we classify and thereby identify and recognize things in the world. Camus does not seem particularly concerned with this distinction, although it is very important to the later Absurdists. But what he does say indicates pretty clearly that it is primarily the first of these two senses that he has in mind—absurdity as a world without reason.

Human beings are purposeful creatures, doing one thing for the sake of another and hence acting always, or usually, for a reason. So, we tend to transfer this way of thinking to the world itself, first interpreting objects in terms of their use to us and then, more generally, in looking for reasonable patterns of behavior on the part of the external world. But when we become more self-consciously critical, this process of "objectification" becomes strained, and we find it increasingly difficult to locate reason in the world. And then we suffer from the experience of absurdity.

The world we thereafter see for the first time as strange, new and alien or inhuman. Stripped of its idealized garb, the dense materiality of the world, the heavy side of absurdity, looms large.

> A step lower and strangeness creeps in: perceiving that the world is "dense," sensing to what degree a stone is foreign and irreducible to us, with what intensity nature or a landscape can negate us. At the heart of all beauty lies something inhuman, and these hills, the softness of the sky, the outline of these trees at this very minute lose the illusory meaning with which we had clothed them, henceforth more remote than a lost paradise. The primitive hostility of the world rises up to face us across millennia. For a second we cease to understand it because for centuries we have understood in it solely the images and designs that we had attributed to it beforehand, because henceforth we lack the power to make use of that artifice. The world evades us because it becomes itself again. That stage scenery masked by habit becomes again what it is. It withdraws at a distance from us.[7]

It is the successful projection of human thought upon the world, naively seeing the world through a transparent conceptual frame we are not even aware of, that gives the world its customary sense of familiarity. This "useful artifice" is what Piaget calls "externalization." Like Narcissus gazing into a pool, we see ourselves reflected in the world, and this gives the world a familiar, secure and satisfying aspect. This is what we need and what we normally get, and it is precisely this which the experience of absurdity terminates.

> The mind's deepest desire... is an insistence upon familiarity, an appetite for clarity. Understanding the world for a man is reducing it to the human, stamping it with his seal...The mind that arises to understand reality can consider itself satisfied only by reducing it to terms of thought... If man realized that the universe like him can love and suffer, he would be reconciled. If thought discovered in the shimmering mirrors of phenomena eternal relations capable of summing them up and summing themselves up in a single principle, then would be seen an intellectual joy of which the myth of the blessed would

be a ridiculous imitation. That nostalgia for unity... But the fact of that nostalgia's existence does not imply that it is to be immediately satisfied.[8]

The separation of thought from reality that the experience of absurdity brings about, therefore results in a sharp dualistic conception of the world, a split between the human and the nonhuman, consciousness and physical reality, essence and existence. Only within such a duality could one analyze the experience of nostalgic longing—the failure of our *desires* to be fulfilled in *reality*, two things which ought to correspond, but don't.

> Of whom and of what indeed can I say: "I know that?" This heart within me I can feel; and I judge that it exists. This world I can touch, and I likewise judge that it exists. There ends all my knowledge, and the rest is construction.[9]

We know our own thoughts, and we cannot deny the existence of an external reality. That is, we have essence on one side and bare existence on the other. But how the two are related to one another we have no idea. And this is obviously a serious gap in our knowledge, for any knowledge of the world (as well as any meaningful experience of the world or any meaningful sense of being) requires seeing existing realities *as* or *in terms of* our conceptual essences. Absurdity, for Camus, is precisely the perception of this unbridgeable gap, that peculiar privative relation between the human desire to understand and the refusal of the world to accommodate us.

> What is absurd is the confrontation of this irrational [world] and the wild longing for clarity whose call echoes in the human heart. The absurd depends as much on man as on the world. For the moment it is all that links them together. It binds them one to the other as only hatred can weld two creatures together.[10]

The last part of this passage is interesting, for it suggests a bond, however tenuous, between the two terms of the absurdist duality. It is the tragic link, referred to earlier, and it is Camus' link with 19th century Romanticism. Absurdity is not a totally neutral vision of reality independent of all thought since it quite clearly implies a perception of the world as *lacking* what human thought demands. And, of course, to see the world in this problematic light is to see the world still through a human, indeed a Romantic point of view. Even as the gap between man and the world widens, the Romantic outlook tries more and more desperately, however hopeless the situation, to establish a sympathetic link with an increasingly alien and indifferent world.

In this Romantic framework, I cry out to the world, but the world refuses to answer my cry and thus rejects and rebuffs me. It is like a lover's quarrel. But, however useless the attempt, I refuse to accept this rebuff and continue looking to the world for that sympathetic response I know I will never receive. Out of loyalty solely to myself and my humanistic ideals, I continue, like Sisyphus, a task which I know is doomed to failure.

Later (chapter three) we will see how Robbe-Grillet tries to untie this last link to human subjectivity, removing the humanly tragic bias and exposing a totally neutral reality. "The world is neither meaningful nor meaningless," according to Robbe-Grillet; "it simply is."

It is this link which leads to Camus' conception of absurdity, which he defines as the relationship between man's desire for meaning and the world's lack of it. It is a two-term relationship; absurdity is a property of neither man nor the world alone, but of their confrontation.

> I said before that the world is absurd, but I was too hasty. This world in itself is not reasonable, that is all that can be said. But what is absurd is the confrontation of this irrational [world] and the wild longing for clarity whose call echoes in the human heart... Absurdity consists in the disproportion between intention and reality... The magnitude of the absurdity will be in direct ratio to the two terms of my comparison... Absurdity springs from a comparison... The absurd is essentially a divorce. It lies in neither of the elements compared; it is born of their confrontation... The world is neither so rational nor so irrational. It is unreasonable and only that... It is that divorce between the mind that desires and the world that disappoints...[11]

Interestingly, this account of absurdity is fully compatible with the meaning of the term in ordinary language, whether French or English, as Camus demonstrates by several examples from everyday experience. In one such example, Camus considers what we mean in ordinary speech when we call absurd a lone man attacking a mob. It is, just as in the philosophical analysis above,

> The disproportion between his intention and the reality he will encounter, of the contradiction I notice between his true strength and the aim he has in view. Likewise we shall deem a verdict absurd when we contrast it with the verdict the facts apparently dictate.[12]

Two important consequences follow from this definition of absurdity. First, as Camus asserts, it is not the world itself which is absurd but only the world in relation to human expectations. Absurdity makes sense only in terms of a human demand or expectation. As he says in a passage quoted earlier, "the absurd depends as much on man as on the world."[13]

In these passages Camus indicates his awareness of an important ambiguity which haunts most accounts of absurdity. Is absurdity the experience *of* reality stripped of all humanly meaningful content, or the experience *that* reality is independent of human thought? Absurdist writing, including Camus', frequently appears to assert the former view of absurdity as a vision of "the naked World" (Sartre). But this is clearly inconsistent. The whole point about the experience of absurdity is that reality transcends conceptual categories that we can't perceive reality as it is in itself.

What Absurdists mean, and what they assert in more careful moments, is that we become aware *that* thought and reality are distinct sorts of things which don't automatically, necessarily or completely match up. The simplest, but also most misleading way of expressing this is to talk of "the separation of thought and reality," which taken in a too literal fashion does suggest the experience of thought on one side and the perception of a naked reality on the other. It is probably true that Absurdists have themselves sometimes been misled by their own form of words into thinking this was what they meant. But in these passages at least, Camus shows that he is aware of the ambiguity and sees which way the account ought to go. On purely philosophical grounds we would have to give Camus very high marks for this section of *The Myth of Sisyphus*.

To say that the world is absurd is not, therefore, the same as saying simply that it is without reason or explanation. "Absurd" is an emotionally loaded word; Robbe-Grillet is quite right about that. To call something absurd is to criticize, condemn or denounce it, and this is to suggest that it ought to be otherwise, that we justifiably expect it *not* to be without reason or explanation. So to say the world is absurd is not just to point out that it is without reason or explanation, but also to perceive that it lacks, or is missing reason and explanation. But what exactly is the difference between something which doesn't have a certain property and something which lacks or is missing that property? This is in part what the existentialist theory of negation is supposed to answer.

In the 1930's English-speaking philosophers had a good laugh over Heidegger's assertion that "negation negates notching)," as the prime example of philosophical absurdity. And out of context it is not perhaps as clear as one would like. But the critics may have been too hasty. The view which first Heidegger and then Sartre tried to develop was that negation was not a fact about the external world, but a peculiarly human way of perceiving things.

Recall the picture-puzzles for children in which one is asked to find what is missing in the picture. You are not asked simply to say what is not in the picture—that would be too easy. If the picture shows the interior of a house, you can truly say that there are no mountains, elephants or locomotives in the picture. But this is not what you are asked to find; you are asked to discover what is missing and this means what *ought* to be there but is *not*. You notice that a table has only three legs and is therefore missing a fourth leg; you notice that the door lacks a handle and so on.

The point is that there is no such thing as something's being missing aside from the human conception (essence) of what ought to be there or what we expect to find there. You glance at the table and discover there are no dessert spoons, or in Sartre's example considered in the first chapter, we look in at a cafe and see that Peter's not there. The only person who can meaningfully say, "Peter's not here tonight" is one who knows that Peter usually frequents this cafe or promised to be present on this particular night. It would be quite pointless, for example, except as a bad joke, for me to remark upon entering the cafe that Fidel Castro's not there.

So when Camus says the world is absurd, he means that it lacks reason, that it is missing explanation. It is a privative description, based on an unfavorable comparison with the human world of reasons and explanations. In itself, Camus says, the world does not *lack* reason, that is, it is not irrational; it simply doesn't have reason, that is, it is simply *not* reasonable. This parallels the ordinary English distinction between what is amoral and what is immoral (that is, immoral is to amoral what irrational is to not reasonable). "Amoral" implies that it is not the sort of thing which *could* be either moral or immoral; whereas "immoral" implies that it is precisely the sort of thing which assuredly *ought* to be, but alas is *not*, moral. The idea of irrationality, then, is based on a privative comparison with a world of human reason-giving; it suggests that the external world *ought* to be reasonable, that we somehow *expect* it to be reasonable.

This point is extremely important in discussing the attempt to solve the problem of absurdity, particularly as we find it in Beckett, by altering the human expectation. As the ancient Stoics, whom Beckett frequently quotes, argued, if a problem depends on human desire and that desire is unreasonable, the problem can be removed by eradicating the desire. The same strategy can also be found in Hindu and Buddhist sources which absurdist writers occasionally call upon for support.

We can't change reality, but we can change our relationship to that reality, especially, as Beckett and occasionally Ionesco, argue, if that expectation is not justified. So long as we demand that the world be meaningful and it is not, we will be frustrated, clinging to the Romantic, heroic posture of *The Myth of Sisyphus* and "A Free Man's Worship." But why *should* the world be reasonable? What right have we to expect this of an inanimate world, especially a world so completely nonhuman as Camus and the other Absurdists insist it is? Is that a reasonable demand? Does it even make any sense? It may turn out to be logically impossible for the thing-in-itself to have meaning!

Is it reasonable to suppose that the world is unreasonable and meaningless because it can only appear meaningful to human beings? If we could imagine a world in which there were no human beings (which Berkeley is right in pointing out we cannot), there would not be the word, concept or category of a tree and hence it would make no sense to call that thing a tree. But that does not mean that in the world as we actually find it that thing is *not* a tree. Similarly, in the absence of people there would be no such thing as Newton's Second Law of Dynamics, as such, but that does not mean we can't explain things in the world as we actually find it in terms of Newton's Law. *Because* we assign meanings and give reasons, and do this consistently and according to rules, the world is a relatively reasonable and meaningful place.

The world we *know* is therefore a world of recognizable, meaningful items bound together according to various reasons, interpretations, and explanations. In themselves it may be true that things are meaningless and reasons have no place, but the world which we know and experience is by definition a world which we interpret and understand in terms of human concepts and essential forms of thought. The world in itself is not something we *could* experience; the world we *can* experience is by that very token a world we experience in terms of concepts and categories of thought.

Thus, to say that the world in itself is meaningless and absurd is really a tautology; it is saying that the world minus reason and interpretation is a world without reason and interpretation. This, of course, is perfectly true, though we ought to add that it is unreasonable to expect or demand that the world in itself *ought* to have reason and meaning. The world in itself can't have reason and meaning, so it's unreasonable to suppose that it *ought* to. In fact, when analyzed closely, it turns out that the idea of a meaningful and reasonable world in itself makes no sense whatever. On the other hand, to say that the world we know and experience is reasonable and meaningful is also a tautology; it is saying that the world which we interpret and explain to ourselves is an interpreted and explainable world.

The second important consequence of Camus' definition is that any attempt to drop one or other of the two terms which define the problem is inadmissible as a solution to the problem, and is indeed only an attempt to ignore or cover it up. We must not deny the problem or pretend it doesn't exist, Camus insists, but face it squarely, and this means accepting both sides of the problem, human understanding and reality. Both parts of the problem must be included in any assessment of absurdity because the problem consists precisely in their relationship to one another. Denying either distinctness *from* one another or their relationship *to* one another is therefore to deny the experience of absurdity.

This forms the basis of Camus' attack on both the existentialist solution of Kierkegaard, Chestov and Jaspers and the phenomenological solution of Husserl, the first for exaggerating the gap between man and the world, the second for pretending it doesn't exist. The existentialists deny the tragic relationship of thought and reality; the phenomenologists deny the distinction between thought and reality. Chestov, for example, argues that because of the absolute gulf between man and the world, we are totally ignorant of the world, that the world is a complete mystery, and thus effectively drops out of consideration.

At the opposite extreme, Camus argues, Husserl simply defines the world as thoroughly and totally comprehensible to man. Thus, for Husserl as for Parmenides, the world becomes synonymous with what is reasonable; while for Kierkegaard, the world is so unreasonable, that we are free to take that "leap of faith," embracing anything we like, however irrational. The truth, Camus insists, lies somewhere between these two extremes.

Absurdity, as we have seen, depends on the hope that the world is intelligible. But if that hope is to remain constant, it must be a reasonable one, and to be a reasonable hope it must be based on at least partial success in understanding the world. Without the possibility of understanding the world the absurd hope would simply be abandoned; without the possibility of failure to understand the world the absurd hope would never be thwarted as it is in the experience of absurdity. Against Kierkegaard's "leap of faith," rejecting reason and embracing irrationality, Camus argues,

Our appetite for understanding, our nostalgia for the absolute are explicable only, in so far, precisely, as we can understand and explain many things. It is useless to negate the reason absolutely. It has its order in which it is efficacious.[14]

As we will see later, this is also an extremely telling argument against Sartre's extremist position in *Being and Nothingness*.

Kierkegaard, therefore, "does not maintain the equilibrium" Camus insists upon as a necessary ingredient in absurdity between the desire to understand and the relative unintelligibility of the world. Kierkegaard, stressing man's frustrated longing to understand everything completely, embraces the subjective side of the problem, turning his back on the world we desire to understand. Husserl chooses the other side of the problem, construing the world as an extension of man's understanding intellect. Husserl thus makes his own leap of faith, determined to find intelligible essence in every object of consciousness—an act, for Camus, of "philosophical suicide."

The absurd mind has less luck. For it the world is neither so rational [as Husserl claims] nor so irrational [as Kierkegaard maintains]. It is unreasonable and only that... In the universe of Husserl the world becomes clear and that longing for familiarity that man's heart harbors becomes useless. In Kierkegaard's apocalypse that desire for clarity must be given up if it wants to be satisfied.[15]

Thus both Kierkegaard and Husserl are guilty in opposite ways of a lack of balance, though Husserl appears to have realized this and in his last period tried desperately, though with questionable success, to redirect phenomenology away from its slide into idealism.[16] The absurd is a balance between two components: a desire for reason and the lack of reason in the world. Kierkegaard embraces the second as a positive statement of faith in the irrational; Husserl, at least in his most productive years, converts the first, the desire for reason, into a proof that the world *is* thoroughly reasonable. In neither case is there that tragic tension necessary to the experience of absurdity.

This is also the foundation of Camus' definition of tragedy, mentioned earlier, and his critique of Sartre for failing to maintain the proper tragic balance between man's hope and the world's reality. If our desire to understand the world were totally thwarted, there would be no problem how we could understand the world, nor, equally, if we always succeeded. The problem arises from the fact that we *have* an understanding of the world which we *recognize* is incomplete, or inaccurate. It is this realization which informs us that there is a difference between what we think the world is like and what the world really is like.

It would never occur to a solipsist that his view of things didn't correspond in some respects with reality. Nor would this occur to an omniscient observer. Only when knowledge breaks down, here and there, do we get the distinction between the world and how we perceive the world. We become aware of reality, not by seeing it as it is in itself, but by becoming dissatisfied with our interpretations of reality.

This is the way the word "reality" functions in our language, as well. Where there are conflicting accounts of a given event, we ask, "What do you suppose really happened? Will we ever know what was going on in reality?" This is the sort of question we all asked after John Kennedy's assassination. What we meant is that although we knew what the reports stated, we weren't convinced these reports "told it like it was," especially as different accounts varied considerably in their reconstructions of that event. We assumed that something of a very definite and concrete nature did occur, and we wondered whether these accounts of that event were accurate. What we meant presupposes a contrast between what seemed to happen and what really did happen. And that presupposes at least this much metaphysics, that there are events in the world and there are accounts or interpretations *of* those events, and that these two can fall apart or at least not "fit" very well.

Much of our ordinary talk about "real" and "reality" presupposes, in other words, something like the Scholastic distinction between thoughts *about* things and an independent reality to which those thoughts may be directed. It also implies the evaluative judgment that unless one intends to tell a lie, day-dream, or talk about mythical entities, one ought not to be satisfied with thoughts which only "loosely" fit reality, but must press toward a better fit.

Notice how important this use of "really" and "reality" is to us in expressing our ordinary views. There is something about us as people that these words articulate that makes possible a sense of dissatisfaction with the status quo, the desire for a better world, speculation about the future, and the gradual development and improvement in any branch of knowledge. People, we may say, are like this. They think they know certain things; they believe the world is like their description of it in certain respects. And they have a certain confidence about this, But they are also aware, here and there, that their account of the world is not perfect, that the world is *not* exactly as they say it is, and occasionally, whether in lying or in simply being mistaken, *not at all* as they say it is. And so they press on trying to perfect their theories and interpretations. This is the situation in which we all find ourselves, and we express ourselves on this score by the use of locutions like the ones above about what "really happened," or what it's "really like."

It may be true, as followers of Husserl or Heidegger would hold, that the world we know is a conceptual, interpreted world, but it is also true that we can and do have a sense of dissatisfaction with the falsity or inaccuracy of some of our representations of the world, and to that extent some sense of the real "thing itself" determines everyman's view of the world and his relation to it. Consider the type of situation portrayed in the Japanese film *Rashomon*. The film concerns a trial in a medieval Japanese court of law to determine the circumstances in which a nobleman is killed by a highwayman who then has sexual relations with the nobleman's bride. Was the man murdered or did he die in a fairly fought duel? Was the wife forcibly raped or did she reject her husband and encourage the highwayman?

Each witness to the event has a different version, depending on his or her biased, self-interested standpoint, the highwayman claiming he killed the nobleman in a duel after the woman encouraged his amorous advances, and the ghost of the nobleman insisting that he was treacherously murdered after being forced to witness the rape of his wife by the highwayman. Yet the judges rightly assume that only one concrete thing happened, that the man was murdered or not, and that some of the witnesses are more nearly accurate in their statements than others. Indeed, without this assumption, the trial, like all trials, would be pointless. This is not to say that the judges can find the truth; sometimes they can't. But at least they *think* they can, and this belief determines their attitudes, behavior and general stance *vis-à-vis* the objective world.

We can also become dissatisfied with the world as we understand it, and any plan to improve upon it or any fictional conception of a different and possibly better world presupposes the contrast between thought and the transcendent object of thought which terms like "reality" help us to fix and preserve. We are capable of recognizing, in other words, both that our thoughts don't (but ought to) fit reality and that reality doesn't (but should) fit our hopes and desires. We see that the world is neither just as we say it is nor precisely as we think it should be, and so we are motivated by a desire not only to improve upon our interpretations of the world, but, through change or in fiction, to improve upon the world as well.

This seems a reasonable account of certain ordinary ways of speaking and acting, and it also provides important insight into us as people, throwing off valuable hints and suggestions for philosophical anthropology. Generally, it seems part of the human situation always to have a limited, partial view of the world *and to know* it is limited and partial. If our interpretations of things are limited and partial, it follows first that the world as we know it is an interpreted world, a human achievement in some sense, and second that there is more to the world than our account of it—in short, a mutual independence of thought and reality.

Thus, Camus, like all Absurdists, is a realist and a dualist, though not in a naive or simplistic way. Here, as elsewhere, Camus shows a more sophisticated awareness of the problem than he is generally credited. It might even be argued that in his rejection of the easy solutions of existentialism and idealistic phenomenology, Camus aligns himself with the most contemporary mood of philosophers returning to the tough, knotty problems of traditional philosophy. On the most literal level it appears that Camus and other Absurdists are arguing that there are two elements, thought and reality, essence and existence, totally distinct and bearing no relation to one another, like Parmenides' two "ways." And, in an effort to speak plainly and simply, this is the most plausible interpretation of many of their assertions taken at face value.

It is also likely that the Absurdists themselves are sometimes taken in by their own plain way of speaking. But here at any rate Camus makes it clear that he sees that this simplistic formula won't do, except heuristically as a very rough preliminary indicator. Without some link between thought and reality we would have no awareness of an external world, much less a worry over the extent of our understanding of it. To see that thought does *not* correspond with reality ironically but clearly presupposes that thought does correspond with reality at least some of the time. A mistaken perception, for example, can only occur in a context of presumably *veridical* perception. Only if the world appears as partially comprehensible can the doubt about its comprehensibility even arise. Nor, equally, if the world were *completely comprehensible*. In that case we would all be naive realists, simply identifying, or better, not distinguishing thought and reality; the world would just *be* what it seems to us to be. Camus is therefore correct in his suggestion that the experience of absurdity must be within a prescribed balance between understanding the world and failing to understand it.

By understanding reality partially and *knowing* it is partial, we see the fundamental difference between an understanding of reality and the reality of which it is an understanding. But the fact that they are necessarily different sorts of things does not mean they are altogether unrelated. A picture of a dog is a very different sort of thing from a dog, but it is nonetheless *related* to a dog by being a picture *of* it. In a similar fashion Plato in *The Republic* confuses the fact that a representation of a bed is not and cannot be a bed with the quite different fact that it may or may not be a good *representation* of a bed. As we will see later, Sartre fails to keep this distinction straight and so is led into confusions.

If we define absurdity as the disproportion between the world and our hopes and expectations, it is assumed that we are talking about reasonable hopes and expectations, hopes and expectations which could only be reasonable on the basis of some actual success, however partial. In the so-called "mystery" plays and novels of absurdist writers (*e.g.*, Ionesco's *Victims of Duty*), this point is successfully exploited dramatically. Some question arises, and a solution is sought; there is no lack of clues, and evidence of all sorts comes to the surface. Various plausible hypotheses emerge which clarify and explain—up to a point. But in the end each breaks down in some crucial flaw, and we are left without a single, comprehensible view of the total situation, as Mr. and Mrs. Martin discover in trying to determine whether they are man and wife in *The Bald Soprano*.

It is not that the world is totally incomprehensible. On the contrary, the world is full of symbolic import; in fact, everything in the world points, suggests, implicates. It is just that it never adds up to a total picture. And it is this partially successful, partially unsuccessful attempt to understand the world which makes us aware that thought and object are different things which may or may not coincide.

It is also from the standpoint of balance that Camus criticizes Sartre's idea of freedom, especially in *Nausea* and the novels of the *Roads to Freedom* trilogy. Man is free, according to Sartre, only in the sense that he is totally and absolutely cut off from the world. Men are unaffected by the world and in that sense are free *from* outside interference. But they are equally *not* free to do anything in the world.

Again, Camus is surprisingly the more sophisticated of the two, and closer to the truth. To be free requires being linked to the world without being completely constrained by the world, as R. M. Hare argues in his famous "paradox of freedom."[17] As Camus points out, on Sartre's view we are neither constrained nor linked, and this amounts to a very odd sort of negative, useless freedom.

> [Sartre's] characters are, in fact, free. But their liberty is of no use to them...For in this universe man is free of the shackles of his prejudices, sometimes from his own nature, and, reduced to self-contemplation, becomes aware of his profound indifference to everything that is not himself. He is alone, enclosed in his liberty.[18]

Thus, Camus' notion of absurdity presupposes a dualistic realism, though no absolute separation. Thought and reality are distinct, though they can be more or less closely related. The two brought into proximity makes for a meaningful, reasonable, familiar world. The two relatively out of joint produces a meaningless world experienced as absurd. It is precisely on this ground that Camus disagrees with Husserl. For Husserl the world is the world constructed by human thought. The world arises with and only with human consciousness. This is the basis of Husserl's famous refutation of Cartesian dualism, and with it the traditional mind-body problem and the supposed problem of knowledge of the external world.

As a human construction the world is thoroughly understandable; it makes no sense, in this scheme, to speak of our understanding falling short of some transcendent reality. Therefore, there cannot be, in Husserl, any tragic reflection on the failure of thought to conform to reality. That failure clearly depends, as Camus is aware, on a duality of thought and a transcendent reality. At the same time, however, Camus is not committed to the view that we are somehow independently conscious both of our own thoughts and of the "naked World" as distinct objects of awareness. In fact he explicitly denies this. What he does say is that we become aware *that* there is a distinction between the two, and this is obviously a very different claim. It is one thing to see someone naked and quite another to see that they are wearing clothing. There is, for Camus, no transcendent reality of which we are completely ignorant; indeed what understanding we do possess is of various facets of reality. We understand reality, but not as it is in itself. Even where we do understand reality, reality and our understanding of it are not the same thing.

Interestingly, Camus' fiction is not as concerned with philosophical themes of absurdity as *The Myth of Sisyphus* and his other nonfiction works, the explanation for which probably has to do with the important distinction Camus draws in his article, "Herman Melville," between traditional novelists, like Melville (whom Camus particularly admires) in which ideas are expressed in images, and more recent novelists, such as Kafka, in which the images *are* the ideas.

> In Kafka, the reality that he describes is created by the symbol, the fact stems from the image, whereas in Melville the symbol emerges from reality, the image is born of what is seen.[19]

What I think Camus means by this is that in the traditional novel the image has been created by lifting real objects out of a context of ordinary perception and putting them to work in a new context in the work of fiction. Because of this, such images operate on at least two planes, the "manifest" plane of ordinary experience, and the "latent" plane of its new philosophical import in the novel. Thus, on one level, we have, in *Moby Dick*, an exciting fishing yarn, while on another level this becomes an image of man's search for the Absolute (or some such thing). In Kafka, on the other hand, the images only work on a philosophical level and thus become pure symbols. It is impossible, for example, to read Kafka's story of a man tickled to death by a newly developed writing machine as a documentary of political torture.

Camus recognizes the limitations to metaphysical themes within the traditional style which he nonetheless prefers. Thus, on the whole, he consciously and wisely, perhaps, avoids metaphysical ideas in his fiction. Sartre, who also works mainly in the traditional manner, may be said for this reason to fail in many of his novels and plays precisely because of this limitation of the traditional novel. By the same token, Ionesco and Beckett have achieved far greater success in exploring metaphysical themes in fiction because they largely abandon the traditional form in favor of a writing style in which, as Camus says, the "reality is created by the symbol."

Where Camus does express philosophical ideas in fiction is probably best seen in *The Stranger*, in which Camus illuminates in terms of concrete human experience what it is like to face the world without any humanly projected illusions. Meursault appears incapable of ordinary human feeling; he is indifferent both to his mother's death and to the death of the Arab he has senselessly, almost accidentally killed. No one can understand Meursault's attitude, and as a result, everyone comes to despise him, not as a murderer, for whom in certain circumstances we might feel a degree of sympathy, but for his cold and unfeeling lack of concern. But Meursault is unfeeling only in the sense that he refuses to conform to the social conventions of what is considered the appropriate feeling, *i.e.*, that one should weep at one's mother's funeral and be contrite after an act of passion which results in another's death, even if that is not what one truly feels.

In this Meursault is an absurdist hero. The experience of absurdity is the experience of the separation of reality from all human projection. Ordinarily we blindly accept the conventional interpretation through which members of a particular society create and are thus able to share a commonly understood reality. To this socially constructed reality we have learned in turn how to respond in socially intelligible and acceptable ways. Achieving this comfortable and socially necessary conformity, of course, requires that each individual relinquish the peculiarities of his or her particular perspective. Most of us do this quite willingly, never realizing that these stereotyped responses are anything but expressions of our own unique and individual selves. Only the absurdist hero realizes this unconscious hypocrisy and, like Meursault, refuses to participate in the pretense.

The theme of the novel is not, then, as some critics have supposed, the dehumanizing effects of European nihilism, for which Meursault would have had the greatest contempt, but rather an odd sort of heroic posture in honestly and courageously facing the truth about a reality stripped of its familiar social guise. In order to locate this idea in images of everyday life Camus must find someone ordinarily capable of such extreme social indifference, and so he chooses someone like Meursault as being more believable than, say, an intellectual of the kind Sartre selects for the central character in *Nausea*.

Of the two Camus' is probably the more successful as a work of literary fiction. In the preface to the American University edition of *L'Etranger* Camus himself wrote,

> The hero of my book is condemned because he does not stick to the rules. In this respect, he is foreign to the society in which he lives, he wanders, on the fringe, in the suburbs of private, solitary, sensual life. And this is why readers have been tempted to look upon him as a piece of social wreckage. A much more accurate idea of the character... will emerge if it is asked just how Meursault refuses to conform. The reply is a simple one: he refuses to lie. To lie is not only to say what is not the case. It also, above all, means saying more than is the case, and, as far as the human heart is concerned, more than we feel. It is what we all do, every day to simplify life. He says what he is, he refuses to hide his feelings, and immediately society feels itself threatened... Meursault..., far from being empty of all feeling,...is inspired by a passion which is deep because it is stubborn, a passion for the absolute and for truth. This truth is still a negative one, the truth of what we are and what we feel, but without it no conquest of ourselves or of the world will ever be possible... *L'Etranger* [is] the story of a man who, with no heroics, accepts to die for truth.[20]

Or, as Meursault himself puts it at the end of the novel,

> Nothing, nothing had the least importance, and I knew quite well why... From the dark horizon of my future a sort of slow, persistent breeze had been blowing toward me, all my life long, from the years that were to come. And on its way that breeze had leveled out all the ideas that people tried to foist on me in the equally unreal years I then was living through... It was as if that great rush of anger had washed me clean, emptied me of hope, and gazing up at the dark sky spangled with its signs and stars, for the first time, the first, I laid my heart open to the benign indifference of the universe. To feel it so like myself, indeed, so brotherly, made me realize that I'd been happy, and that I was happy still.[21]

The Stranger is not without its problems, however. In order to make the central character believable, Camus has selected a person whose indifference to social norms is completely unlearned, unthinking, sensual and instinctual. In this way Camus avoids Sartre's problem in *Nausea* of selecting an absurdist protagonist, Roquentin, who is so intellectually conscious throughout the novel of the metaphysical implications of his absurd situation that the character is largely unbelievable—except as an unemployed philosophy instructor. But by solving this problem Camus finds himself faced with the opposite problem. If Meursault is totally unaware of the absurdist grounds for his indifference, can he really be said to be an absurdist? Is every antisocial person an absurdist hero who "refuses to lie," who is "inspired by a passion for the absolute and for truth," and who "accepts to die for truth?"

Clearly, the person who meets these descriptions is one whose indifference and stubborn antisocial character spring from his realization of the gap between his own individual perspective and the socially packaged world offered up by his society—someone, in short, like Sartre's Roquentin. But then would such a character be believable as an ordinary human being, representative of many of his type in society? Camus' solution to this dilemma in *The Stranger* is to gradually increase Meursault's awareness of the reasons for his stubborn refusal to conform to socially approved norms so that toward the end of the novel Meursault's reflection on his plight, while in prison, eventually becomes a philosophical account of absurdity.

But problems still haunt either end of this psychological transition. In the beginning of the novel is it believable that anyone but a psychopath could be so genuinely and instinctively indifferent to social pressures without an alternative intellectual rationale? And is it believable toward the end of the novel that such an instinctual man could so quickly become a philosopher? Perhaps, as we shall see later on, these problems simply cannot be completely overcome within the framework of the traditional realist novel, the novel form in which, as Camus says, philosophical ideas are expressed in images.

In summary, Camus provides us with a remarkably clear and reasonably accurate definition of absurdity as the perception of the divorce of thought from reality, the clashing dissonant relation between these two terms. This offers a convenient point of departure for our discussion of further developments of this fundamental concept by other absurdist writers that we shall consider in subsequent chapters. One such development is the characterization of the object stripped of human meaning. Camus has little to say about this, far less than Sartre, Ionesco and Beckett, though on the whole he seems to perceive a world without meaning as a heavy, dense materialism. Nor does Camus appear nearly as concerned as other Absurdists with the problem of language detached from the world.

Indeed Camus' position is Romantic in many ways. We reach out to communicate with the world and are tragically rebuffed, but even this rebuff is a kind of communication. Language, for Camus, is never completely detached from the world, floating free, "on holiday," as Wittgenstein once said.

Chapter Two: Camus

It is also in Romantic terms that Camus occasionally speaks of a kind of solution to absurdity which we should mention in closing. At times Camus refers to an experience of natural beauty which overcomes the tragic frustration of trying to remake the world in our own image. In this Romantic and aesthetic, and almost mystical vision, the world is accepted on its own terms, neither meeting nor denying our demands upon it, but transcending those demands altogether. Since those demands are not frustrated, the tragic problem of absurdity is overcome, though apparently only in rare moments for Camus. Later we will see this solution developed, first in Ionesco and then more thoroughly in Beckett, as a positive, hopeful and constructive side to absurdity.

At first Camus finds only a wary truce between man and nature as between two watchful enemies.

> Every day he went off into the mountains and came back speechless...When he reached the distant summit and saw the immense countryside stretching out before him, he felt not the calm peace of love but a kind of inner peace which he was signing with this alien nature, a truce concluded between two hard and savage faces, the intimacy of enemies rather than the ease of friendship.[22]

But there is also an experience Camus mentions in the *Notebooks* in which the self-important humanistic and romantic demands made upon the world are transcended and the sheer beauty and wonder of the world absorbs all consciousness, replacing everything—including the humanistically inflated importance of ourselves, standing arrogant, hurt, and defiant against the world.

> We lead a difficult life, not always managing to fit our actions to the vision we have of the world... But a day comes when the earth has its simple and primitive smile. Then, it is as if the struggles and life within us were rubbed out. Millions of eyes have looked at this landscape, and for me it is like the first smile of the world. It takes me out of myself... It denies me a personality, and deprives my suffering of its echo. The world is beautiful and this is everything. The great truth which it patiently teaches me is that neither the mind nor even the heart has any importance...The world reduces one to nothing...Without anger, it denies that I exist. And, agreeing to my defeat, I move toward a wisdom... except that tears come into my eyes, and this great sob of poetry which swells my heart makes me forget the truth of the world.[23]

Notes

1. Albert Camus. "Three Interviews," in *Lyrical and Critical Essays*, Philip Thody, ed., Ellen Conroy Kennedy, trans. (New York: Alfred A. Knopf, 1969), p. 346.
2. Albert Camus, *Notebooks 1935-1942*, Philip Thody, trans. (New York: Alfred A. Knopf, 1969), p. 25.
3. Albert Camus, "On the Future of Tragedy," in *Lyrical and Critical Essays*, *op. cit.*, p. 304.
4. Albert Camus, "On Jean-Paul Sartre's La Nausee," *Ibid.*, p. 201.
5. Ibid.
6. Albert Camus, *The Myth of Sisyphus*, Justin O'Brien, trans. (New York: Vintage Books, 1955), pp. 3-7.
7. *Ibid.*, p. 11.
8. *Ibid.*, p. 13.
9. *Ibid.*, p. 14.
10. *Ibid.*, p. 16.
11. *Ibid.*, pp. 16-37.
12. *Ibid.*, p. 21.
13. *Ibid.*
14. *Ibid.*, p. 28.
15. *Ibid.*, p. 36.
16. Major criticisms of Husserlian idealism include Rudolf Boehm, "Husserl und der Klassische Idealismus," in *Vom Gesichtspunkt der Phenomenologie*, (Martinus Nijhoff, 1968); Joseph Kockelmans, Edmund Husserl's *Phenomenological Psychology* (Duquensne University Press, 1967); Ludwig Landgrebe, *Major Problems in Contemporary European Philosophy* (Ungar, 1966); Maurice Merleau-Ponty, *Phenomenology of Perception* (Humanities Press, 1962); Anna-Teresa Tymieniecka, *Why is There Something Rather the Nothing* (Van Gorcum, 1966); Theodor Celms, *Der Phaenomenologische Idealism Husserls* (Riga, 1928); Roman Ingarden, *Der Streit um die Existenz der Welt* (Max Niemeyer Verlag, 1964-1966); Paul Ricoeur, Husserl, *An Analysis of his Phenomenology* (Northwestern University Press, 1967).
17. R. M. Hare, *Freedom and Reason* (Oxford: Oxford University Press, 1963), p. 1.
18. Albert Camus, "On Sartre's Le Mur and Other Stories," *Lyrical and Critical Essays*, *op. cit.*, p. 205.
19. Albert Camus, "Herman Melville," *Ibid.*, p. 293.
20. *Ibid.*, p. 251-52.
21. Albert Camus, *Notebooks 1935-1942*, *op. cit.*, p. 45.
22. *Ibid.*, p. 5.
23. *Ibid.*

Chapter Three: Sartre

Sartre is by far the most philosophical of the writers we will consider. Besides being a novelist, a playwright, a critic and a social commentator, Sartre was also a professional philosopher. There is in Sartre's writings, therefore, the clearest link between philosophical ideas and fictional images—in Camus' opinion, as we have seen, far too great a link. That is, in Sartre there is a deliberate and direct translation of philosophical ideas into fiction. In other Absurdists one finds suggestions of philosophical import in the fiction and then discovers some corroboration here and there in nonfiction works which are partially but not exclusively philosophical in nature.

With Sartre, on the other hand, one can locate the same idea developed fictionally, say in *Nausea* or *No Exit*, as had previously been articulated philosophically, say in *Being and Nothingness*. What is doubtful about Sartre's literary works, as Camus points out, is that the ideas have not been worked out fictionally, but are simply philosophical ideas dressed up as fiction. On the assumption that fictional content must be transformed by fictional form and not simply translated into it (see chapter one), Sartre's literary output is not as artistically compelling as that of Camus, Ionesco or Beckett. Indeed, as we will see, it is only with radical changes in the form of the novel and play that the metaphysical content of Ionesco's and Beckett's work becomes so persuasive and exciting as art.

Nonetheless, from a philosophical point of view, the comparison of Sartre's philosophical writing with his fiction proves both interesting and illuminating. Our plan in this chapter, then, will be to look first at *Being and Nothingness* and then at *Nausea*, the most philosophical of his fiction works, to see how absurdity is first defined and then concretely located within human experience.

Prior to *Being and Nothingness*, Heidegger introduced two new notions of nothingness into an already bewildering maze of traditional conceptions, and these new notions are important in understanding Sartre. In the first sense nothingness is the gap between man and the world (consciousness and what we are conscious of) which, in our discussion, is simply another name for absurdity in its simplest form. In Heidegger's second sense, nothingness is the evaporation of objects from the world, which we understand in the context of our discussion as the light aspect of the response to absurdity. The first is an epistemological awareness of, the second an emotional response to the distinction between thought and object, essence and existence.[1] *Being and Nothingness* is an exploration of the first; *Nausea* a fictional account of the second.

But this notion of a gap between man and the world presupposes a metaphysical and epistemological dualism in Sartre which is highly problematic. Philosophically, Sartre is, or was when he wrote *Being and Nothingness*, a phenomenologist, and the hallmark of phenomenology is its repudiation of dualism, especially the mind-body dualism of Descartes. This, along with the attendant problems of freedom and determinism, and knowledge of the external world, pretty well define the scope of modern philosophy.

A widespread conception of the task of philosophy at the turn of the 20th century in Britain, America and on the Continent was the rejection of dualism. Prominent examples include Dewey's concept of "experience" as an inseparable synthesis of thought and the object of thought, and Moore's famous "refutation of idealism" based on a similar synthesis, though independently derived. But above all, this defines the task of phenomenology in its early years. How then can Sartre be both a phenomenologist and a dualist?

Like Dewey and Moore earlier, phenomenologists distinguish thought and object simply as two poles or sides of a single organic unity, the intentional act. Since each requires the other, and neither can exist apart from the other, there is a distinction but no dichotomy between thought and its object. In Hume's language, they are distinguishable but not separable. This might be symbolized (T-0). Sartre accepts this notion and makes use of it in his own refutation of Cartesian dualism: thought can't be removed from its object in any fundamental way since without its object there is no thought. Where there is thought there is an object of thought; if you think you must think something, an argument Plato had used much earlier to prove the existence of Ideas (to think about ideal justice, there must be an ideal justice, even though it can't exist in the spatio-temporal physical world).

But Sartre also wants a notion of the object as being more independent of thought (that is, "real," in the traditional sense), and this leads to a sharper split between thought and object. A real object, of course, can exist independently of any thought, and in the case of mistakes, fantasies and the like, thought can go its own way independently of reality. The object in this sense we will call the real object and symbolize its relation to the other object (the intentional object): (T-0) - R.

In terms of our earlier discussion, the intentional object designates being as essence, while the real object corresponds to being as existence. It is around this ambiguity between the intentional object and the real object that difficulties arise in trying to understand Sartre. To think is to think about something. So you can't think without a something to think about. But is this "something" the object as it appears to you or the object as it is independently of your, or anyone else's, thought of it? Sartre wants both, and he distinguishes the two in *Being and Nothingness* as the "phenomenon of being" (the intentional object) and the "being of phenomena" (the real object).

In this sense, then, Sartre is a realist and a dualist. To a certain extent this is, like Camus, a deliberate rejection of the tendency in Husserl and Heidegger toward idealism, but it is also, at least partly, a dualism despite himself. Sartre would really like to have it both ways—avoiding both idealism and dualism. Indeed the major stated purpose of *Being and Nothingness* is to differentiate nonhuman being (being-in-itself) from human being (being-for-itself) without falling into Cartesian dualism. But, somewhat like Locke toward the end of the *Essay*, Sartre has considerable difficulty demonstrating at the end of *Being and Nothingness* that the two regions of being *are* held together in any sort of meaningful synthesis. Since the two are said to be synthesized only in the weak sense that both can be included in a third, very broad category, Sartre cannot be said to have succeeded.

Dualistic pairs always belong to some common category, if only in the sense that this is what they are dualistic pairs of. As Ryle points out in *Concept of Mind*, Cartesian dualism requires placing both Mind and Body in the same category of substance (a category *mistake*, on Ryle's view). Since this sort of synthesis is required by dualism, it is not a sufficient shield against the charge of dualism. Descartes himself could claim this sort of synthesis of mind and body; since both are substances, he might argue, substance joins them together in a new unity. The two terms of any duality exist necessarily but trivially within the larger vacuous sphere of whatever it is their dichotomy has split in two. In Sartre's case it is the most vacuous of all categories, "pan," all there is.

What is required for a genuine synthesis that would avoid dualism is a sense in which the two functionally require or interact with each other, as in the thought-object synthesis of intentionality. Thought needs an object because the very nature of thought is to be the thought of an object; and an object of thought needs thought because in order to be an object of *thought* it must, by definition, be capable of being thought. Indeed, as we have seen all along, this is the sort of synthesis required to have a meaningful world, and a full sense of being, along the lines derived from Aristotle, namely, a genuine link between our conceptions and reality, that is, between essence and existence. But this synthesis is nowhere to be found in Sartre, nor can we imagine how he could overcome the radical dualism of Being-in-itself and Being-for-itself.

There is no great mystery about a dualist trying to avoid dualism. It happens frequently. Spinoza solved Cartesian dualism by treating Descartes' two created substances, mind and matter, simply as attributes of a single substance. But then a new dualism sprang up within his philosophy, between the one substance and its many modes. Dualisms are very hard to get rid of; certainly they don't disappear simply by fiat. Many philosophers today are reluctantly coming to the conclusion that the grandiose plans of the 1950's for ending all dualisms once and for all must now be abandoned as overly simplistic. Thus, despite Sartre's attempt, the old dualism of Descartes, Locke and Kant between thought and reality, essence and existence simply reemerges in *Being and Nothingness* as the duality of Being-in-itself and Being-for-itself.

The phenomenologists have not then avoided the ancient dilemma we noted earlier in discussing Aristotle between idealism and realism, or, since realism implies dualism, the dilemma between idealism and dualism. Thus far the synthesis of essence and existence has only been achieved within an idealist standpoint. In rejecting dualism Husserl and Heidegger gravitate toward idealism, while Sartre, in rejecting idealism, inevitably moves toward dualism. Because of the inseparability of thought and object in the intentional act, the object of thought becomes necessarily intelligible, through and through. Thus Camus' criticism we saw earlier that it is *too* "rational." For Husserl everything can be separately bracketed and made an object of investigation. Thus, anything, including reality, being, and the world, can become a meaningful object of thought. For Sartre, on the contrary, the being of phenomena, the ultimate ground of what appears to us in consciousness, cannot be bracketed and therefore transcends understanding, somewhat like Aristotle's prime matter.

Heidegger's theory of being follows Husserl in rejecting the traditional contrast between real and ideal being, reality and appearance. Heidegger's notion of being concerns the contrast between *meaning*, which includes both real *and* apparent being, on one side, and *nothingness* on the other side. Being is whatever can be comprehended *as something*; that is, interpreted in terms of some conceptual framework. Even fictional entities, dreams and mirages are understood as *something*. They have identifiable essence, if not real existence. Being, for Heidegger, in other words, is essence or being-as. Nothingness, for Heidegger, is not, therefore, nonexistence, but non-essence, that is, the *meaninglessness* of things.

Like Sartre, John Wild disagrees with Heidegger that being is coextensive with meaning. While Wild admits that the world we are *aware of* is a humanly interpreted world, coextensive with meaning, he argues that this is only possible against the broader back drop of a "world-horizon" which includes both understood reality and reality which awaits, or needs to be understood.

> Being is not necessarily joined with meaning as the major stream of Western thought, and also Heidegger, have supposed. Contrary to these teachings they may fall apart, and they may have fallen apart in the world of our time.[2]

It seems to me the realists, Sartre, Wild and Camus, are right. We need a concept of a reality which is *not* understood to explain the world we do understand. Husserl and Heidegger are right to insist on the *priority* of intelligible being, the priority, that is, of being as the synthesis of thought and reality. But they are wrong in ignoring the important question of the relation of the understood world to an independent reality. As the Zen Buddhists say, we must not mistake the finger which points for the moon to which it points. Meaning and being, essence and existence, are not identical. Thus, unfortunately, all the problems of dualism remain; how can we determine whether our interpretations of the world really "tell it like it is?"

At the outset of *Being and Nothingness* Sartre states his aim as overcoming the appearance-reality dualism by "the monism of the phenomenon."[3] Nonetheless, as he admits, his account eventually reverts to "a new dualism: that of finite and infinite,"[4] by which he means something like appearance and reality, things as we understand them and things as they are in themselves. As John Stuart Mill said, an object appears in perception in only one finite way at a time, though we are aware that there are infinitely many more ways in which the object could appear. There is, therefore, an ambiguity in Sartre's notion of being which he tries to clear up at the beginning. Being refers either to understood being ("phenomenon of being") or to a transcendent reality which always stands outside thought ("being of phenomena"). The phenomenon of being is being as it *appears*, that is, describable being, being under some human interpretation, while the being of phenomena is indescribable, it *just is*. In the latter sense,

> Being is neither one of the object's qualities, capable of being apprehended among others, nor a meaning of the object...The object does not *possess* being, and its existence is not a participation in being...It is. That is the only way to define its manner...It is being-for-revealing and not revealed being...Knowledge cannot by itself give an account of being; that is, the being of phenomena cannot be reduced to the phenomenon of being.[5]

In terms of our discussion, the phenomenon of being is essence and the being of phenomena is existence. Insofar as we can talk about it, locate it among other concepts and even define it, being has a comprehensible essence (like substance in Aristotle). But insofar as being transcends the thinking subject, it cannot enter thought in any way (like Aristotle's notion of prime matter).

The problem, like that of Plato and Aristotle before him, is in reconciling these opposed conceptions. As Klaus Hartmann puts it in his penetrating book, *Sartre's Ontology*,

> The resulting division of beings (existents) is into subjective being and the being of phenomena. Sartre's ontology is based on this division...It must contain an elucidation of the relation between members of this disjunction.[6]

But this is going to be very difficult to accomplish. Ironically, by identifying the understood object as the intentional object, Sartre opens an even wider gap between the *real* object and thought. Through his distinction of the intentional object and the real object, Sartre has made it a matter of necessity that the intentional object be thoroughly understood while the real object remain completely beyond understanding, thus widening the gap between thought and reality and making any reconciliation well-nigh impossible.

As Sartre tries to show in *Nausea*, because of the mutual split between thought and the real object, the object could literally be anything, while we, on the other side of the dichotomy, can also be anything and are hence absolutely free. In other words, the two are so far apart, neither exerts the slightest influence or limitation on the other. This is reminiscent of Stoic freedom, based on a similarly extreme Socratic duality of mind and body. We can say what we like of reality, but reality pays not the slightest heed. And whatever the world is like, we are free from any interference from it. In Husserlian language, Sartre resists the idea that the world itself can be bracketed. As Mary Warnock says,

> He objects...to the whole idea of the phenomenological "epoche," the putting of the world inside brackets...For, he argues, things in the world just will not submit to being bracketed. They exist, fully, and as obstacles to ourselves...It may well seem that Sartre's objection to Husserl is rather like Dr. Johnson's refutation of Berkeley's idealism, the refutation by kicking a stone.[7]

Thus the realist split in Sartre's ontology between thought and reality, essence and existence, or as he calls it in *Being and Nothingness*, "Being-for-itself" and "Being-in-itself." The entirety of Sartre's elaborate analysis of this distinction turns on the relatively simple relation of "transcendence." "Consciousness is consciousness *of* something. This means that transcendence is the constitutive structure of consciousness."[8] If thought is *of* an object, then it transcends that object. That is, there are things in the world and there are conceptions and interpretations *of* things.

This doesn't mean that thoughts are not things too, but that they always operate on a second level directed at other things on the first level. Similarly with representational pictures or stories, insofar as the stories are *about*, or *of* something besides themselves, they have a self-transcending nature. All the rest of the contrast between being-in-itself and being-for-itself is implied in this transcendence.

Thought is always directed or related, for example, to something beyond itself; reality is not. It also follows from the notion of transcendence that thought exists *only in* this relation to the object; it has no self-existence, which the real object does. Similarly, thought has no nature or content of its own. Again, it is strictly parasitic on the object. As Sartre insists, thought is not the presence of the object to an already existing thought, but the reverse, the presence of thought to an object of thought. This is just the reverse of the idealist worry over the impermanence of the object, that is, whether it exists if we are not thinking of it. For Sartre, the problem is whether there is anything to thought apart from its transcendence to the object.

This resembles Hume's analysis of consciousness. Do we have an idea of what thinking is like, Hume asks? No; whenever we introspect upon our thinking we find only various objects of thought. Similarly, Moore in his refutation of idealism argues that consciousness is nothing but the form of our thought; the content is always the object of thought. Of course, thought could itself become an object of thought which Sartre sometimes seems to ignore. But even so, *as such*, it is no longer thought but the object of thought. The active thinking cannot be the object of its own act of thought. Finally it follows from the idea of transcendence that in thinking of an object we must think of it in terms of what it is not. That is, to think of X is to think of X as A, and *not* B, C or D.

Thought attributes categories to the object, and hence conceives it in terms of its comparison with other objects; it is like some but not like others. Hence attribution to an object always implies negation. To say X is a tree is to say it is not a stone, or a chimpanzee, and so on. Also, since there is always more to the object than can appear to consciousness at any one instant, what the object *is* at any given moment is related by thought to what it can become but is not at the moment. The tree is perceived in terms of its possibilities for firewood, potential farm plot, and so on. Essential to thought, therefore, is its relating the object to what it is *not* (other objects and future possibilities), a theory very similar to empiricist accounts, like that of C. I. Lewis, for relating the sensation of a momentary appearance to the perception of an object. None of this holds true of the real object, which has no interest in its relation to anything. Indeed, in itself it *has* no relations to anything beyond itself. We relate things according to *our* interests; there are no relations in reality.

Hence, being-in-itself, having no intrinsic connections with anything else, is essentially without meaning or reason. It just is; wholly gratuitous, and, in an odd way, atomistic in its absolute isolation from everything else. Hence we can never know the real object; to know X is to convert it into an essence, looking at only one aspect among many, and relating what is essentially non-relational. This is an ancient legacy, as we have seen, but more immediately it is the legacy of the Kantian epistemology, that we can only understand reality by humanizing and thereby distorting it.

All Sartre's descriptions of the distinction between being-in-itself and being-for-itself revolve around these characteristics, though, for reasons we will examine shortly, Sartre focuses on the *negative* character of thought—hence the title of the book, *Being* (being-in-itself) *and Nothingness* (being-for-itself). Being-in-itself, Sartre argues, is transphenomenal, that is, it is independent of thought.

> It is the being of this table...It requires simply that the being of that which *appears* does not exist *only* insofar as it appears. The transphenomenal being of what exists *for consciousness* is itself in itself...The primary characteristic of the being of an existent is never to reveal itself completely to consciousness...Consciousness can always pass beyond the existent, not toward its *being*, but toward the *meaning of this being*...[Thus we] distinguish two absolutely separated regions of being...Being...in itself..., at bottom beyond the *self*..., Being...opaque to itself precisely because it is filled with itself...The being of *for-itself* is defined, on the contrary, as being what it is not and not being what it is...Being[-in-itself] is isolated in its being and...does not enter into any connection with what is not itself...It *is*, this is what consciousness expresses in anthropomorphic terms by saying that [it]...is superfluous (*de trop*)...uncreated, without reason for being, without any connection with another being.[9]

Real being, then, is meaningless. Meaning comes only with human attribution, and this is possible only with the assignment of one thing to another, hence relations; and relations are only possible with negation. Hence for Sartre, negation is the essential character of human consciousness. Much of Sartre's way of putting this is inexcusable mystification; but much of it can be translated into a sensible, important and largely correct analysis of human thought. A clearer, though possibly less exciting, account of this aspect of consciousness has already been given by the American pragmatists, with whom both Sartre and his mentor, Heidegger, show great affinity. Whatever the source, let's look at this sensible "grain of truth" in Sartre's difficult claims about man's nothingness.

Human thought is seldom, if ever, a blank staring, as Descartes seems to have thought. We are purposeful creatures, doing one thing for the sake of another. And this capacity translates into human perception and thought. We tend to see an object in terms of its function or use, in terms of what it can and cannot do for us. Every momentary perception of an object, therefore, is filled out by expectations in terms of what is not present, but which could become so if we act or fail to act in certain ways. Crossing a street I catch a glimpse of a car coming toward me. It is not idle curiosity that I see it as a car. I see the car *now* in terms of what will happen to me in the immediate future if I do not take care to get out its way. Once out of the way, I catch sight of a bus, a bus which is a potential means of getting me to my destination if I take the appropriate action to get on it.

Upon reflection, we can see that the "infinitude" of an object, as opposed to the "finitude" of its present appearance, consists largely if not entirely of these purposive or anthropomorphic possibilities. But oddly perhaps, this means that we see things mostly in terms of what they are not. As Hume said, an object is composed mainly of imagination. As a thought experiment, consider how much of your thought each day is concerned with things which do not exist (past, future, hopes, plans, dreams, etc.). X is of interest to me mainly in terms of what it may bring in the future. But by definition the future does not exist, so my interest in the object is in terms of what it is not, but might become if I take the appropriate action. It is only through this aspect of human thought that "nothing" and "not" enter the world.

As we saw in our cafe example in the last chapter, there is no nothing in reality, there is nothing only relative to human expectation. Likewise, of course, there is no essential something without some limitation, or "determination," as Hegel calls it, and this too implies the concept of "nothing." To be A is *not* to be B, C, or D. As Sartre says.

> Non-being always appears within the limits of a human expectation...The world does not disclose its non-being to one who has not first posited them as possibilities.[10]

> There is not the slightest emptiness in being, not the tiniest crack through which nothingness might slip in. The distinguishing characteristic of consciousness, on the other hand, is that it is a decompression of being. Indeed, it is impossible to define it as coincidence with itself.[11]

As Sartre acknowledges, Heidegger had already analyzed consciousness along these lines, though *positively*, in terms of man's "being-in-the-world" through throwness, concern and projection, using objects as tools (*das Zeug*) "for the sake of" our projects and concerns. For Heidegger man is essentially a being whose existence is to understand and interpret himself and his world. "*Dasein* is an entity which, in its very Being, comports itself understandingly toward that Being."[12] This basic feature of man Heidegger calls his "being-in-the-world." Man is the kind of thing which must live in a familiar, interpreted world. Being-in-the-world, then, is composed of various human concerns, and this presupposes our ability to relate to objects in terms of our interests and needs, being able to see them as objects which can meet or thwart those needs.

This is our primary cognitive relation to things in the world, according to Heidegger; not a theoretical curiosity, but a practical concern with objects which "manipulates things and puts them to use."[13] Thus in our everyday attitude we see things as tools, instruments "for writing, sewing, working, transportation, measurement"; things are "essentially 'something in-order-to'..."[14] Thus, we project from our human standpoint a purposive relation on things, fixing them as means to some human end, an "assignment or reference of something to something."[15] We understand a pencil, for example, by relating it to the purpose or end of writing; this is how it takes its place in the phenomenal world of our concern.

> As understanding, *Dasein* projects its Being upon possibilities...The projecting of the understanding has its own possibility—that of developing itself [which] we call "interpretation," the working out of possibilities projected in understanding...We "see" it as a table, a door, a carriage, or a bridge...In the mere encountering of something, it is understood in terms of a totality of involvements and...assignment-relations...In the projecting of the understanding, entities are disclosed in their possibility...[16]

Sartre, however, prefers to describe this process by its negative, rather than its positive, designation.

> The characteristic of Heidegger's philosophy is to describe Dasein by using positive terms which hide the implicit negations. Dasein is "outside of itself, in the world," it is "its own possibilities," etc. All this amounts to saying that Dasein "is not" in itself...[17]

Why does Sartre prefer this negative characterization? Sartre is quite right that negation is only possible with human thought. "What must man be in his being in order that through him nothingness may come into being?[18] As a transcendental analysis of the possibility of negation, Sartre's account is basically correct. He is also correct in his analysis of thought in terms of possibilities, which in turn imply negation. And there are other interesting ways in which negation enters the picture which we ought to consider briefly.

In the transcendence of consciousness thought is revealed as *not* being reality and reality is revealed as *not* being thought.

> If man adopts any particular behavior in the face of being-in-itself...it is because he is not this being. We discover non-being as a condition of the transcendence toward being.[19]

> What is present to me is what is not me...The thing, before all comparison, before all construction, is that which is present to consciousness as not being consciousness.[20]

> Being is revealed as not being the for-itself...It appears outside the for-itself, beyond all reach, as that which determines the for-itself in its being.[21]

Also, because thought is mere transcendence, it adds *nothing* to being. "It does not enrich being, for knowledge is pure negativity. It only brings it about that there is being. But this fact...is not an inner determination of being—which is what it is—but of negativity."[22] Elsewhere Sartre describes thought as a decompression of being. There is also *nothing to* thought but its aboutness in relation to the object. When we are conscious of something we may or may not be conscious of being conscious of it. Even where we are, there is no content to this consciousness *of* consciousness but its character of "aboutness" or transcendence. Where we are conscious of something without being conscious of that consciousness, our consciousness is totally absorbed in its object, losing itself therein in a way Heidegger calls our "fallenness" in the object, reducing itself to *nothing*.

> A psychological and empirical exemplification...is...the case of *fascination*. In fascination...the knower is absolutely nothing but a pure negation; he does not find or recover himself anywhere—he is *not*. The only qualification which he can support is that he is not precisely this particular fascinating object...I am precisely the immediate negation of the object and nothing but that.[23]

And finally, as we saw in Aristotle, we can understand an object only by reducing it from a real being to an understood being. That is, only by reducing existence to essence. Thus thought loses itself in the object, and the object loses its reality in thought.

> But while being in-itself is contingent, it recovers itself by degenerating into a for-itself. It *is*, in order to lose itself in a for-itself. In a word, being *is* and can only be.[24]

> *That which* is annihilated in consciousness...is the contingent in-itself...As soon as I consider this totality in in-itself, it nihilates itself under my regard...This perpetually evanescent contingency of the in-itself which, without ever allowing itself to be apprehended, haunts the for-itself and reattaches it to being-in-itself -this contingency is what we shall call the facticity of the for-itself.[25]

We can't grasp being-in-itself, yet it "haunts" us, taunts us like the carrot just out of reach of the donkey in one of Sartre's more colorful illustrations.[26] Facticity is the link with the experience of nausea, to which we will return shortly. It is the contingency of the thing-in-itself which suggests to us that we too are materially contingent and can become nothing. We can't grasp the thing-in-itself, but by way of contrast with understood being, we have some regulative concept, or "limiting concept," as Sartre describes it, of pure facticity—that reality is not this or that, but just *is*.

> It is impossible to grasp facticity in its brute nudity, since all that we will find of it is already recovered and freely constructed. The simple fact "of being there," at that table, in that chair is already the pure object of a limiting-concept and as such cannot be grasped.[27]

In short, we can't think existence, but *knowing* that we can't makes us aware that there *is* existence beyond the reach of thought, and as Sartre goes on to show in *Nausea*, while we can't *think* existence, we can experience it in moments of "nausea."

These, then, are some of the many interesting ways in which thought can be described in terms of negation. But there are positive ways as well. And, of course, each of these negative ways can also be described positively, as Sartre admits in discussing Heidegger's positive characterization. And while it is true that negation enters the world only with human thought, so does being in the full sense of meaningful, understood being enter the world with and only with human conceptualization. The for-itself is no less responsible for the phenomenon of being than it is for nothingness. Why the insistence, then, on the negative as primary? Partly out of a sense of cleverness, perhaps, a love of the paradoxical contrast of logical opposites (*e.g.*, "Being and Nothingness"). But it is also meant to address itself to a long and honorable philosophical tradition since Parmenides, and more recently enlivened by Hegel, of whom Sartre's analysis is a deliberate parody. This traditional interest in negation is of paramount importance for our investigation of absurdity.

Recall our earlier remarks about Plato and Parmenides. Nothing is first perceived as a direct contradiction of Being. Since there *is* no nothing (this being a contradiction in terms), there can be nothing sensible to say about it. Therefore, Parmenides argued, statements about nonbeing (and indeed any negative statements) are simply meaningless. Plato, finding this unacceptable, tried to translate nonbeing-statements (negative statements) into positive statements about difference. To say that Theaetetus is not tall is to say that he falls within a different class of persons (small and medium-sized persons). But Plato's analysis has extremely far reaching implications for the theory of meaning, for it applies to the very nature of assertions and not just to negative assertions. What Plato has given us is nothing less than an analysis of assertion. Paraphrased, Plato can be seen as saying that to think is to think A of X and this is to think of X as not being B, C or D.

So, "nothing" became associated first with difference and then with assertion and finally with consciousness in general as a kind of private, inner and silent assertion. To describe something is to delimit its many possibilities. Otherwise you haven't said anything. This is what underlies the problem of synthetic *a priori* knowledge, the problem how to have significant, informative knowledge with absolute certainty. Upon reflection, it looks like we cannot have such a thing because to be absolutely certain, the object of discussion must be as limited in itself as our description of it, and this could only result in trivial tautologies. To say anything significant is, by definition, to attribute to it one of many possible properties.

Thus the range of possibilities for the object must always be larger than what you attribute to it. But this is precisely what makes error possible, that is, what you assert is possible but not true turns out to be the case. So, significant certainty turns out to be a contradiction in terms. Another way of putting this is to say that just as the term "reality" shows that there is more to existence than there is to essence (that is, that the world transcends what we think of it), so the term "nothing" shows that there is more to essence than to existence (that imagination can outrun the status quo). Horatio is right, there is more in heaven and earth than is dreamed of in philosophy: but the reverse also holds. We can never equate the two in an idealistic union.

This is the rich philosophical pedigree of the concept "nothing," but of course "nothing" still retains its ordinary, naive, gut-level sense of sheer void, so that all these statements that "consciousness is nothing" have the flavor of mystery and paradox, which appears to be deliberate in Sartre, suggesting death, annihilation. The terms Sartre uses are borrowed directly from Hegel. In Hegel's famous analysis, Being (in-itself, or reality) is the thesis; Nothing (for-itself, or consciousness) is the antithesis; and Daseyn, or Determined Being (being-as, or conceived being) is their synthesis. Thus for Hegel, as for Aristotle, being in the full sense is a synthesis of essence and existence. For Sartre, however, there is no synthesis of thought and reality, essence and existence, and so the two remain deeply divided, as Hartman points out.

It is the perception of this split that accounts for the experience of absurdity and nausea. Being-in-itself appears as totally alien to consciousness, a mere thing. What we do understand of it turns out to be our own descriptive concepts and labels.

> Being is revealed as not being the for-itself...It appears *outside the for-itself*, beyond all reach, as that which determines the for-itself in its being. But the fact of revealing being as a totality does not touch being any more than the fact

Chapter Three: Sartre 53

of counting two cups on the table touches the existence or nature of either of them.[28]

The presence of for-itself to being reveals being as a thing.[29]

Being is everywhere opposite me, around me; it weighs down on me, it besieges me, and I am perpetually referred from being to being; that table which is there is being and *nothing* more; that rock, that tree, that landscape—being and *nothing* else. I want to grasp this being and I no longer find anything but *myself*...for in order to know being such as it is, it would be necessary to be that being.[30]

Being is without reason, without cause, and without necessity;...'there is' being because the for-itself is such that there is being.[31]

(That is, there is a concept of being only through human thought; the concept of existence belongs to essence, while existence itself transcends all concepts whatsoever.)

So, part of the experience of absurdity is the experience of being as fundamentally alien from human consciousness. As such being-in-itself is seen as threatening and repugnant. In *Being and Nothingness* this experience which Sartre calls "nausea" is limited to my experience of my own body as an alien being-in-itself, threatening, negating my self, my consciousness for-itself. But it is threatening not only in the sense that it reveals how I am not it, but in the more primitive sense described by Bertrand Russell in "A Free Man's Worship" that I depend on this body, however different I am from it internally, and that my very being is at the mercy of something totally alien from me. In *Nausea*, however, the sense of nausea is expanded to include revulsion toward all physical objects divorced from human content or meaning.

Despite the phenomenological style, there is an unmistakable materialism in *Being and Nothingness*, a kind of epiphenomenalism of the mind dependent on a material body of an alien nature, rising and falling with it (which makes Sartre's later Marxism less difficult to reconcile with his earlier phenomenological existentialism). We have already mentioned the weakness of Sartre's attempted synthesis of these two different types of being at the end of the book.

But after our description of the In-itself and the For-itself, it appeared to us difficult to establish a bond between them, we feared that we might fall into an insurmountable dualism.[32]

A well-founded fear. In a trivial sense Pan includes both, just as "being" includes both if they are different sorts of being. But this is not enough for the kind of synthesis Sartre needs. He needs to show that, though different, each requires the other. And this Sartre is not willing to admit. In direct opposition to Hegel, Sartre argues that while being-for-itself depends on being-in-itself, the reverse does *not* hold—being-in-itself does *not* depend on being-for-itself. In his famous argument about Classical and Romantic art, Hegel assumes the reverse, that while you can't have a material form without spiritual content, you can have pure spiritual content without any material form. What this amounts to is idealism.

Sartre's position is the materialist converse of this.

> But although in one sense consciousness considered in isolation is an abstraction, and although phenomena...are similarly abstract insofar as they cannot exist as phenomena without *appearing* to a consciousness, nevertheless the being of phenomena as in an in-self which is what it is cannot be considered as an abstraction...Therefore while the relation of the for-itself to the in-itself is originally constitutive of the very being which is put into the relation, we should not understand that this relation is constitutive of the in-itself but rather of the for-itself.[33]

It is definitely a one-way street. Consciousness depends on reality, but reality does not depend on consciousness (only the *intentional* object depends on consciousness). This makes a mockery of the synthesis of for-itself and in-itself in the totality of Pan, as Sartre comes close to admitting in one interesting passage.

> As for the totality of the for-itself and the in-itself, this has for its characteristic the fact that the for-itself makes itself *other* in relation to the in-itself but that the in-itself is in no way other than the for-itself in its being.[34]

It is this absolute division which is manifested in the experience of absurdity. Not only an alien world, but a world completely indifferent to any human conception or explanation. The world can literally do anything and we are conversely infinitely free.

Looking beyond the influence of *Being and Nothingness* on *Nausea* to a more critical accounting, we must agree with Camus that this total indifference is wildly contrary to plain fact. Our explanations reflect to some extent the limitations of the world on itself and the world most certainly imposes many restrictions and limitations on my freedom to act in the world. (Indeed, this may be the only clear sense we have of "facticity.")

The source of Sartre's enormous error would seem to be his confusion of the fact that consciousness and reality are different sorts of things, which they surely are, with the quite different claim that they therefore have no relation to one another. By the transcendence relation, reality can never be *knowledge of* reality. But that doesn't mean they can't be related in the knowledge relation. In any act of thinking it is possible to understand an aspect of reality, and this is genuine, correctible knowledge of an alien reality, which can be progressively improved upon. As Camus points out, we *can* know reality; the only thing we cannot know is reality as it is *in itself*. This confusion in Sartre's

> strange conception of the *en soi* [in-itself]...as an absolute plenum with no potency, and indeed no real relations to anything beyond...Heidegger suggests such a view by his conception of subhuman existence as a determinate being-on-hand..., something finished and simply there, in violent contrast to the unfinished potentiality of *Dasein*. In Sartre, this contrast between a subhuman *en soi* that is fully in act, and a human *pour soi* [for-itself]...that is purely potential nothingness, is magnified to an exaggerated opposition that warps his whole ontology.[35]

Wild is right. Objects can't do just anything. Independently of all human interpretation, a piece of glass is more likely to break than a piece of rubber. There are limitations and some of these are reflected in thought (*i.e.*, are understood by us). Recalling our discussion of the last chapter, it is ironic how much more sophisticated and incisive is Camus' position, though far less philosophical in style. As Hartmann points out,

> The same qualities do not appear everywhere. The availability of certain qualities and discrete units cannot be referred simply to our negation of being. Discreteness must somehow be grounded in being-in-itself.[36]

And as Hartmann argues, this problem is due to the lack of synthesis of the two terms which Sartre borrows from Hegel's opposition of Being and Nothing.[37] The opposition of subject and object in Sartre's ontology coincides with the opposition at the beginning of Hegel's *Logic*, but remains arrested there.

> Sartre's ontology...is unable to account for what there is per se from an objectively ontological perspective, namely, individual things and individual persons.[38]

Here, Sartre takes the side of Kantian realism against Hegelian idealism, pushing Kant's position to an extreme. Thought converts pure existence into essence. Kant and Sartre interpret this to mean that thought thereby falsifies existence and that pure existence is therefore always completely unknown (like Aristotle's prime matter). Hegel interprets this same fact to mean that existence is evolving into essence. We don't distort it; it changes! Hence the idealist synthesis in Hegel which Sartre, along with Kant, Locke and Aristotle, could not find within a realist framework.

Nausea is the attempt to translate the metaphysics of absurdity into human experience. Since we cannot think existence we must locate it within some precognitive experience. In the novel Sartre tries to show how the world looks and feels to someone, namely Roquentin, suffering "nausea," the concrete experience of absurdity. The structure of the novel turns on the progressive dissolution of objects, as perceived by Roquentin and systematically recorded daily in his diary, step by step, from individual ordinary physical things to a vast, all-encompassing emptiness. In the first stage words become divorced from things which nonetheless retain their discrete, distinct, individual, thingly guise.

In the second stage the lines of demarcation between individual objects begin to dissolve and objects melt together into a curious kind of fog. And finally, in the third stage, this fog diffuses still further into sheer emptiness, though this is only suggested briefly at the very end of the novel. Within this description of the perception of objects divorced from meaning Sartre weaves the correlative notions, so important in his later fiction, of freedom and adventure.

The manifest "story line" of the novel is very thin. Antoine Roquentin's present stage of life comes to an end as he abandons his two remaining illusions of a meaningful existence—completing his historical research on the 18th century figure, M. Rollebon, and recapturing his sense of romantic adventure with his old lover, Anny. The novel ends as Roquentin prepares to leave the provincial capital, Bouville, where he had been living the past few years, for Paris to begin a new life as a fiction writer.

The dominant themes of the novel move on a very different plane, however, as Roquentin records in painstaking detail a devastating change which has occurred in his experience of the world around him.

> I must tell how I see this table, this street, the people, packet of tobacco, since those are the things which have changed. I must determine the exact extent and nature of this change.[39]

It is a change of immense importance, yet words seem incapable of describing it. Indeed, described in words, there is no detectable change at all!

> For instance, here is a cardboard box holding my bottle of ink. I should try to tell how I saw it before and now how I [do]. Well, it's a parallelopiped rectangle, it opens—that's stupid, there's nothing I can say about it.[40]

It is not Roquentin who has changed but, somehow, the objects themselves. Whatever change has occurred in Roquentin's outlook must indeed be explained in terms of the changed status of objects in the world.

> The Nausea is not inside me: I feel it *out there* in the wall, in the suspenders, everywhere around me. It makes itself one with the cafe, I am the one who is within it.[41]

Roquentin then begins describing a series of experiences with particular, everyday physical objects in which the disturbing quality of these objects gradually emerges. At first, in the case of the stone on the beach, it is a very confused experience, difficult to understand and describe.

> I saw something which disgusted me, but I no longer know whether it was the sea or the stone. The stone was flat and dry, especially on one side, damp and

muddy on the other. I held it by the edges with my fingers wide apart so as not to get them dirty...[42]

Later, with the glass of beer, it becomes clearer to Roquentin that the difficulty in putting into words what he is trying to describe is precisely that it is something beyond words and distinct from linguistic description

> Everywhere, now, there are objects like this glass of beer on the table there. When I see it, I feel like saying: "Enough..." I have been *avoiding* looking at this glass of beer...I don't want to see it..." Well, what's the matter with that glass of beer?" It's just like all the others. It's beveled on the edges, has a handle...I know all that, but I know there is something else. Almost nothing. But I can't explain what I see.[43]

It is not, of course, the objects themselves which have literally changed, but like the absurd experience generally, the semantic relation of words to objects. Words can only describe how one glass of beer is like other glasses of beer, *i.e.*, what they share in common, beveled edges, handle, etc.—the universal essence of "a glass of beer." Words are in principle, then, incapable of describing the individual existence of this particular glass of beer. Of all the things we feel it is difficult to put into words, existence is the one thing, and indeed the only thing, where this is literally impossible.

In our ordinary experience we look at the existing object in terms of its essence, we see that as a glass of beer, one among many, an instance of its "type," and thus "avoid" looking at *this* glass of beer. We see the essence in the existing individual, we do not see its existence, that is, we do not see it as the unique individual it is. "Everything is what it is and not another thing," as Joseph Butler once remarked, but we don't see things this way; we see them as something other than themselves, as glasses, stones, etc. We *think* we have been looking at the individual object, while all along we have seen only its general identity or essence.

This is the basis of Roger Fry's distinction in *Vision and Design* between *seeing* things in ordinary perception and *looking at* them in an aesthetic context.

> The needs of our actual life are so imperative, that the sense of vision becomes highly specialized in their service. With an admirable economy we learn to see only so much as is needful for our purposes; but this is in fact very little, just enough to recognize and identify each object or person; that done, they go into an entry in our mental catalogue and are no more really seen. In actual life the normal person really only reads the labels as it were on the objects around him and troubles no further...It is only when an object exists in our lives for no other purpose than to be seen that we really look at it...Biologically speaking, art is a blasphemy. We were given our eyes to see things, not to look at them. Life takes care that we all learn the lesson thoroughly, so that at a very early age we have acquired a very considerable ignorance of visual appearances...The subtlest differences of appearance that have a utility value still continue to be appreciated, while large and important visual characters, provided they are

useless for life, will pass unnoticed...Children have not learned it fully, and so they look at things with some passion. Even the grown man keeps something of his unbiological, disinterested vision with regard to a few things. He still looks at flowers, and does not merely see them...The vision with which we regard such objects is quite distinct from the practical vision of our instinctive life. In the practical vision we have no more concern after we have read the label on the object; vision ceases the moment it has served its biological function.[44]

But this begins to make clearer the disturbing aspect of objects as *mere objects*. As a glass of beer, or a piece of writing paper, objects are assigned useful purposes and so occupy a friendly place in the world of our common needs and interests. In his popular radio broadcast just after the second world war, later published as "Existentialism and Humanism," Sartre makes clear the functionalist, purposive nature of the human perception of the essence of an object.

> If one considers an article of manufacture—as, for example, a book or a paper-knife—one sees that it has been made by an artisan who had a conception of it...and...pre-existent technique of production which is a part of that conception and is, at bottom, a formula. Thus the paper-knife is at the same time an article producible in a certain manner and one which, on the other hand, serves a definite purpose, for one cannot suppose that a man would produce a paper-knife without knowing what it was for. Let us say, then, of the paper-knife that its essence—that is to say the sum of the formulae and the qualities which made its production and its definition possible—precedes existence...[45]

In this same article Sartre tries to show how we extend this functionalist way of understanding objects to non-manufactured objects, and indeed to everything we come in contact with. "Here, then, we are viewing the world from a technical standpoint...When we think of God as the creator, we are thinking of him...as a supernatural artisan,"[46] an idea first expressed in Plato's *Timaeus*. As an example of this extension of purposeful explanation, whose overtness strikes us as cute, or clever, consider the kind of children's book that begins: "The cow is there to give us milk; the hen is there to give us eggs; the pig is there to give us bacon," in which the world's resistance to purposeful rendering, especially in the last case, is conveniently glossed over. Stripped of their familiar role, objects become mere things totally indifferent to our purposes and existing as limits to our freedom to act purposefully.

But if the mere thinghood of the object, its existence, is necessarily beyond words, how does Sartre, or Roquentin, describe it in the novel? This poses a very serious problem. After we have kicked or pounded the object, or repeated emphatically, "it just is!," what is there to say about existence? Perhaps we should simply remain silent.

Sartre's solution is to describe the object in terms other than its customary utilitarian, functional description. He does not refuse to describe the object entirely, but simply in its most customary fashion. The streetcar seat is

Chapter Three: Sartre

described, for example, as the body of a dead bloated donkey floating down the river and its rough knap as the claws of tiny animals. This device resembles poetic imagery in which we are invited to see familiar objects in unfamiliar ways. Insofar as we find this possible we are tacitly being persuaded that the object is not tied exclusively to any one description, thus loosening, however slightly, that naive link between word and object. These alternative descriptions provide a *sense* of the object transcending its *usual* description, and thereby, an indirect sense of its existence transcending *all* description.

Obviously words cannot describe what lies beyond words, but there are uses of words which can suggest indirectly a non-semantic reality. In *Being and Nothingness* this non-semantic reality is referred to as the "being of phenomena" which does not enter into any internal "relationships," a "being-in-itself" which just is—an interesting use of words to refer to what cannot be verbally described. So in *Nausea* the object beyond all description is nonetheless described though in unusual, metaphorical ways, and from unusual points of view.

> Today, I was watching the riding boots of a cavalry officer who was leaving his barracks. As I followed them with my eyes, I saw a piece of paper lying beside a puddle. I thought the officer was going to crush the paper into the mud with his heel, but no: he straddled paper and puddle in a single step. I went up to it: it was a lined page, undoubtedly torn from a school notebook. The rain had drenched and twisted it, it was covered with blisters and swellings like a burned hand; the red line of the margin was smeared into a pink splotch; ink had run in places. The bottom of the page disappeared beneath a crust of mud. I bent down, already rejoicing at the touch of this pulp, fresh and tender, which I should roll in my fingers into greyish balls. I was unable...Objects should not *touch* because they are not alive. You use them, put them back in place, you live among them: they are useful, nothing more. But they touch me, it is unbearable. I am afraid of being in contact with them as though they were living beasts.[47]

Of course, inanimate objects are not living animals, but this metaphor, this way of seeing them does bring out their indifference to us, the separate "lives" they lead once they have been removed from the perspective of their utility to us as human beings. Nor is a streetcar seat a *dead* animal, though this too serves to evoke the sense of a physical reality completely untouched by the animating spirit of human consciousness, a dull, leaden material existence heavy as a corpse.

Since sight and hearing are the most intellectual and hence semantically linked senses, it is primarily through touch that Roquentin becomes aware of the brute existence of things. We *see* them in terms of their generalized significance or identity; but when we *feel* them we sense that there is more to an object than the label by which we classify it.

> Suddenly, there it is: the Nausea...My hand is clutching the handle of the dessert knife. I feel this black wooden handle. My hand holds it. My hand. Personally, I would rather let this knife alone: what good is it to be always touching something? Objects are not made to be touched. It is better to slip between them, avoiding them as much as possible...[48]

Included among the objects thus divorced, alienated from descriptive, semantic meaning is Roquentin's own body and the parts of his body. In *Being and Nothingness* this is the entire focus of nausea, while in *Nausea* it is only a part, though a significant part of that experience.

> I see my hand spread out on the table. It lives... it is me. It opens, the fingers open and point. It is lying on its back. It shows me its fat belly. It looks like an animal turned upside down. The fingers are the paws.[49]

Similarly on the streetcar seat, it is touch which reveals the thing qua thing, which in transcending the utilitarian identity of the object appears as a thing with a will of its own, opposing mine, like an animal.

> I lean my hand on the seat but pull it back hurriedly; it exists. This thing I'm sitting on, leaning my hand on, is called a seat. They made it purposively for people to sit on, they took leather, springs and cloth, they went to work with the idea of making a seat and when they finished, *that* was what they had made. They carried it here, into this car and the car is *now* rolling and jolting with its rattling windows, carrying this red thing in its bosom. I murmur: 'It's a seat,' a little like an exorcism. But the word stays on my lips: it refuses to go and put itself on the thing. It stays what it is, with its red plush, thousands of little red paws in the air, all still, little dead paws. This enormous belly turned upward, bleeding, inflated—bloated with all its dead paws, this belly floating in this car, in this grey sky, is not a seat. It could just as well be a dead donkey tossed about in the water, floating with the current, belly in the air in a great grey river, a river of floods; and I could be sitting on the donkey's belly, my feet dangling in the clear water. Things are divorced from their names. They are there, grotesque, headstrong, gigantic and it seems ridiculous to call them seats or say anything at all about them: I am in the midst of things, nameless things. Alone, without words, defenseless, they surround me, are beneath me, behind me, above me. They demand nothing, they don't impose themselves: they are there.[50]

The object is now divorced entirely from its name, and from all human words, concepts and descriptions. As such it is essentially indifferent to linguistic description; it could be described as anything.

> I was in the park just now. The roots of the chestnut tree were sunk in the ground just under my bench. I couldn't remember it was a root any more. The words had vanished and with them the significance of things, their methods of use, and the feeble points of reference which men have traced on their surface. I

was sitting, stooping forward, head bowed, alone in front of this black, knotty mass, entirely beastly, which frightened me.[51]

And even whole streets.

> I *know* it's the Rue Boulibet but I don't recognize it. Usually, when I start down it I seem to cross a deep layer of good sense: squat and awkward, the Rue Boulibet, with its tarred and uneven surface, looked like a national highway when it passes through rich country towns with solid, three-story houses for more than half a mile; I called it a country road and it enchanted me because it was so out of place, so paradoxical in a commercial port. Today the houses are there but they have lost their rural look: they are buildings and nothing more.[52]

In our ordinary experience words and object are joined together into an indistinguishable unity. In the nauseous experience of absurdity, on the other hand, the two split apart. This creates a change in the object; it also creates a change in the word. We, say, for example, that an object is black, and "black" looks like the name of a distinct quality, just as "seat" looks like the name of a distinct object. But, of course, black, is only a generalized kind of quality, applying to many different sorts and degrees of black. Just as objects become mere objects in the experience of absurdity, so do words become mere words, that is, mere sounds and marks detached from their meaningful connection to the world.

> Black? I felt the word deflating, emptied of meaning with extraordinary rapidity. Black? The root *was not* black, there was no black on this piece of wood—there was...something else: black...did not exist. I looked at the root: was it *more than* black or *almost* black? But I soon stopped questioning myself because...I had already felt their cold, inert qualities elude me, slip through my fingers.[53]

How can a black root not be black? How can a seat not be a seat? The point concerns the semantic relation telescoped in the little word "is" in "is black" and "is a seat." In the sense in which this relation is understood to name distinct ontological entities (whether objects or qualities) the relation does not hold and in *that* sense the object is *not* black or a seat. But, of course, in the sense in which this particular object and quality are classifiable within the broad abstract concept of "seat" and "black," it is a seat and black. The main thing is to see that black is not an objective entity ("black did not exist"), but only a humanly constructed essence or label. In the experience of nausea, objects refuse to accept their labels, and labels refuse to attach themselves to objects. Detached from one another both word and object take on a disturbing strangeness. In a more playful way, children will similarly disassociate word from object by repeating a word over and over again until its "existence" as a mere sound is detached from its meaning, and it begins to sound funny.

Names for the qualities of objects are therefore in precisely the same fix as names for the objects themselves, mere idealized abstractions, not proper names of any actual existence.

> The sounds, smells, the tastes. When they ran quickly under your nose like startled hares and you didn't pay too much attention, you might believe them to be simple and reassuring, you might believe that there was real blue in the world, real red, a real perfume of almonds or violets. But as soon as you held on to them for an instant, this feeling of comfort and security gave way to a deep uneasiness: colours, tastes, and smells were never real, never themselves and nothing but themselves...[The black] *looked* like a colour, but also...like a bruise or a secretion, like an oozing—and something else, an odour, for example, it melted into the odour of wet earth, warm, moist wood, into a black odour that spread like varnish over this sensitive wood, in a flavour of chewed, sweet fibre...But this richness was lost in confusion and finally was no more because it was too much.[54]

As Bergson points out, it is the very nature of conceptual, semantical understanding of an object to break it up into discrete, namable units, even though the object itself is not so sharply divisible. Linguistically and conceptually even the color spectrum is composed of discrete, individual colors, even though, as a continuum, the spectrum is not, by definition, so divisible.

> Our mind, which seeks for solid points of support, has for its main function in the ordinary course of life that of representing *states* and *things*. It takes, at long intervals, almost instantaneous views of the undivided mobility of the real. It thus obtains *sensations* and *ideas*. In this way it substitutes for the continuous the discontinuous, for motion stability, for tendency in the process of change, fixed points marking a direction of change and tendency. This substitution is necessary...to positive science.[55]

And, he might have added, necessary for *all* ordinary understanding and discourse. One of the ways in which poetry differs from prose is its device of mixing descriptions which ordinarily belong to different sense modalities (called syncretism) in a way which calls to mind the pre-conceptual experience of a more homogeneous, continuous world, a world in which, as in Sartre's example, we *see* the moisture, warmth, earthy smell of the tree root.

If words do not attach essentially to objects but are imposed from without by men, then objects can be described as anything. But if so, then, so far as we know, objects can be anything. Hence, the all-pervasive contingency of physical existence. The reasons, explanations we offer in order to relate objects together into a pattern of systematic understanding, whether in science or common sense, are, just like the words we use, mere human projections. The experience of nausea is the realization that all words, descriptions and explanations are merely human constructs which have nothing whatever to do with real existence, though they serve a valuable utilitarian function.

In this sense, two divided realms of thought and object (being-for-itself and being-in-itself, essence and existence) are completely free from one another. Objects are free from our labels and we are free, as thinking beings, from objects. However we interpret the world the world remains what it is; and no interpretation of objects can determine that which is interpreting them (human thought), since the interpretation (essence) must spring from the interpreter (human existence). In this one case, and only in this case, existence precedes essence. In order for the world to have any influence on me, it must be related to me.

But relations exist only in human thought, not in reality. Therefore, sociological, psychological and physical determinism are merely theories. As such they are determined by me; I am not determined by them. The result is a world of total freedom.

> I understood the Nausea...I did not formulate my discoveries to myself. But I think it would be easy for me to put them in words now. The essential thing is contingency. I mean that one cannot define existence as necessity. To exist is simply to be there...Contingency is not a delusion, a probability which can be dissipated; it is the absolute...All is free, this park, this city and myself.[56]

As a result, anything can happen.

> What if something were to happen? What if something suddenly started throbbing? Then they would notice it was there and they'd think their hearts were going to burst...For example, the father of a family might go out for a walk, and, across the street, he'll see something like a red rag, blown towards him by the wind. And when the rag has gotten close to him he'll see that it is a crawling, skipping, a piece of writhing flesh rolling in the gutter, spasmodically shooting out spurts of blood.[57]

Since objects cannot be in any way related to one another they can only be conceived as atomistic.

> We were a heap of living creatures, irritated, embarrassed at ourselves, we hadn't the slightest reason to be there, none of us, each one, confused, vaguely alarmed, felt in the way in relation to the others. *In the way*: it was the only relationship I could establish between these trees, these gates, these stones. In vain I tried to count the chestnut trees, to locate them by their relationship to the Velleda, to compare their height with the height of the plane trees: each of them escaped the relationship in which I tried to enclose it, isolated itself, and overflowed. Of these relations (which I insisted on maintaining in order to delay the crumbling of the human world, measures, quantities, and directions)—I felt myself to be the arbitrator; they no longer had their teeth into things.[58]

Things are always more than the names, descriptions, and relations in terms of which we try to fix them in the orbit of our human concerns. The world transcends and overflows any human understanding of it. The irony is that we can experience reality, being-in-itself, but cannot describe it in any way whatever. Even words like "reality," "being," "existence" and "nothingness" can do no more than express the *feeling*, or *experience* of nausea and how it differs from our ordinary experience of the world. It cannot describe a world beyond description.

As Sartre makes clear in *Being and Nothingness*, even nothingness is a human concept which comes into the world with and only with human thought. In *Nausea* this is translated into Roquentin's experience of absurdity.

> I knew it was the World, the naked World suddenly revealing itself, and I choked with rage at this gross, absurd being. You couldn't even wonder where all that sprang from, or how it was that a world came into existence, rather than nothingness. It didn't make sense, the World was everywhere...There had been nothing *before* it. Nothing. There had never been a moment in which it could not have existed. That was what worried me: of course there was no reason for this flowing larva to exist. But it was impossible for it not to exist. It was unthinkable: to imagine nothingness you had to be there already, in the midst of the World, eyes wide open and alive; nothingness was only an idea in my head...This nothingness had not come *before* existence, it was an existence like any other and appeared after many others.[59]

The same absurd thought-object gap applies equally to any historical explanation of the world, in particular to Roquentin's historical account of Rollebon. Roquentin now sees that here, too, nothing can be verified; it is all a matter of subjective projection.

> I am beginning to believe that nothing can ever be proved. These are honest hypotheses which take the facts into account: but I sense so definitely that they come from me, and that they are simply a way of unifying my own knowledge...Slow, lazy, sulky, the facts adapt themselves to the rigour of the order I wish to give them; but it remains outside of them. I have the feeling of doing a work of pure imagination.[60]

This is more apparent in the case of those things we use as historical evidence for our hypotheses. Roquentin is examining a letter actually written by Rollebon. As evidence this object links Roquentin to Rollebon and the past in an elaborate interconnected web linking this piece of evidence to thousands of others.

But it exists as evidence only within a human point of view, a historical perspective concerned with the past. In itself, it is just a piece of paper with dried ink marks on it. It is only within the human gaze that it can mean something more. As people we can make it mean more by projecting our historical concerns upon it, but in itself it is just a thing—not even a thing from the past, but a thing existing *now*, sitting there on Roquentin's desk. In copying out a particular sentence from the letter, the whole elaborately constructed facade of history collapses before Roquentin's eyes.

"Care had been taken to spread the most sinister rumours..." I had thought out this sentence, at first it had been a small part of myself. Now it was inscribed on the paper, it took sides against me. I didn't recognize it any more...It was there, in front of me; in vain for me to trace some sign of its origin...I looked anxiously around me: the present, nothing but the present...The true nature of the present revealed itself: it was what exists, and all that was not present did not exist. The past did not exist. Not at all. Not in things, not even in my thoughts...Now I knew: things are entirely what they appear to be...and behind them...There is nothing.[61]

As we pointed out in our analysis of Sartre's conception of human thought in terms of "nothing," whatever depth or meaning the world has is creatively achieved by connecting what actually exists here and now with what does not exist, but is expected to do so or can be made to do so through human agency. Here Sartre has exerted enormous influence on New Realists, like Robbe-Grillet, who try to remove all human interpretation from description and present the flat, unemotional surface of existence. The sense of the historical past is simply the most vivid illustration of this distinction of "manifest-latent" content. Rollebon doesn't exist, nor indeed any of the past except as a current interest in our minds today.

I had said that the past did not exist. And suddenly, noiseless, M. de Rollebon had returned to his nothingness. I held his letters in my hands,...He is the one, I said,...who made these marks...Too late: these words had no more sense. Nothing existed but a bundle of yellow pages.[62]

So, too, with the idea of romantic adventure in life which Roquentin had been hoping in vain to recapture in his relationship with Anny. When he finally meets Anny, after a long separation, he discovers that she has given up completely the search for a sense of adventure and is now quite content to merely exist—like a pet animal, eating, sleeping, and passively enjoying whatever of life's pleasures happen to come along. He also discovers that the old adventure with Anny had been deliberately constructed by Anny, like a work of art.

Now Roquentin comes to see that there is no adventure in reality; adventure is nothing more than a human decision to dramatically link up events in our own minds. The events themselves have nothing to do with one another, certainly nothing dramatic or adventurous.

This feeling of adventure definitely does not come from events...It's rather the way in which the moments are linked together...You suddenly feel that time is passing, that each instant leads to another, this one to another one, and so on: that each instant is annihilated, and that it isn't worthwhile to hold it back, etc., etc. And then you attribute this property to events which appear to you in the instants; what belongs to the form you carry over to the content.[63]

The experience of nausea is unusual because of the constant pressure of normalcy against it, the pressure to see the world in terms of our meanings, explanations and purposes. Absurdity appears for a moment and then is as quickly gone, replaced by the mundane, friendly ordinary face of the world.

> But suddenly it became impossible for me to think of the existence of the root. It was wiped out, I could repeat in vain: it exists, it is still there..., it no longer meant anything. Existence is not something which lets being thought of from a distance; it must invade you suddenly, master you, weigh heavily on your heart like a great motionless beast—or else there is nothing more at all...Suddenly they existed, then suddenly they existed no longer: existence is without memory; of the vanished it retains nothing—not even a memory.[64]

The experience of existence must be pre-linguistic, pre-conceptual, visceral, and, since it is by definition beyond words and concepts, it is also beyond the reach of memory. It is a total assault on the person, an all-or-nothing proposition.

> I realized that there was no half-way house between non-existence and this flaunting abundance. If you existed, you had to *exist all the way*, as far as mouldiness, bloatedness, obscenity were concerned.[65]

Either we feel raw existence, that is, in Sartre's language, either we "exist," or else we sink back into words, concepts, into essence. Since the two are absolutely opposite, we cannot do both at once.

> There was so much, tons and tons of existence, endless: I stifled at the depths of this immense weariness. And then suddenly the park emptied as through a great hole, the World disappeared as it had come, or else I woke up—in any case, I saw no more of it; nothing was left but the yellow earth around me, out of which dead branches rose upward. I got up and went out. Once at the gate, I turned back. Then the garden smiled at me. I leaned against the gate and watched for a long time. The smile of the trees, of the laurel, meant something.[66]

Throughout the novel, Roquentin's experience of absurdity becomes more frequent and prolonged and more and more encompassing. Roquentin's attitude toward the nausea experience is also increasingly ambivalent. Nausea is the understanding of bare existence, and to understand this is to truly "exist" as a human being. On the one hand this frees us from the illusions, naiveté, and pretense of ordinary experience, but on the other hand it is a revolting, disgusting experience. There is an ambiguous envy in Roquentin's attitude toward those who remain within the blissful ignorance of the mundane outlook, comfortably projecting meaning onto the world, unaware that they are doing so.

> Each one of them has his little personal difficulty which keeps him from noticing that he exists.[67]

I would so like to let myself go, forget myself, sleep. But I can't, I'm suffocating: existence penetrates me everywhere, through the eyes, the nose, the mouth...And suddenly, suddenly, the veil is torn away, I have understood, I have seen...[68]

By seeing existence through the eyes of essence, ordinary people do not "exist," that is, do not confront pure existence face to face as Roquentin does, and it is this fascination with the "naked World" that draws Roquentin farther and farther into "the Nausea."

Never, until these last few days, had I understood the meaning of 'existence.' I was like the others...I said, like them, 'the ocean is green; that white speck up there is a seagull.' But I didn't feel that it existed...; usually existence hides itself. It is there, around us, in us, it is us, you can't say two words without mentioning it, but you can never touch it. When I believed I was thinking about it, I must believe that I was thinking nothing, my head was empty, or there was just one word in my head, the word 'to be.' Or else I was thinking of *belonging*, I was telling myself that the sea belonged to the class of green objects, or that the green was a part of the quality of the sea. Even when I looked at things, I was miles from dreaming that they existed: they looked like scenery to me..., they served me as tools, I foresaw their resistance...If anyone had asked me what existence was, I would have answered, in good faith, that it was nothing, simply an empty form which was added to external things without changing anything to their nature. And then all of a sudden, there it was, clear as day: existence had suddenly unveiled itself. It had lost the harmless look of an abstract category: it was the very paste of things..., the root, the park gates, the bench,...all that had vanished: the diversity of things, their individuality, were only an appearance, a veneer. This veneer had melted leaving soft, monstrous masses, all in disorder—naked, in a frightful, obscene nakedness.[69]

In this last passage we see the first sign of the curious transformation of heavy and dense, proliferating absurd matter into a soft, melting mush, or, the symbol in Nausea, fog. If words are divorced from objects, the objects can be described as anything. But if so, then they can *be* anything, so far as we *know*. But if they can be anything, then they are nothing definite. Without human consciousness there are no lines of demarcation, between objects, and without lines of demarcation there are no divisions distinguishing one object from another. And so their overt heaviness dissolves into the lightness described by Ionesco which we referred to at the outset.

What is peculiar in Sartre's treatment is the imposition of an intermediary fog or soup between the extremes of heavy, atomistic, mere things and pure emptiness which we find in Beckett and the later Ionesco.

Fog had filled the room: not the real fog, that had gone a long time ago—but the other, the one the streets were still full of, which came out of the walls and pavements. The inconsistency of inanimate objects! The books were still there, arranged in alphabetical order on the shelves with their brown and black backs and their labels...But...how can I explain it? Usually, powerful and squat, along with the stove, the green lamps, the wide windows, the ladders, they dam up the future. As long as you stay between these walls, whatever happens must happen on the right or the left of the stove...Thus these objects serve at least to fix the limits of probability. Today they fixed nothing at all: it seemed that their very existence was subject to doubt, that they had the greatest difficulty in passing from one instant to the next. I held the book I was reading tightly in my hands: but the most violent sensations went dead. Nothing seemed true; I felt surrounded by cardboard scenery which could quickly be removed. The world was waiting, holding its breath, making itself small—it was waiting for its convulsion, its Nausea,...I murmured: *Anything* can happen, *anything*.[70]

They did not want to exist, only they could not help themselves. So they quietly minded their own business; the sap rose up slowly through the structure, half reluctant and the roots sank slowly into the earth. But at each instant they seemed on the verge of leaving everything there and obliterating themselves.[71]

Much of this can be articulated, I think, in terms of dialectical stages in the order of our learning process. At first the cognitive identity of individual objects becomes detached, but the objects still exist as distinct entities and their spatial and temporal relations still hold the world together as a rational, if somewhat abstract, system of spatio-temporal relationships of physical objects. But, of course, this is only the thin edge of the wedge. As Kant pointed out several centuries earlier, even to think of things as objects, and to relate them together - spatially and temporally is no less a human achievement and a human imposition than the acts of labeling and classifying. This is Borges' thesis in his "New Refutation of Time" referred to in the first chapter. Aspects of the world are not themselves related into semi-permanent objects, but it is we who create these relationships. Similarly, objects are not themselves related to one another spatially or temporally, but it is we who assign these relationships to them for our own human purposes in making the world a more familiar and manageable place. Thus we realize that space, time and objecthood are human projections upon the world and that reality is something other than this, and, as these relationships cease to apply, objects begin to melt and dissolve into a soft, amorphous jelly.

It is through the extreme separation of thought and existence, ironically, that Roquentin finds a kind of solution to the problem of absurdity at the end of the novel by renouncing existence and embracing the world of pure essence as his only refuge. The problem with absurdity is the distance between things and our descriptions of them. But as Descartes discovered, this distance cannot touch pure thought, or purely cultural objects, such as circles, songs, and fictional stories. These "objects" only exist in description, so there is no gap in their case between description and object, and hence no absurdity.

This notion first appears in the contrast of a circle with the exposed root of the chestnut tree.

Absurd, irreducible; nothing—not even a profound, secret upheaval of nature —could explain it,...neither ignorance nor knowledge was important: the world of explanations and reasons is not the world of existence,...A circle is not absurd, it is clearly explained by the rotation of a straight segment around one of its extremities. But neither does a circle exist. This root, on the other hand, existed in such a way that I could not explain it. Knotty, inert, nameless,...in vain to repeat: "This is a root"—it didn't work anymore. I saw clearly that you could not pass from its function as a root, as a breathing pump, to that, to this hard and compact skin of a sea lion, to this oily, callous, headstrong look. The function explained nothing: it allowed you to understand generally that it was a root, but not *that* one at all.[72]

In the language of *Being and Nothingness*, the circle belongs to the human world of being-for-itself, while the tree root belongs to the nonhuman world of being-in-itself. Hence between the root and our human, functionalist account of it there is always a gap which thought can never fill, a gap which doesn't occur in the case of the circle since both the circle and our explanation of it occupy the same thought side of the great divide between thought and object. As Plato first pointed out in his account of the divided line in *The Republic*, when we transcribe an ideal object onto paper we never equate the marks on paper with the object to which those marks refer. The circle drawn on the blackboard is not "the circle." Printed numerals are not numbers, etc. There are many objects of human culture which we recognize *through* physical objects whose existence nonetheless transcends those physical objects. Poems, novels, music do not exist entirely in the pages on which they are printed.

In examining Rollebon's sentence Roquentin realized that the historical meaning can only exist in the mind, in an activity of mind Sartre later termed the unrealizing function of mind. A person who couldn't unrealize, that is, one who saw physical marks on paper *only* as physical marks on paper could never see a piece of paper as a description of a historical event, or as a drawing of a ship at sea, or as a poem about a lost love.

Similarly, in the case of music. The existence of the music cannot be identified completely with any physical object, such as a score, or a phonograph record. In one of Sartre's most intriguing examples Roquentin contemplates an old jazz recording of "Some of These Days." Like circles, the song doesn't "exist"—that is, does not exist over and above human interpretive thought.

> It does not exist...if I were to get up and rip this record from the table which holds it, if I were to break it in two, I wouldn't reach it. It is beyond—always beyond something, a voice, a violin note. Through layers and layers of existence, it veils itself, thin and firm, and when you want to seize it, you find only existants, you butt against existants devoid of sense. It is behind them; I don't even hear it, I hear sounds, vibrations in the air which unveil it. It does not exist because it has nothing superfluous: it is all the rest in relation to it, which is superfluous. It is.[73]

If the tree root is in itself pure existence, then the music in itself is pure essence. It does not "exist"; it "is." And in the same sense Roquentin says, in the following sentence, "And I, too, wanted to be." Just as we can "exist" in absurd awareness of existence, so we can "be" in an ideal world of pure essence. Renouncing both naive absorption in the world and the "existence" of nausea, Roquentin here turns his back on objective reality in favor of a world of pure thought which absurdity cannot touch.

Thus, in the end, instead of renouncing writing altogether, Roquentin gives up historical writing for fiction as the ideal escape from physical existence. Unlike the historians, who pretend to be writing about the real world, things as they really happened in the past, the fiction writer cuts all ties with the existing world in favor of a world within his own mind. Unlike the historian, therefore, the fiction writer frees himself from the absurd gap between description and reality, essence and existence. It is senseless to try to corroborate a fictional account with reality because fiction doesn't refer to any actual reality. As Rilke urges in *Duino Elegies*, if we cannot return to a humanly interpreted world in which we see physical reality through human eyes, then it is better to turn to objects of pure thought.

If we can no longer achieve the essence-existence synthesis, we had better strive for essence alone. At least this beats nausea.

> Another type of book, I don't quite know which kind—but you would have to guess, behind the printed words, behind the pages, at something which would not exist, which would be above existence. A story, for example, something that could never happen, an adventure. It would have to be beautiful and hard as steel to make people ashamed of their existence.[74]

If this sounds like idealism, which it surely does, we are brought back to our initial dichotomy—either dualism or idealism, there is no resolution of this dilemma in Sartre.

Of course, Sartre's position is not really idealistic since the ideal world into which he retreats is still contrasted with the real world of sheer existence (which the idealist would not countenance). But can he, or anyone, reject existence in favor of a world of pure essence? Only if the two are as utterly distinct as Sartre contends they are. But, as Camus shows us very clearly, they are *not* absolutely separated from one another. Though none of our interpretations match reality completely or exactly, some obviously come closer than others.

For all its admitted inadequacy, to describe a seat as a seat is better than describing it as a sunflower. Words are not the same as objects, but they can *describe* objects, and though words can never describe objects *completely*, or exhaustively, they can be *relatively* successful. Nor is fiction entirely removed from the ordinary world of existence. A story is constructed of elements (people, cities, streets, rivers, beer glasses, etc.) lifted out of a context of real existence, and the mood or theme of the story reflects back on that real world from which those elements were borrowed. The story of the wicked witch, for example, is based on the idea children already have of old women in the real world, and may in turn create a negative bias in the child's mind against those elderly women he or she comes in contact with in everyday life.

It is interesting that the succeeding generation of writers who were greatly influenced by Sartre, such as Robbe-Grillet and Butor, criticize Sartre, not for his misguided *attempt* to describe reality stripped of all human meaning, but for his (and Camus') *failure* to provide this neutral description. Thus the New Realists press on toward what I have argued is the illusory goal of a neutral description of the thing-in-itself, pure existence stripped of all essence.

Robbe-Grillet, for example, holds that while all previous writers believe they are realists, none of them actually are. All so-called realism is simply a form on anthropomorphism. *Old* forms of writing *seem* unrealistic simply because we have become familiar with their stylistic conventions and thus aware of them *as* conventional, and hence as unrealistic. *New* forms of writing appear *realistic* because they abandon these tired, worn-out conventions which we recognize as conventional in favor of conventions which are too new to be recognized as conventional. Later, of course, the new conventions lose their transparency and we see them for what they are—conventions, not reality.

We will see this theme of alternating transparency and opaqueness of stylistic conventions developed further in Ionesco and Beckett.

> All writers believe they are realists...All of them are right...; each one has different ideas about reality...It is easy, moreover, to understand why literary revolutions have always been made in the name of realism. When a form of writing has lost its initial vitality..., when it has become a vulgar recipe, an academic mannerism which its followers respect only out of routine or laziness, without ever questioning its necessity, then it is indeed a return to the real which constitutes the arraignment of the dead formulas and the search for new forms capable of continuing the effort. The discovery of reality will continue only if we abandon outworn formulas...What is the use...if it only concludes in a new formalism soon as sclerotic as the old one was?...Nothing in art is ever won *for good*...But the movement of these evolutions and revolutions constitutes its perpetual renaissance.[75]

Thus, it is a mistake to impose on reality that form of anthropomorphism which was so admired in older writers like Balzac, who established the mood or tone of a story by anthropomorphized descriptions of inanimate objects, such as the furniture in a room. Traditional critics

> make it the sole...criterion of all praise as of all reproach, to identify...a precise reflection on man, his situation in the world...with a certain anthropocentric atmosphere, vague but imbuing all things, giving the world it's so-called *significance*, investing it from within by a more or less disingenuous network of sentiments and thoughts.[76]

The new critic, on the other hand, will reject all human projection, or anthropomorphism.

> He sees [things], but he refuses to appropriate them, he refuses to maintain any suspect understanding with them, any complicity; he asks nothing of them...[77]
>
> The world around us turns back into a smooth surface, without significance, without soul, without values;...we find ourselves once again facing things.[78]
>
> Instead of this universe of "signification" (psychological, social, functional), we must try then, to construct a world both more solid and more immediate. Let it be first of all by their presence that objects and gestures establish themselves.[79]

Although this sounds remarkably like the program of Sartre and Camus to honestly face reality stripped of all human projection, all human illusions, Robbe-Grillet criticizes Sartre and Camus for *continuing* that romantic projection of human concerns onto the world, the "pathetic fallacy" of traditional fictional narrative. And, of course, Robbe-Grillet is correct. As we have seen, the tragedy of absurdity can only arise from the privative comparison of reality with man's hopes and desires. Only with the expectation of what we *want* of reality does reality's indifference to that expectation strike us tragically as a *rejection*, or *refusal*. It is this lingering romantic humanism in absurdist writing that Robbe-Grillet attacks. In *The Stranger*, for example, he says,

> *existence* in it is characterized by the presence of interior distances, and...*nausea* is man's unhappy visceral penchant for these distances...Is this really to take the "side" of things, to represent them from "their own point of view"?[80]

For Robbe-Grillet absurdity is still too humanly attached. It presupposes a suspect metaphysical synthesis of essence and existence. We must overcome the tendency toward this metaphysical romanticism, transcending the absurd longing for meaning toward a genuinely neutral confrontation with reality, which is neither rational nor irrational, but simply a-rational.

> Is it a question of what is called the *absurd*? Certainly not...It is, that's all. But there is a risk for the writer: with the suspicion of absurdity the metaphysical danger returns. Non-sense, a-causality, and the void irresistibly attract higher worlds and super natures...[81]

But *can* we escape all human subjectivity and projection in our approach to reality? I am convinced we cannot, but the reader can judge for himself whether or not Robbe-Grillet succeeds in the following passages, or whether, like Sartre and Camus, he simply projects his own attitude of human indifference. In *Le Voyeur*, for example, he seems to continue the kind of neutral, geometrical description Sartre begins in *Nausea* of the ink-bottle box (..."it's a parallelepiped rectangle, it opens—"), though in this case it is a description of a waterfront pier.

The stone rim—an oblique, sharp edge formed by two intersecting perpendicular planes: the vertical embankment perpendicular to the quay and the ramp leading to the top of the pier—was continued along its upper side at the top of the pier by a horizontal line extending straight toward the quay.[82]

Does this describe the "naked World" or does it express Robbe-Grillet's cold, hard-edged, purely visual attitude toward things? Or, let the reader judge for himself the neutral objectivity of this more general statement of a "stubborn, defiant" realty.

But the world is neither significant nor absurd. It *is*, quite simply...And suddenly the obviousness of this strikes us with irresistible force. All at once the whole splendid construction collapses; opening our eyes unexpectedly, we have experienced...the shock of this stubborn reality we were pretending to have mastered. Around us, defying the noisy pack of our animistic or protective adjectives, things *are there*.[83]

Notes

1. Mary Warnock, *Existentialism* (London: Oxford University Press, 1970), p. 1.
2. John Wild, *The New Empiricism* (Englewood Cliffs: Prentice-Hall, 1962), p. 427.
3. Jean-Paul Sartre, *Being and Nothingness*, Hazel Barnes, trans. (New York: Philosophical Library, 1956). p. xlv.
4. *Ibid.*, p. xlvii.
5. *Ibid.*, p. xlix.
6. Klaus Hartman, *Sartre's Ontology* (Evanston: Northwestern University Press, 1966), p, 33.
7. Warnock, *op. cit.*, p. 196.
8. Sartre, *op. cit.*, p. lxi.
9. *Ibid.*, pp. lxiii-lxvi.
10. *Ibid.*, p. 7.
11. *Ibid.*, p. 76.
12. Martin Heidegger, *Being and Time*, John McQuarrie and Edward Robinson, trans. (London: S.C.M. Press, 1962) p. 78.
13. *Ibid.*, p. 95.
14. *Ibid.*, p. 97.
15. *Ibid.*
16. *Ibid.*, pp. 188-192.
17. Sartre, *op. cit.*, p. 18.
18. *Ibid.* p. 24.
19. *Ibid.*, p. 44.
20. *Ibid.*, pp. 173-175.
21. *Ibid.*, p. 181.
22. *Ibid.*, p. 179.
23. *Ibid.*, p. 177.
24. *Ibid.*, p. 81.
25. *Ibid.* pp. 82-83.
26. *Ibid.*, p. 202.
27. *Ibid.*, p. 83.
28. *Ibid.*, p. 181.
29. *Ibid.*, p. 197.
30. *Ibid.*, p. 218.
31. *Ibid.*, p. 619.
32. *Ibid.*, p. 617.
33. *Ibid.*, pp. 171-172.
34. *Ibid.*, p. 624.
35. Wild, *op. cit.*, p. 143.
36. Hartmann, *op. cit.*, p. 40.
37. *Ibid.*, p. 39.
38. *Ibid., p. 135.*

39. Jean-Paul Sartre, *Nausea*, Lloyd Alexander, trans. (New York: New Directions, 1964) p. 1.
40. *Ibid*.
41. *Ibid*., pp. 19-20.
42. *Ibid*., p. 2.
43. *Ibid*., p. 3.
44. Roger Fry, *Vision and Design* (London: Chatto and Windus, 1920).
45. Jean-Paul Sartre, "Existentialism and Humanism," Philip Mairet, trans., in Morton White, ed., *The Age of Analysis* (New York: Mentor Books, 1955), p. 122.
46. *Ibid*., p. 123.
47. Sartre, *Nausea, op. cit*., p. 10.
48. *Ibid*., p. 122.
49. *Ibid*., p. 98.
50. *Ibid*., p. 125.
51. *Ibid*., pp. 126-127.
52. *Ibid*., p. 169.
53. *Ibid*., p. 130.
54. *Ibid*., pp. 130-131.
55. Henri Bergson, *An Introduction to Metaphysics* T.E. Hulme, trans. (New York: The Liberal Arts Press 1949), p. 50.
56. Sartre, *Nausea, op. cit*., p. 131.
57. *Ibid*., p. 159.
58. *Ibid*., p. 128.
59. *Ibid*., p. 134.
60. *Ibid*., p. 13.
61. *Ibid*., pp. 95-96.
62. *Ibid*., p. 96.
63. *Ibid*., p. 56.
64. *Ibid*., pp. 132-133.
65. *Ibid*., p. 128.
66. *Ibid*., p. 135.
67. *Ibid*., p. 111.
68. *Ibid*., p. 126.
69. *Ibid*., p. 127.
70. *Ibid*., pp. 76-77.
71. *Ibid*., p. 133.
72. *Ibid*., p. 129.
73. *Ibid*., p. 175.
74. *Ibid*., p. 178.
75. Alain Robbe-Grillet, "From Realism to Reality," in *For A New Novel*, Richard Howard, trans. (New York: Grove Press, 1965), pp. 158-159.
76. Robbe-Grillet, "Nature, Humanism, Tragedy," *ibid*., PP. 51-52.
77. *Ibid*. , p. 52
78. *Ibid*., p. 71.

79. Robbe-Grillett, "A Future for the Novel," *ibid.*, p. 21.
80. Robbe-Grillet, "Nature, Humanism, Tragedy," *op. cit.*, p. 68.
81. Robbe-Grillet, "From Realism to Reality," *op. cit.* pp. 163-164.
82. Robbe-Grillet, "A Future for the Novel," *op. cit.* p. 19Za.
83. *Ibid.*

CHAPTER FOUR: IONESCO

Ionesco develops many of the themes of absurdity discussed in previous chapters, but with a greater balance between the heavy and light phases of absurdity and with a decided movement, in the evolution of his work, from the oppressive heaviness of absurdity toward its euphoric lightness, a movement we will see carried still further in Beckett.

Most of his work appears to revolve around these predominantly metaphysical themes, as Ionesco himself has frequently pointed out.

> Two fundamental states of consciousness are at the root of all my plays. Sometimes one dominates, sometimes the other; sometimes they are mingled. These two basic feelings are those of evanescence on the one hand, and of heaviness on the other;...of light and of heavy shadows...All of us have felt at times that the world is made of some dreary substance, that walls no longer have any thickness. We seem to see through everything in a universe without space, made up only of light and color; all our existence, all the history of the world becomes at this moment useless, senseless, impossible. When one does not succeed in going beyond this first step of disorientation..., the sensation of evanescence results in a feeling of anguish, a sort of dizziness...But all this can just as well become euphoric: Anguish is suddenly transformed into liberty; nothing is important any longer but the wonder of being...This state of consciousness is very rare...I am most often under the dominance of the opposite feeling: Lightness changes to heaviness...; the world weighs heavily; the universe crushes me. A curtain, an insuperable wall comes between me and the world...; matter fills everything, takes up all space; annihilates all liberty under its weight; the horizon shrinks and the world becomes a stifling dungeon...[1]

Practically all of Ionesco's work relates directly or indirectly to a recurring experience which he had as an adolescent and which he refers to frequently as the most crucial of his life.

> I felt everything was emptying away...It was like a release, things lost their weight around me, I was cutting adrift from things and they were losing all

arbitrary, conventional significance, all that enormous mass of meanings of all sorts...amidst which I had been trapped, that labyrinth of tangled paths in which I had lost my way. Everything was now pervaded by a dazzling light, and...I became aware, with limitless joy, that everything exists...in a heavenly light, delicate, fragile...Yet in one instant things became once again heavy, opaque and dark...I myself seemed to grow heavy again, dense, heavy as lead, a mere thing that emptiness can eat away.[2]

Unlike Sartre and Camus, Ionesco has developed a style of writing which more perfectly matches the absurdist content. Instead of *asserting* that consciousness has become detached from reality, Ionesco *demonstrates* this in a use of language which is itself detached and disjointed. Rather than *describe* the psychological moods of oppressive heaviness and evanescent lightness, Ionesco *buries* his characters beneath masses of furniture or has them walking on air. Rather than argue, as Roquentin does in *Nausea*, that things can become anything, eggs actually metamorphose in Ionesco's plays into people, who then become slabs of meat, etc. The *form* of expression, in other words, has become inseparable from its content. As Camus put it, the philosophical ideas have been thoroughly integrated into concrete images.

Ionesco himself puts it this way.

> The philosopher thinks by philosphizing, the painter thinks by painting...A playwright is a man who thinks by writing his dramas or comedies...The dialogue and movement of the stage are the author's particular way of exploring reality...The language of literature...is by no means an illustration or vulgarization of some other, superior language...It's often the artist's language which stimulates and organizes the thought of others, which creates new ways of seeing the world.[3]

This new form gives Ionesco's work a power and directness lacking in even the best fiction of Sartre and Camus. Ionesco makes the point himself in an almost brutal way, though modestly omitting his own name from those with whom he contrasts Sartre and Camus.

> [Sartre and Camus] were talking about absurdity and death, but...they never really lived these themes,...they did not feel them within themselves in an almost irrational, visceral way...All this was not deeply inscribed in their language...With Adamov and Beckett it really is a very naked reality that is conveyed through the apparent dislocation of language.[4]

Unfortunately, however, this very synthesis of form and content makes it exceedingly difficult to "translate" or even understand his plays. As a result the metaphysical thrust of his work is often misunderstood as a sociological concern with the failure of human communication in modern society, despite Ionesco's repeated protestations to the contrary.

In the first part of this chapter we will work through this misunderstanding as a convenient way of exploring Ionesco's conception of the absurd. Language, of course, is an important theme in all of Ionesco's work, and the dislocation of language is certainly the single most striking feature of his unusual style. In addition, it is this aspect of his work which dominates his earliest period (the first three plays, especially *The Bald Soprano*) which established Ionesco as a writer of the first rank. Add to this the fact that the communication theme was introduced to the English-speaking public by no less a critic than Kenneth Tynan, and we can begin to appreciate the tenacity of this persistent interpretation. In the 1950's Ionesco was introduced to many who had never read or seen his plays as a nihilist obsessed with the breakdown of society following the second World War. Ionesco himself offers a very different interpretation of his own work.

Like all great art, Ionesco's plays operate on many different, interpenetrating levels at once—social, psychological, historical, religious and philosophical. Thus, for example, the image of heaviness can legitimately be understood in some of his plays as social conformity (*Victims of Duty*, *A Stroll in the Air*, *Jack* and *The Lesson*), and in others, as human brutality (*The Killer*, *Amedee*, *The Lesson* and *Victims of Duty*), and in some of these plays, as both. Nonetheless, it is the metaphysical dimension which forms the underlying structure of the plays in the light of which the other, subordinate themes must be understood.

It is not ordinary human communication which has broken down, but only, as in *Nausea*, the ultimate metaphysical failure of words to communicate reality absolutely, as it is in itself. It is not a historical change which has suddenly affected the ability of people to communicate verbally which concerns Ionesco, but a profound reflection on the absolute limits of any language to describe reality completely, as it is in itself.

In *The Observer* 1958 Tynan ("Ionesco, Man of Destiny?")said that Ionesco's plays, in particular *The Bald Soprano*, represented a rejection of reality where all communication was impossible and words were completely meaningless. In *Conversations with Eugene Ionesco* (not translated into English until 1971) Ionesco roundly refutes this interpretation of his work. We are *not* socially isolated, but do quite easily communicate with one another.

> About the crisis of language today: actually no such crisis exists...There's no such thing as the impossibility of communication, except as a single case: between me and myself. Socially, everything is communicable...Words are there, clear and precise, to say what there is to be said. We deliberately conceal our thoughts, while revealing them...What there is to be said can be said. What needs to be said, that which is existence and not just a thing, this alone refuses to be said.[5]

As in *Nausea* it is only that *extraordinary* reflection on the relation of thought and language to reality which necessarily evades linguistic description. *Ordinary* communication is not only possible but easily accessible. In *The Bald Soprano*, Ionesco says,

> I wasn't concerned with the impossibility of communication or with solitude. Quite the contrary. I am in favor of solitude...It's easy to communicate. Man is never really alone; and if he's unhappy, it's because he's never really alone.[6]

What Ionesco is expressing in this play and others is the totally transparent absorption of most people in their blindly projected linguistic and conceptual formulae on the world, a projection which makes the world familiar, commonplace and mundane, an absorption in the world which makes ordinary communication possible but which also makes us blind to what Sartre called "existence." In Ionesco's work he contrasts the naive state of ordinary consciousness with the sheer wonder and novelty of the world when we become conscious of that projection, distancing ourselves from it so that forms of communication cease to be naively accepted and become, for the first time, strange and opaque. From that point of view it seems amazing that people can live and communicate so easily and nonchalantly within such a conventional world.

> There is a degree of communication between people...They understand one another. That's what's so astounding...If, intentionally, you put yourself completely outside everything, on one floor above what's going on, if you look at people as though they were part of a show and you yourself were a being from another world looking down on what's happening here, then you wouldn't understand anything, words would be hollow, everything would be empty. You can get this feeling if you block your ears when you're watching people dancing...Their movements are senseless. I write plays to express this feeling of astonishment.[7]

Clearly, the failure of communication is not to be understood on an ordinary mundane level, but as a theatrical device for *exposing* that mundane outlook in which words naively attach to objects, and to reveal in its place that wonderful and terrifying "naked Reality" which appears once the ordinary, comfortable acceptance of linguistic conventions has been stripped away.

> Once people have accepted existence; once they've moved inside it, everything stops being amazing or absurd. Once they've accepted the idea of being on the inside they start to communicate. When you step outside, move away and take a good look, you stop communicating.[8]

As with Roquentin in *Nausea*, on the ordinary mundane level there is no problem naming and describing a streetcar seat, a tree root or a glass of beer. This is done as a matter of course precisely because the relationship of words to objects is never called into question, but is naively taken for granted, words simply attaching to objects. Once that relation is called into question both the word and the object take on a new look quite independently of its association with the other. As we noted in the first chapter, a meaningful world is the product of the synthesis of essence and existence, while their separation is the cause of absurdity and meaninglessness. Only in that extraordinary experience of their separation do objects appear strange and words lose their meanings.

> I wanted this play [*The Bald Soprano*] to express the feeling of strangeness that the world inspires in me. The characters are completely emptied of their content; so are their words. For instance, you may say, or hear, the word "horse." You can understand the phrase, "I am getting on my horse." But it's possible for the word to get emptied of its content, for you no longer to hear anything but the sound, "horse, horse, horse." Sometimes it's not only the sound, it's all reality that's emptied of its content.[9]

Thus, far from *deploring* the failure of ordinary communication, Ionesco is trying to *create* it! He attempts to jar us out of a familiar world where ordinary communication is possible into a strange, new world in which language stands at a distance from reality.

At the same time, however, absorption in a commonly accepted world which makes ordinary communication possible thwarts the revelation and communication of genuinely personal insights into the world. Thus the conditions which make ordinary communication possible are precisely those which prevent the more profound disclosure between individuals—that truly personal communication which Sartre argues is simply impossible. Carried to an extreme, *complete* acceptance of and absorption in the linguistic conventions which make projection possible reduces all language to the level of the cliché and robs language of any personal discovery or individual interpretation. To focus sharply on the transparency of unthinking, naive projection of conventional, mass meaning, Ionesco has reduced the characters in *The Bald Soprano* to this impersonal level of cliché.

> They don't want to communicate, they have no desire to...They don't think...They inhabit the world of the impersonal, the world of the collective...In short, the characters in my plays are people who pronounce slogans to save themselves the trouble of thinking.[10]

In the language of *Nausea*, they don't "exist." By reducing his characters to total transparency, Ionesco shocks his audience into a virtual state of complete opacity in which we see, perhaps for the first time, the conventionality of our own language, our thought, our feelings—even our most "private" feelings, and we see clearly that words are not attached to objects but exist altogether independently. On a more superficial level the distancing affected by Ionesco's plays might make us see only the arbitrary constructions of obviously conformist clichés, making us feel superior to people who engage in this form of trite conversation, but on a deeper level we see that this affects all forms of thought and speech, from the most banal to the most profound. All are human constructions, reality transcends them all.

Even the theory of absurdity, oddly enough. This is not "the one truth" which shows all other theories to be shallow or false, but is itself simply one more humanly constructed interpretation of the world from a particular human standpoint. All views of the world are absurd in this sense, even the absurdist view, as Ionesco is well aware. "It is absurd to say that the world is absurd."[11] As Camus also was aware, to call the world absurd presupposes some absolute stance from which to make this judgment, a stance explicitly denied by the absurdist point of view.

> If I denounce the absurd, I transcend the absurd by the very fact of my denunciation. For by what right should I declare a thing to be absurd, unless I had before me the image...of something that was *not* absurd.[12]

But this is the very transcendence which the absurdist position denies. "We cannot soar above it all, we cannot be superior to the Divinity...That's a piece of folly."[13]

Thus, Ionesco's view of communication is considerably richer and more complex than is generally recognized. Although ordinary communication takes place within, and even requires, that naive absorption in social stereotypes in which linguistic forms are simply transparent, ideal communication, Ionesco believes, exists only within a tension between conventional forms of expression and individual perception. In order to reveal some new aspect of reality, a form of speech must break with the stereotype and explore the world from a fresh, individual perspective.

But this new form of expression will remain unintelligible and opaque until it is translated into more conventional symbols or until the new form of communication becomes commonly accepted. But in either case, the freshness of the original insight tends to get lost in a new stereotype. In order to break through *this* stereotype to a new vision of reality, new forms of expression must be sought, and so the cycle begins again. It is within this tension of old and new, originality and cliché, transparent and opaque that Ionesco holds important communication takes place.

A form of expression which is traditional is scarcely noticed as a form of speech but becomes a transparent window through which the object appears. But a form of expression which is new and not yet accepted, like Ionesco's own plays, attracts attention to itself, becoming therefore opaque and difficult to understand. With understanding and acceptance of the new conventions comes communication, but this eventually leads to the cliché.

> Things are incommunicable in the beginning because they have not yet been communicated, and incommunicable in the end because the expressions that prop them up have been worn out.[14]

> When a thing or an idea is fashionable, it's often mere repetition—a cliché emptied of its content, its truth, its discovery. On the other hand, obviously every work is rooted in time...the time it's written in...which is why all worthwhile literary works stand at the crossroads between time and eternity.[15]

It is not the form of speech itself which is either meaningful or meaningless, but the way in which it is received by human speakers. The very same form of words can be at one time a breathtaking revelation and at another time a banal cliché. Meaningful forms of thought and language must therefore be constantly refreshed, revitalizing themselves, since, however significant, they eventually gravitate toward the accepted, the familiar and the trite. In *Present Past, Past Present* Ionesco speaks of the evolution of all forms of speech from revelation to cliché as the product of the inevitable transparency which occurs when forms of thought and speech become conventionalized.

> [We are] lost in the impersonal world of the "one"; it is necessary, therefore, to put everything in question again, it is necessary to reconsider the very basis of speech, to go back to axioms...But each new system of expression, once it has become a convention, or an acquisition, or a cliché, or an ideology, loses its essential truth. Life becomes a word.[16]

For Ionesco the primary purpose of art is to guide this necessary reviving of language, in which words no longer revolve around themselves, but become instruments for new ways of seeing the world.

> Every work of art is the materialization of an almost indescribable personal experience, it is putting a language in question again, it is a rediscovery or a discovery of the world seen by the poet for the first time. The poet cannot invent new words...of course. But the handling of the words...renews them. The reader...must in turn be able to receive this new virginity.[17]

Of course, as Ionesco realizes, the same degenerating process must affect his own work, and indeed is already occurring.

> Alas, all the sincerity, all the authenticity, all the truth, everything that I have lived and felt all by myself is already disappearing in clichés, expressions that belong to the public patrimony and to men in general.[18]

Elsewhere Ionesco remarks on the way in which the radical dislocating techniques of absurdist writing is fast becoming an accepted convention.

> What once looked like the dislocation of language now seems very clear to us. The way of expressing a certain disaster is starting to congeal again and increasing the distance between us and the disaster. This disjointed language has reconstructed itself in another way; or rather, the dislocation, having as it were congealed, now looks to us like a new coherence...perhaps I should say, like a new crust, an armour. This is why the great themes have always to be reworked, relived, re-examined.[19]

As Robbe-Grillet also points out, even the attempt to reject the "profound transcendent" in favor of the "immediate significance" of things risks...transcendence (metaphysics loves a vacuum, and rushes into it like smoke up a chimney); for, within immediate significance, we find the absurd, which is theoretically non-significance, but which as a matter of fact leads immediately to a new transcendence; and the infinite fragmentation of immediate meaning thus establishes a new totality, quite as dangerous, quite as futile.[20]

Language can communicate, then, but it need not; and meaningful discourse is certainly not automatic. Thus Ionesco frequently distinguishes ordinary polite talk from meaningful discourse.

One can speak without thinking; for this we have clichés...The only true thought is living thought.[21]

Sometimes he marks the distinction as that between "language in general" and the "spoken word" of the individual.

There is language in general, on the one hand, and the spoken speech of the individual, on the other. I am not in language in general. I am in the spoken word.[22]

And, like Camus, he often contrasts the inadequacy of words with the power of images.

It's as though by writing books I had worn out all symbols without getting to the heart of them. They no longer speak to me with living voices. Words have killed images or concealed them...Words are not speech.[23]

Images are so concise, so profound and complex, and words are so inadequate to translate living thought.[24]

Words "hide" or "mask" reality because, through the adoption of linguistic conventions, we confuse word and object, the word then replaces the object and words begin to stand between us and the world they are meant to reveal. The situation is not hopeless, however, since words can reveal aspects of reality if they are understood as what they are, namely conventions for focusing on a particular aspect of the world as seen from a particular human point of view.

What is needed, then, is a new understanding of the relationship of thought and language to reality, which Ionesco suggests in several of his prose works. First we must realize that we cannot grasp reality as it is in itself, that reality and our understanding of it are always and necessarily distinct.

The world in itself is not knowable. Because there is only *consciousness of the world*, which means that for Husserl, as for Kant, reality in itself cannot be grasped...; it exists but it does not exist *for me*.[25]

Like the other Absurdists, Ionesco is thus a realist and a dualist. There is a reality independent of us and there are human forms of thought and speech which highlight facets of that reality from predetermined human points of view. But word and object, thought and reality are never identical and never completely coincide; each transcends the other.

> The philosopher thinks by philosophizing. The painter thinks by painting; painting is the form of his thought, it is his thought...This simply proves that reality, or the world, appears under a multiplicity of aspects to the many and various temperaments of men,...In my view, a playwright is a man who thinks by writing his dramas or comedies...Knowledge...is also construction...since any knowledge, any encounter between self and the world is a projection of the self into...the world, a projection, that's to say a pattern, a shape, an architecture...A whole world is built up, or disclosed, as the artist writes it and thinks it.[26]

Our *view* of the world, then, is a human creation, but if, in our blind acceptance of that view, we forget its human invention, we confuse word and object and get locked into the staid, linguistically demarcated world from which Ionesco's plays seek to release us.

It is important to realize that for Ionesco, unlike Sartre and Camus, this release can be a joyous, euphoric experience, acting as a counterbalance to the leaden heaviness of absurdity we found in Sartre. Once we realize the creativity of human thought and its distinction from reality, we see things as divorced from their names and hence as alien and heavy, but, for Ionesco at any rate, we can also experience this as a release from a static, regimented, collectivized world into a fresh vision of reality as absolutely transcending all linguistic boundaries, demarcations, limits and therefore as limitless and in that sense, empty or transparent.

The parallels to mystic exaltation are unmistakable and will be discussed later. In one of his autobiographical recollections of that crucial boyhood experience to which much of his later work relates he writes,

> Once, long ago, I was sometimes overcome by a sort of grace, a euphoria. It was as if...every notion, every reality was emptied of its content. After this emptiness, after this dizzy spell, it was as if I found myself suddenly at the center of pure, ineffable existence; it was as if things had freed themselves of all arbitrary labels...It did not seem to me that I was the victim of a nominalist crisis; on the contrary, I think that I became one with the one essential reality, when, along with an immense, serene joy, I was overcome by what I might call the...certainty of being, the certainty that the social order, politics, language, organized thought, systems and systematizations...were pure nothingness...[27]

In this last sentence, we get a clear idea of the forces of social conformity opposing the vision of euphoric lightness which occupy a central place in many of his plays.

As a result of this vision, he goes on to say, word and object become detached, each standing out from the other, revealing both as strange and new. Sometimes this dislocation of word and object was brought about in the kind of game children often play, repeating a word over and over again until it sounds "funny," that is, until the word-sound separates itself off from its customary meaning.

> Often this began in an unexpected way, when I would pronounce the most ordinary word; paper for example. It was as if the word disappeared, a word that had replaced a reality that it had imprisoned and hidden...I became totally conscious that meanings, that words are arbitrary, mere labels.[28]

As human meaning recedes from reality, the systematic architecture it imposes on reality also retreats, resulting in a kind of emptiness, not empty like a new house, but, as toward the end of *Nausea*, empty of all human demarcations separating objects, marking them off from one another.

> Walls collapsed, definitions were dislocated...The names of things drew apart from things...Our reality broke up into thousands of pieces, went up in smoke, then the smoke blew away, and there was nothing now but this immense sun...Everything that I had thought to be solidly built was only castles of cards that had tumbled down.[29]

> It began with the feeling that space was emptying itself of its material heaviness...Notions were freed of their content. Objects became transparent, permeable; they were no longer obstacles and it seemed as if one could pass through them...I felt as if I had received a blow right in the heart...dissolving the limits of things, breaking down definitions, abolishing the meaning of things...as the light seemed to make the walls and the house I was walking by disappear.[30]

But the exhilarating experience of lightness can be just as suddenly replaced by our everyday, mundane experience of the world.

> It lasted a few seconds...[then] the miraculous evidence vanished. The sky became just a sky...Things, the walls, took on their usual form again...All that was left was this world of...shadows,...the everyday world took its usual place again.[31]

A major theme in Ionesco's latest plays is how to achieve and retain this experience of lightness.

Returning to the point from which we started, we do have more or less adequate means of communicating with one another, exploring, describing, enumerating the things in our world. But it is this very facility which hides us from the fact that the world transcends all these systems of explanation. Ionesco's work is designed to bring about that unusual experience in which we see the humanly based conventionality of all our thoughts and interpretations and see the world as transcending altogether human modes of expression.

> There are times when the world seems emptied of all expression, all content. There are times when we look at it as though we'd just that moment been born, and then it looks astonishing and inexplicable. Of course, we have plenty of explanations to hand!...Only these systems fade the moment we have this primordial feeling...[32]

The concept of the original freshness of our perception of the world is, of course, a Romantic view. As children everything is new and wonderful; then, as Wordsworth pointed out, as we grow older we take things for granted and the wonderful freshness of the world is lost in a dull familiarity. "The end of childhood is when things cease to astonish us. When the world seems familiar...one has become adult."[33] Yet as adults we recover an odd sort of second childhood, in which we pretend that the world is really just as comfortable and familiar as our projected systems of thought and language have made it out to be.

> Then, I believe most human beings forget what they have understood, recover another sort of childhood that, for some of them, for a very few, can last all their lives. It is not a true childhood, but a kind of forgetting.[34]

In this essentially Romantic terminology, the purpose of Ionesco's plays is quite simply to recover that lost insight of the child. As he records in an old diary, after adolescence Ionesco himself experienced the dazzling light vision less and less frequently, though, throughout his adult life, he could occasionally recover it.

> I sometimes wake up, become conscious, realize that I am surrounded by things and by people, and if I look closely at the sky or the wall or the earth or the hand writing or not writing, I have the impression that I'm seeing it all for the first time, then, as it were, the first time, I wonder, or I ask, "what's that?"[35]

This is often followed by the experience of evanescent lightness.

> Then...a sudden light, a great blinding light floods over everything, obliterating all meaning, all our preoccupations, all those shadows, that's to say all those walls that make us imagine limits, distinctions, separations, significances.[36]

The experience of reality is not, then, the experience of some new Transcendent Absolute beyond this ordinary world, but simply the plain, ordinary world stripped of its conventional conceptual and linguistic formulae.

> Nothing seems more surprising to me than that which is banal; the surreal is there, within grasp of our hands, in everyday conversation.[37]

But because we normally identify reality with *conceptually interpreted* reality, this new experience can equally be described as unreal or a-real.

> A second possible attitude: to consider reality as something beyond reality, to be aware of it not as surrealistic but as unfamiliar, miraculous, a-real. Reality of the unreal, unreality of the real.[38]

The constant theme in all of Ionesco's plays, then, is metaphysical absurdity, the separation of language from reality and a vision of that reality stripped of its familiar linguistic garb.

> So what strikes me as absurd, utterly extraordinary, is existence itself...The moment there's a gap between ideology and reality, there's absurdity...In fact language does nothing but contradict at every moment an extremely simple and visible reality, as if everyone were refusing to see this reality.[39]

It is not the falsity of linguistic description which contradicts reality, but its transparency. By examining the transparent familiarity of ordinary conventionalized thought and language from the standpoint of absurdity, the ordinary acceptance of the world stands out visibly opaque and extraordinary. What is unique to Ionesco's vision of absurdity is its positive, euphoric, light side as a counter-balance and solution to the Sartrean heaviness of nausea. To gain a more thorough grasp of this aspect of Ionesco's thought we must turn to the plays themselves.

There is a steady progression in the evolution of Ionesco's plays from the heavy to the light side of absurdity. The first group of plays, from 1948 to 1951, deals largely with the problems of language communication which we have been discussing. The second group, from 1951 to 1953, are mostly concerned with the mechanical proliferation of heavy, oppressive matter. In the third group, 1953 to 1957, we begin to see a greater emphasis on the mystical quality of emptiness or lightness which Ionesco refers to so often in his autobiographical notes, as well as the transition of heavy to light and back again to heavy. And, finally, in his latest period, 1963 to 1974, the dominant theme is sheer lightness alone.

Ionesco's first play, *The Bald Soprano*, was first performed in 1948. In the play the Martins pay a social call on the Smiths. They discuss the most trivial banalities until firemen arrive to put out an imaginary fire. There is also the Smith's maid, Mary, who appears from time to time, somewhat like the chorus of Greek tragedy or the jester in Elizabethan drama, to make telling comments on the absurd behavior of the two couples.

Three major themes can be detected in this play, all of which have to do with the limitations of human discourse. The first, and most obvious, is the degeneration of language into clichés. The Smiths announce in deadly earnest to one another that they are man and wife, live in this house, have two children, and so on. Ionesco says he got this idea for the play from studying an introductory phrase book in English as a foreign language, where such dialogue takes place. In one stage version (which Ionesco liked so well he later had it incorporated into the play), the end of the play returns to the beginning scene of the Smith's conversation, suggesting that this dreary nonsense goes on and on *ad nauseum*. By distancing ourselves from this exaggerated version of ordinary polite conversation ("How are you?" "Fine, and you?" "Not bad." "How's the family?" etc.), the play presents a hilarious spoof of insincere, unthinking, generalized collective talk which communicates absolutely nothing about the individuals themselves.

But a more important theme which many reviewers, including Tynan, failed to detect at first, is the more subtle metaphysical notion of how truly amazing ordinary things actually are. The play is not simply a condemnation of people who pretend that the commonplaces of their lives have monumental importance—though that element is certainly present; it is also an attempt to show that from an aloof, distanced perspective these commonplaces are truly astonishing. What is amazing is that people generally take them for granted. As Ionesco said of the play some years later, "Nothing seems more surprising to me than that which is banal." The play is not perhaps so successful in conveying this second theme, however.

The third theme is the inability of logical, rational thought to completely reveal reality as it is in itself. In the play Mr. and Mrs. Martin construct an elaborate and ingenious logical proof that they are married to one another. They establish that each is married and has a daughter, and that since this daughter has one red and one white eye, it must be the same daughter and that they are therefore the parents of this daughter, and so man and wife. In itself the dialogue is a powerful comment on people whose consciousness of the world has been totally absorbed in generalized patterns of thought, speech and action. They lack that personal intuition which would make any such argument completely unnecessary.

But after their discovery, Mary enters and, as an aside to the audience, points out that through one tiny flaw in the Martin's argument, the conclusion is falsified, and they are not in fact married to one another after all.

> Mary: I can let you in on a secret. Elizabeth is not Elizabeth, Donald is not Donald. And here is the proof: the child that Donald spoke of is not Elizabeth's daughter...Whereas Donald's daughter has a white right eye and a red left eye, Elizabeth's child has a red right eye and a white left eye! Thus all of Donald's system of deduction collapses when it comes up against this last obstacle which destroys his whole theory...But who is the true Donald? Who is the true Elizabeth? Who has any interest in prolonging this confusion? I don't know. Let's not try to know. Let's leave things as they are.[40]

There is a similarly indecisive conclusion to the debate later in the play as to whether the fireman rang the door-bell. The most obvious point of this, of course, is the fallibility of rational systems of proof and argumentation. The conclusion rests on the truth of all the premises; if only one of these proves false, the whole theory collapses. This coincides with Ionesco's stated intention of exposing the inadequacy of our verbalized understanding of reality by picking apart its weaknesses one by one.

Nonetheless I think the important point is a more subtle one. What is amazing about the proof is that is goes as far as it does toward establishing Donald's and Elizabeth's matrimony, though not quite all the way. As Camus said, we are able to understand a great deal about the world, and explain and prove a great many things within it, but we can never get to the absolute bottom of things, and this shifts our attention, not to the foolishness of logical or scientific explanation, but to the broader metaphysical theme of the absolute distinction of word and object, thought and reality. This is what has become known as the "mystery" element in absurdist fiction. A problem is posed, its solution seems immanent but at the last moment breaks down, and we are left with an unexplained problem.

The point, again, is not that things are totally unexplainable or meaningless, but that they are not completely or absolutely explainable. The fallacy in Donald's argument, after all, is established by Mary's equally logical proof. The mystery element is a successful literary device for suggesting a notion of reality just beyond our grasp, like the carrot Sartre refers to just beyond the reach of the donkey. This is one solution to the dilemma how to describe the thing in itself which by definition cannot be described—the absurdist writer simply shows *that* forms of thought never completely capture or exhaust the object, that the object therefore always transcends our attempts to explain it. It is not that explanations are false or inaccurate, but that they are not identical with the things they do explain. Explanations are useful human devices for relating bits of experience into a humanly intelligible order, but they are human projections; they are not identical with the very fabric of reality.

In the other two plays of the first period, *The Lesson* and *Jack*, Ionesco develops the idea of the tyranny of language cut off from reality. When words cease to expose an aspect of reality from a personal human point of view, words can take on a menacing life of their own. In his second play, *The Lesson*, 1950, an eager and attractive young female student visits a professor for a private lesson. At first the professor is shy, retiring and polite; but gradually he assumes command and verbally dominates the girl who is reduced from a pleasantly bright girl to a mumbling imbecile.

As the professor grows in strength and the student gradually weakens, she expresses a growing drowsiness and fatigue which is the first of Ionesco's images of absurd heaviness, appearing in this early play as a response to human tyranny through linguistic conformity. Finally, the professor murders the girl, in one version with the word "knife," in another, through a violent sexual attack. The maid, who, as in *The Bald Soprano*, appears from time to time, warns the professor he is going too far, and, as she announces the professor's next student, informs the audience that this is his 50th victim, which brings down the curtain.

In *Jack or the Submission*, 1950, the central theme is the subjugation of the individual to the collective mentality of the group as expressed in linguistic conventions. At first Jack refuses to accept conventional values; in particular, he refuses to say "I love fried potatoes" and to accept a conventional marital relation with Roberte, his family's choice. His parents and sister plead with him to be reasonable.

> Jack: There's nothing I can do about it, I was born like this...I've done all that was in my power!
> Mother Robert: What an unfeeling heart...
> Father Robert: He's an intransigent stranger...

To emphasize the interchangeable uniformity of group thinking, many of the characters in this and others of Ionesco's plays have the same name, *viz.*, Robert or Roberte.

At first, like Camus' stranger, Jack refuses to conform to this collective mentality. But then he reluctantly retracts and agrees to love fried potatoes. Then an interesting twist occurs which robs Jack, not only of the negative heroism of Camus' stranger, but of the rewards of social conformity as well. Jack begins to articulate his own personal view of things (he prefers girls with three noses, for example); Roberte accepts his vision of the world, sprouting the desired number of noses (the first indication of the proliferation image of the later plays), and they begin to plan their own individualized life together. Finally Jack realizes he has been trapped; they are simply constructing new conventions.

> Jack: I refused to accept...They assured me that someone would devise a remedy. They promised me some decorations,...they swore they would give me satisfaction...I made other criticisms in order finally to declare to them that I preferred to withdraw,...they implored me to hope...I fell for it!
> But everything was false...Ah, they had lied to me...and how to escape? They boarded up the doors, the windows with nothing, they've taken away the stairs...Anything is preferable to my present situation. Even a new one. [*i.e.*, with Roberte][41]

This is an interesting dramatization of Ionesco's notion discussed earlier of the inevitable degeneration of individual insight into conventionality. Jack's unique, individual solution, with which he was lured into a compromising, partial acceptance, has become the familiar rut everyone else is in. In this statement of Jack's we see another early attempt to articulate dramatically the heaviness of absurdity under the guise of social conformity blocking the passage to freedom. Here the central problem of absurd heaviness is suggested which the later plays develop and then try to solve. Linguistic conformity, as a symbol for social conformity generally, ties us to a narrow, stereotypical view of the world alien to our deepest individual instincts. Our only world is a world devised by others. In *Jack* there seems no escape, no way to withdraw. Later, the theme of lightness is explored as a solution to Jack's dilemma.

The image of proliferating matter as a symbol for the heavy side of absurdity, which appears tangentially in the earlier plays, is the central focus for Ionesco's second group of plays. The first of these plays, *The Future is in Eggs*, or *It Takes All Sorts to Make a World,* 1951, continues the story of Jack and Roberte, who hatches endless eggs which turn into people and then into sausages, slabs of meat, etc. This is reminiscent of Roquentin' s vision that anything can happen, that objects could become anything. It is first a way of breaking down our familiar acceptance of the way things "naturally" or inevitably are, exposing how remarkable, unaccountable ordinary things really are from the absurdist point of view. But it is also the image of matter protruding, blossoming everywhere, filling everything, choking us, crowding us out, which Sartre refers to as "nausea."

The Chairs is the first and best of Ionesco's plays dealing with this theme. In the play an old couple are preparing for the old man's retirement ceremony. He is an insignificant, ordinary lighthouse keeper who has never received the recognition he feels he deserves. But now everyone, including the Emperor, is coming to the lighthouse to hear his complete and final revelation to the world. He has hired a professional orator to speak for him. During most of the play the old woman brings in more and more chairs for imaginary, nonexistent guests until the room is choked with piled-up furniture. The orator finally does arrive, but turns out to be mute, resorting finally to some meaningless gibberish which he writes on a blackboard—which ends the play.

Here again critics tended to fasten on to the most obvious element in the play, the failure of the old couple and their pathetic, delusory attempt to reverse their failure in one final act. But clearly the dominant dramatic element in the play is the proliferation of the chairs. This forms a perfect image of the mutually empty and full, light and heavy aspects of absurdity. The chairs are empty of people and this, like any object of human use momentarily not in use, such as an unoccupied house, simply reinforces their brute materiality, their heaviness. As Ionesco said of the play,

> The subject of the play was nothingness, not failure. It was total absence: chairs without people...It was both multiplication and absence, proliferation and nothingness.[42]

Objects devoid of human meaning, human understanding, especially chairs which are designed for and so cry out for human use, are full of a nonhuman, alien matter, but they are equally empty of any human significance. The chairs are dramatically successful because they represent a concrete instantiation of the existentialist notion of negation discussed in the second chapter. We notice the absence of something just in case we have come to anticipate its presence. An empty auditorium or playing field is more poignantly empty than a hay field, for example, because it is meant to be occupied by people. In *The Chairs* this sense of absence is heightened by the invisible guests the old man seats and talks to. As Ionesco wrote to Sylvain Dhomme, the director of the play in its first performance,

The subject of the play is not the message, nor the failure of life, nor the moral disaster of the two old people, but the chairs themselves; that is to say, the absence of people, the absence of the emperor, the absence of God, the absence of matter, the unreality of the world, metaphysical emptiness. The theme of the play is nothingness...The invisible elements must be more and more...real...until nothingness can be heard, made concrete.[43]

A similar theme is developed in *The New Tenant*, 1953. A man moves into an unfurnished apartment; movers begin bringing in furniture to the room. More and more furniture arrives until the tenant is completely buried beneath it.

Victims of Duty, 1952, is one of Ionesco's most successful and complex plays. Choubert, a playwright, and his wife, Madeleine, answer the door one evening to a detective in search of a former neighbor neither of them knows. Instead of leaving immediately, the detective enters, begins asking a few polite questions and like the professor in *The Lesson*, gradually subjects Choubert to an intense "third degree." There is a mystery to be solved and the detective is determined to get to the bottom of it.

In a psychoanalytic manner he demands that Choubert go "deeper" and "deeper" into the recesses of his mind until he comes up with the solution The tone of the play is established by Choubert toward the beginning.

Choubert: All the plays that have ever been written...have never really been anything but thrillers...Every play's an investigation brought to a successful conclusion. There's a riddle, and it's solved in the final scene.[44]

This is the detective's attitude toward life in general.

Detective: I remain Aristotlelially logical, true to myself, faithful to my duty...I don't believe in the absurd, everything hangs together, everything can be comprehended in time.[45]

This establishes the dramatic conflict of the play—whether things can be exhaustively explained or not. This theme operates on two levels, as a reflection on life in general and more particularly as a comment on the realistic theater of rational plot, consistent character, etc. If life is not logical then neither should the theater be logical. The form of a play must match its content. Nicolas, a character in the play who appears to speak for Ionesco, makes this plain.

Inspiring me with a different logic and a different psychology. I shall introduce contradiction where there is no contradiction and where there is no contradiction...we'll get rid of the principle of identity and unity of character.[46]

In the play Ionesco does in fact experiment with changing identities and even interchangeable identities of the main characters, but only occasionally, not consistently throughout. From the detective's point of view everything has a solution; if we don't know the answer, we must find it. But the "deeper" Choubert goes the more confusing, mysterious the problem becomes.

Like Jack, Choubert feels a social obligation to cooperate fully with this duly appointed civil servant, so he submits to the interrogation. But this leads, not to any solution of the detective's question, which Choubert knows nothing about, but to a vision of oppressive heaviness—to the heavy side of absurdity. And this heavy weight drags him down deeper and deeper.

> Choubert: I shall be alone in the dark, in the mud.[47]

This represents the trap of conformity which Jack found himself in. To absorb oneself in the socially formed picture of the world is to become immersed in all the goals, problems, aims implied in that picture.

Thus our obligation to uphold the social order is rooted in our acceptance of the world as dictated by the society's linguistic and cultural conventions. But in *Victims of Duty* there appears the first suggestion of a means of escape. Lower down Choubert begins to feel lighter than air, evanescent, transparent.

> Choubert:...the lightening rends the thick gloom, and there on the horizon, behind the storm, a gigantic curtain of darkness is heavily lifting, gleaming through the shadows, still as a dream in the midst of the storm, a magic city,...a bubbling spring...and flowers of fire in the night,...a palace of icy flowers, glowing statues and incandescent seas, continents blazing in the night, in oceans of snow!...Joy...Fullness...emptiness...hopeless hope.[48]

This image of clarity and light (the "magic city") is more fully developed in the "radiant city" of *The Killer*. Now, instead of a heavy mass sinking deeper and deeper, Choubert begins rising higher and higher about to "take off" toward "escape." Interestingly, Madeleine and the detective strenuously object that Choubert is evading his duty. Still, Choubert rises higher and higher in the air.

> Choubert: The air I breathe is lighter than air. I am lighter than air. The sun's melting into light...I can float through solid objects. All forms have disappeared. I'm going up and up...shimmering light...I can fly.[49]

But then he loses his nerve ("Oh!...I don't dare") and falls back heavily to earth again. Choubert cannot completely withdraw from his social conformity and the social obligation that goes along with it.

> Detective: You...forget yourself, forget your duty. That's your great fault. You're either too heavy or too light.[50]

The image of flying through air as a symbol of lightness is taken up again in *Amedee* and *A Stroll in the Air*, while the proliferation image is carried forward in *Victims of Duty* by Madeleine's strangely multiplying teacups and by the endless quantities of bread the detective stuffs into Choubert's mouth, an interesting image also of the mindless "swallowing" of social conventions, as well as the effort simply to shut Choubert up.

In the third group of plays Ionesco concentrates on the transition between heavy and light. In *The Killer*, the play moves from light to heavy; in *Amedee* the movement is from heavy to light. *The Killer*, 1957, one of Ionesco's best efforts, was adapted from an earlier short story "The Photograph of the Colonel." In the play Berenger accidentally wanders into a marvelous section of the city which he has never seen before, "the radiant city." It is dazzling, light, airy and beautiful. The architect of the radiant city shows Berenger around, with the assistance of Dany, the architect's secretary who soon becomes Berenger's lover. To get an idea of the visual effect of the radiant city, we might look at Ionesco's stage directions for the set.

> Atmosphere for Act I will be created by the lighting only. At first...the light is grey, like a dull November day...Then, suddenly, the stage is brilliantly lit; a very bright, very white light; just this whiteness, and also the dense vivid blue of the sky...The blue, the white, the silence and the empty stage should give a strange impression of peace.[51]

To Berenger the city is perfect; it is the outward manifestation of his life-long hopes and dreams, something he always suspected but was never sure could really exist.

> Berenger: I knew that somewhere in our dark and dismal city...there was one [district] that was bright and beautiful...with...sunny streets and avenues bathed in light...This radiant city within a city.[52]

Throughout his life Berenger had found a contradiction between what he felt within himself and what he discovered in the world outside himself. Word and object, thought and reality never coincided; the external world never supported his internal vision. In short, Berenger has always suffered the heaviness of absurdity as symbolized in the ugly and brutal city surrounding the radiant district.

But now within the radiant city he finds the perfect coincidence of thought and reality, inner and outer, the synthesis of essence and existence which Aristotle recognized as necessary to a meaningful world and which the Romantics tried in vain to recapture after the collapse of the medieval world view.

> Berenger: To project this universe within some outside help is needed; some kind of material, physical light...Gardens, blue sky, or the spring, which corresponds to the universe inside and offers a chance of recognition, which is like a translation or an anticipation of that universe or a mirror in which its own smile could be reflected...in which it can find itself again and say: that's what I am in reality and I'd forgotten, a smiling being in a smiling world...Come to think of it, it's quite wrong to talk of a world within and a world without,

separate world; there's an initial impulse, of course, which starts from us, and when it can't project itself, when it can't fulfill itself objectively, when there's not total agreement between myself inside and myself outside, then it's a catastrophe, a universal contradiction, a schism.[53]

The radiant city is, of course, the euphoric vision of emptiness Ionesco reports having experienced in adolescence. In an interesting monologue Berenger relates an almost identical childhood experience to the architect.

Berenger: Suddenly the joy became more intense, breaking all bounds!...The light grew more and more brilliant...My own peace and light spread in their turn throughout the world, I was filling the universe with a kind of ethereal energy...Everything was a virgin, purified, discovered anew...surprise...yet...familiar...I'm sure I could have flown away, I'd lost so much weight,...I was overcome with the immense sadness you feel at a moment of tragic and intolerable separation...and I felt lost among all those people, all those *things*.[54]

But if the city is so perfect, Berenger cannot understand why no one is living there. Just as Berenger's (and Ionesco's) childhood experience of evanescent, euphoric emptiness always reverts back to leaden heaviness, so there is something within the radiant city which chokes its light and weighs it down. And this, of course, is the killer, a homicidal maniac who lures his victims by showing them a photograph of the colonel.

After Dany falls prey to the killer, Berenger sets out to track him down. As in the absurdist mystery technique discussed earlier, Berenger follows many false leads through ugly city images of darkness, angry mobs, political harangues until quite by accident he stumbles onto the killer who kills Berenger. Throughout, heaviness is effectively represented by brutal images of city life—darkness, confusion, violence and aggression. Through a striking series of images the play presents the clear progression of light to heaviness, the final inability of lightness to maintain itself. By presenting a sustained image of lightness in the first act, the play suggests a solution to the heaviness of absurdity, a solution nonetheless negated by the presence of the killer who spoils the radiant city.

The first play to move in the opposite direction, *toward* that solution, is *Amedee, or How to Get Rid of It*, 1953. Like Choubert, Amedee is a playwright, who has written only one line, however, in fifteen years of a play about an old man and woman (cf. *The Chairs*). The problem Amedee and his wife, Madeleine, face is how to get rid of an enormous corpse which is mysteriously growing and spreading out in all directions, threatening to push them out of their small apartment. It is not clear how he died, but there is a suggestion of murder or violence, possibly performed by Amedee himself, whose "dead" marriage he feels responsible for, which, combined with the proliferating corpse, poses a striking image of absurd heaviness.

The image of proliferating matter is strengthened by the burgeoning mushrooms which sprout all over the apartment. In *Point of Departure* Ionesco explains how the theme of proliferating matter is an image of the dead materiality of objects stripped of human meanings.

> Words, obviously devoid of magic, are replaced by accessories, by objects. Countless mushrooms sprout in the apartment of the characters Amedee and Madeleine; a corpse, stretches with 'geometric progression,' also grows there, turning out the occupants. In *Victims of Duty* hundreds of cups are piled up to serve coffee to three people; the furniture in the *New Occupant* [*i.e.*, *The New Tenant*], after blocking the staircase of the apartment building..., ends up by burying the character who wanted to settle in the apartment; in *The Chairs*..., dozens of chairs, with invisible guests, fill the stage; in *Jacques* [*Jack*] several noses grow on the face of a young girl.[55]

Other images of heaviness we have seen are those of conformity, brutality and fatigue, which, in addition to the student in *The Lesson*, Amedee also expresses in the first act. "I feel so tired, so tired...worn out, heavy."

Amedee finally agrees to take the corpse out at midnight and get rid of it. To pass the time until then, Amedee begins pulling in images through the window by an invisible rope, and as he does, the characters both fall into a hypnotic reverie which transforms them into their opposites—Amedee II, who dreams of lightness, and Madeleine II, who meditates on heaviness. This is another of Ionesco's experiments with breaking down the Aristotelian unity of character.

> Amedee II: If only you wished...Nature would be so bountiful...wings on our feet, our limbs like wings...our shoulders wings...gravity abolished...no more weariness.
> Madeleine II: Night...always night...Alone in the world!
> Amedee II: An insubstantial universe...Freedom...Ethereal power...Balance...airy abundance...world without weight...You could lift the world with one hand.[56]

Now the roles are reversed, Amedee is himself again, returning to the reflection of heaviness, while Madeleine II takes up the lightness reverie of Amedee II.

> Amedee (himself): Time is heavy. The world dense.
> Madeleine II: Stone is just space. Walls are void. There is nothing...nothing...[57]

Then the roles begin to reverse yet again.

> Amedee: It's heavy. Yet it's so badly stuck together...Nothing but holes...the walls are tottering, the leaden mass subsides!
> Amedee II: We love each other. We are happy. In a house of glass, a house of light.

Madeleine II: He means a house of brass, brass...house of night.[58]

As Amedee prepares to remove the body, light pours in through the windows and Amedee's spirits are lifted.

> Amedee: Look, Madeleine...all the acacia trees are aglow. Their blossoms are bursting open and shooting up to the sky. The full-blown moon is flooding the Heavens with light, a *living* planet...He [the corpse] won't be able to see all this...And space, space, infinite space![59]

On the stage the enormous corpse is an ideal image of leaden heaviness, its sheer bulk resisting all efforts of human will to budge it and, more important, privatively calling to mind in the strongest terms, as do the chairs, the absence of the living, breathing, active person. There is also a suggestion of violence and brutality in the cause of death and of an amorphous, unresolved guilt.

As Amedee drags the massive corpse through the apartment and out into the street, the corpse begins to open out like a balloon, rising above the ground carrying Amedee up into the sky. Notice how Ionesco describes this scene in his stage directions.

> (Suddenly a surprising thing happens. The body wound around Amedee's waist seems to have opened out like a sail or a huge parachute; the dead man's head can be seen appearing above the rear wall, and Amedee's head can be seen appearing above the rear wall, drawn up by the parachute...Amedee is flying up and out of reach of the policeman.)[60]

All of this is, of course, extremely difficult to stage and requires a great deal of imagination and technical assistance. Like Lewis Carroll, Ionesco often creates his most striking images by converting puns and idiomatic forms of ordinary speech into concrete physical reality, "fishing for thoughts," "going deeper into the recesses of our minds," "feeling high," "swallowing social conventions," "a dead marriage," "a skeleton in the closet." Since dreams also accomplish this, the actual dramatization of these images on stage has the vivid, surreal impact of dreams, especially the well-nigh universal dream of flying, or walking on air, which, just as in most of Ionesco's plays, usually ends by falling back to earth again.

Amedee describes the weight he has lost, which enables him to soar above the city, as his "responsibility," and, as in *Victims of Duty*, those on the ground, including his wife, Madeleine, and the authority figure of the policeman, plead with him to return to his filial and civic duties. But in *Amedee* the central character at last succeeds in transcending the heavy weight of absurdity toward its mystical lightness.

In his latest group of plays Ionesco is concerned with the tremendous effort required to cut the ties that bind us to the dead, heavy earth and release us into the bright, pure atmosphere of light Ionesco sees as man's only hope. Though the solution to the heaviness of absurdity is clear and is apparently simply a matter of our willing it ("If only you wished"), enormous forces of social and worldly pressure militate against it, making it difficult to achieve for more than a fleeting moment.

Like Beckett's *Endgame*, which we will discuss in the next chapter, *Exit the King* (English translation 1963) deals with the problem of how to give up, finally and completely, as Berenger, Amedee and Choubert have tried unsuccessfully, all those links to the naive world we have constructed through human projection, a world we realize is our own construction (and "so badly stuck together") and a world we know is responsible for the dark, heavy side of life, but one we nonetheless cling to as our most familiar and comfortable refuge. In *Exit the King* the image for this effort to relinquish our tenacious hold on the world is the King's reluctance to die.

In some old notes for the play, not actually incorporated in the final version, the Queen states this theme very clearly.

> Queen: How could you get so rooted in this world? You cling to it...you dig your nails into these clouds, this unreal stuff which you take for reality, for rock. You see, it's...breaking up it's dissolving into clouds, flakes, snow, water, steam, smoke. You cling to it. Try to loosen your hold, little by little...Break the habit of living. How could you forget that all this is just a brief passage.[61]

As human beings, we project our human concerns upon the world, but we are not ordinarily aware that we are doing so. As a result our projected meanings become objectified, externalized, attaching to objects and we read our own meanings and significances into the external world around us. This is what draws us to the world, and makes it an interesting, intelligible, familiar place, and finally ties us to it.

Because of this projection, the world is perceived, not only as meeting our needs, but more importantly as thwarting those needs. Thus, the anthrocentricity of our world-view leads to unhappiness. So long as a comfortable anthropomorphism can be maintained, the satisfaction of needs is seen to exceed or at least balance the ways in which those needs can be thwarted, but when, in the experience of absurdity, thought and desire separate from reality and that comfortable world-view begins to break up, as ours has been for the past several hundred years, all that remains is the hope without the fulfillment, seeing the world anthropomorphically as failing or refusing to satisfy man's deepest needs. The solution, therefore, lies, not in looking for something in reality to meet our desires, but in giving up entirely that anthropomorphic view in which the world is seen as neither meeting nor failing to meet those needs.

By realizing our projecting nature we see the distinction of word and object, thought and reality, which we have defined as absurdity, and this makes it possible to disengage ourselves from our particular socially informed view of the world, and indeed from *any* view of the world as absolutely coinciding with reality. It is now possible to see reality as utterly transcending all human values, meanings, interests and concerns. But it is not, unfortunately, quite as easy as all that, since our entire biological and social natures rebel against it, and so the King hangs on, wanting to let go but not quite able to do so.

In a clear reference to the crisis of absurdity referred to above, the play opens in a state of natural and political disaster. The country is in chaos; something must be done. The Doctor to the King expresses the general setting of the play, "Yesterday evening it was spring...Now it's November." Berenger, the King, whom we already know from earlier plays to have some autobiographical links to Ionesco, has lost all power over his subjects and indeed over his own body. He is dying. To his politically ambitious first wife, Marguerite, this is interpreted simply in terms of an irreversible loss of personal and political power which the King must now realistically accept.

To his more loving second wife, Marie, this is an opportunity for a positive affirmation of detachment from the world of human projection. As in *Amedee* and *Victims of Duty* the problem of relinquishing our hold on the conventionally projected world is expressed in terms of social responsibility and power. His death thus represents both the loss of power and his own personal fulfillment, and his wives present him with these two alternatives. Marguerite is a pessimist and a realist who, seeing no ultimate solution, advises Berenger to accept the inevitable loss of the only values in life, power over oneself, others, the world. Marie is an optimist and an idealist who urges the King toward a radical break with this world. Interestingly, Berenger can choose between these two possibilities. As in *Amedee*, the difficulty of the solution, ironically, is not made easier by the fact that it is simply a matter of choosing.

Within the play it is Marie who speaks most eloquently, and most philosophically.

> Marie (to King): Stop torturing yourself! "Exist" and "die" are just words, figments of your imagination. Once you realize that, nothing can touch you, Forget your empty clichés. We can never know what it really means, "exist" or "die"... *Now* you exist, you *are*. Forget the rest. That's the only truth. Just be an eternal question mark...And remember: that you can't find the answer is an answer in itself...Dive into an endless maze of wonder and surprise, then you too will have no end, and can exist forever. Everything is strange and indefinable. Let it dazzle and confound you!...Escape from definitions and you will breathe again!
>
> Open the flood gates of joy and light to dazzle and confound you. Illuminating waves of joy will fill your veins with wonder. You found that fiery radiance within you. If it was there once, it is *still* there *now*. Find it again. Look for it in yourself.[62]

The striking resemblance to mystical, and particularly Buddhist religious language is no accident. Mystics have always regarded the meaninglessness of the world as a solution, rather than a problem. Our problems in life, according to the mystic, are all due to our attachment to objects which results from confusing word and object, mistaking the pointing finger for the moon to which it points, in the famous Zen epigram. By realizing that confusion, knowing that thought and reality, mind and object are ultimately distinct, attachment can be terminated, resulting in a joyous, euphoric state of freedom and release.

In *Conversations with Eugene Ionesco,* Ionesco acknowledges a considerable debt to mystic writers, who "rejected the physical world with all its brightness, its colour and light, what remains paradoxically is light, brightness, vividness."[63] From this religious point of view, the confusion of word and object which causes our unhealthy attachments to the world spring from the projection of our own wishes, desires, aims and purposes onto the world. In *Fragments of a Journal* Ionesco discusses the role of desire.

> Desire is the most serious obstacle to our deliverance. Freudianism can thus, to some extent, be reconciled with Buddhism. Not with Zen, for to wish to free oneself is still a form of will one should seek to free oneself from wishing...If we succeeded in shedding light on Desire...then Desire would disappear. If we could learn the real reasons for our reasons, there would no longer be any reasons for anything. All knots would be slackened, we would surrender ourselves and lapse into indifference and nothingness. Indifference would moreover, allow us to live, that's to say it might make life less unendurable. Not longing to live, not longing to die, just letting things drift. Zen, as a metaphysical "couldn't-care-less" attitude.[64]

We will see this Buddhist conception of a solution more fully developed in Beckett.

The same theme of flying above the earth into empty lightness is taken up again in *A Stroll in the Air* (1963). The central character is again Berenger, again a writer. He has come with his wife, Josephine, and daughter, Marthe, to a cottage in the English countryside for a holiday. For the intellectual the last hold on the world is the desire to wrap it all up in a verbal formula, to talk *about* heaviness, emptiness, the absurdity of life. The last thing to be seen as absurd is the theory of absurdity. In the play Berenger is tired of trying to explain everything in words; and he wishes to be released from this compulsion.

> Berenger: I've always known I never had any reason to write...Once upon a time, though I'm really a nihilist, there was some strange force inside me that made me...write. I can't go on any longer...For years it was a consolation to me to be able to say there was nothing to say. But now I feel far too sure I was right...writing isn't a game for me any more...It ought to lead to something else, but it doesn't.[65]

The play's first image of the transparent, empty lightness to be sought by way of escape is the "anti-world," the opposite and negation of our ordinary, mundane world which in the other plays has been challenged and bracketed by the dislocation of language. In the anti-world objects appear and disappear from within "the void." Berenger and Marthe see it; his wife, Josephine, does not. As in several of the earlier plays, in particular *Victims of Duty,* it is the wife who, along with authority figures, like the professor, detective, fireman, policeman, emperor, king, represent an insistence upon conformity to social obligations which tie us to the heaviness of absurdity and work against release. Not all women play this heavy role, however, witness Marie and Marthe.

As in *Amedee* and *Victims of Duty*, to see the anti-world, like the experience of lightness generally, is to a large extent an act of personal will.

> Berenger: There's no proof that it exists, but when you think about it, you can find it in your own thoughts. The evidence is in your mind. There's not just one Anti-world. There are several...universes, and they're all interlocking.[66]

The anti-world is an image of the humanly creative construction of particular world views from different interested human perspectives. All of these views come from "the void" in the sense that reality in itself transcends all those conceptual and linguistic forms which give our interpreted world its discernible shape and pattern. Reality is void, not like an empty bag, but empty of linguistic and conceptual distinctions and demarcations.

> Berenger: And to think there are people who imagine the void is like a huge black hole, a bottomless pit: and yet the void is neither black nor white and to be bottomless, it would need acres and acres and acres of space...The void is neither white nor black, it doesn't exist, it's everywhere.[67]

The void is simply the transcendence of reality from linguistic boundaries. Compare this statement of Ionesco with that of the great 9th century Zen master, Huang-po, in his discussion of the void.

> Men are afraid to forget their own minds, fearing to fall through the void with nothing on to which they can cling. They do not know that the void is not really the void but the real realm of things.
>
> Though basically everything is without objective existence, you must not come to think of anything nonexistent, and though things are not nonexistent you must not form a concept of anything existing. For "existence" and "nonexistence" are both empirical concepts no better than illusions.
>
> [Reality] is neither long nor short, big nor small, for it transcends all limits, measures, names, traces and comparisons. It is that which you see before you—begin to reason about it and at once you fall into error. It is like the boundless void which cannot be fathomed or measured.
>
> So let your symbolic conception be that of a void...Eschew all symbolizing whatever, for by this eschewal, is "symbolized" the Great Void in which is neither unity nor multiplicity—that Void which is not really void, that Symbol which is not a symbol.[68]

It is interesting but not really surprising to find in this revolutionary 20th century theory of absurdity significant parallels with some of the most ancient philosophical thought both East and West.

As Berenger experiences the joy of this emptying experience and the sense of novelty at the fresh reality revealed thereby, he begins to walk on air, at first only a few feet above the ground, but then soaring high above the hills and village, his wife pleading with him all this while to be sensible and walk on the ground like everyone else. To Berenger it's as though he is returning to an earlier experience which he had almost forgotten.

> Berenger: I've never been so relaxed; I've never felt so happy. I've never felt so light, so weightless...When I look around me, it's as though I was seeing everything for the first time. As though I'd just been born...Like some feeling of joy that's been forgotten yet still familiar, like something that's belonged to me from the beginning of time. You lose it every day and yet it's never really lost. And the proof is that you can find it again...It's all very concrete...a sort of divine intoxication.[69]

The need to "fly," as well as the ability to fly, is not an extraordinary quirk of the half-insane, but part of the inmost nature of all human beings. As the Buddhists say, the Buddha-nature is the true nature of everyone whether he or she knows it or not. The reason most of us are not aware of it is that we *forget* our true nature.

> Berenger: Man has a crying need to fly...It's as necessary and as natural as breathing...Everyone knows how to fly. It's an innate gift, but everyone forgets...It would be better for us to starve than not to fly. I expect that's why we feel so unhappy.[70]

In one sense it is very easy; all that is really required is the desire.

> Berenger: it's perfectly simple. All you need is the will to do it.[71]

In another sense, however, it is exceedingly difficult. Reflecting on all the darkness, injustice, cruelty of the human social order, Berenger, like Choubert, loses faith and falls back to earth "sad," "depressed," and "deflated."

In his latest published work to be translated into English, a novel called *The Hermit* (1974), Ionesco returns to the light-heavy experience with which it all began 25 years earlier.

> Joy was suddenly realizing, in a way I might describe as supernatural, that the world is there, that you are there in the world, that one exists, that I exist. Now everything seemed to prove the inexistence of things and my own existence. I was afraid of disappearing...I had the impression that the little seismic disturbances, imperceptible but fairly numerous, had made the world extremely fragile. Everything was disintegrating, everything seemed on the verge of sinking into an ordinary void. The universe where reality was less and less resistant...I felt myself teetering in a world about to topple. Strange how everything is simultaneously so present and so absent, so hard so thick, and so fragile...The nausea of nothingness. And then the nausea of surfeit...I walked down the street...touching the walls, simultaneously fearing that they might crush me or that they might vanish.[72]

There was a kind of trembling in the walls and ceiling that surrounded me, luminous vibrations in the blinding light. The walls and the roof seemed to be breaking up; their lines became blurred. They lost their density and seemed to me to turn into something increasingly transparent, penumbras, evanescent shadows...Then I saw them shrivel up and slowly recede into the distance. They melted like so much transparent smoke into the luminous distance, then disappeared. Before my eyes, the desert stretched, vast beneath the brilliant sky, the burning sun, to the very horizon. There was no longer anything but sand sparkling in the light. My room seemed to be suspended, silent, a tiny dot in all the immensity...Now the wall disappeared in turn...Where the wall had been images began to form and slowly reform. It grew very bright...A long pathway. At the end, a light brighter than daylight. The light came nearer, encompassing everything. How could my room contain it?[73]

Notes

1. Eugene Ionesco, "The Point of Departure," Leonard C. Pronko, trans., in *Theatre Arts*, June 1958, p. 17.
2. Ionesco, *Fragments of a Journal*, Jean Stewart, trans. (London: Faber and Faber, 1976), pp. 41-42.
3. *Ibid.*, pp. 129-130.
4. Ionesco, *Conversations with Eugene Ionesco*, transcribed by Claude Bonnefoy, Jan Dawson, trans. (New York: Holt, Rinehart, and Winston, 1971), p. 122,
5. Ionesco, *Fragments of a Journal, op, cit.*, pp. 74-75.
6. Ionesco, *Conversations with Eugene Ionesco, op. cit.*, p. 61.
7. *Ibid.*
8. *Ibid.*, p. 62.
9. *Ibid.*, p. 93.
10. *Ibid.*, p. 114.
11. Ionesco, *Fragments of a Journal, op. cit.*, p, 83.
12. Ionesco, "Dialogues avec Ionesco," transcribed by Lerminier, in Richard N. Coe, *Ionesco* (London: Oliver and Boyd, 1961), p. 73.
13. Ionesco, *Fragments of a Journal, op. cit.*
14. Ionesco, *Conversations with Eugene Ionesco, op. cit.*, p. 157.
15. *Ibid.*, pp. 120-121.
16. Ionesco, *Present Past, Past Present*, Helen Lane, trans. (New York: Grove Press, 1971), p. 169.
17. *Ibid.*, pp. 169-170.
18. *Ibid.*, p. 191.
19. Ionesco, *Conversations with Eugene Ionesco, op. cit.*, p. 123.
20. Alain Robbe-Grillet, "From Realism to Reality in *For A New Novel*, Richard Howard, trans. (New York: Grove Press, 1965), p. 166.
21. Ionesco, *Fragments of a Journal, op. cit.*, p. 30.
22. Ionesco, *Present Past, Past Present, op. cit.*, p. 139.
23. Ionesco, *Fragments of a Journal, op. cit.*, p. 61.
24. *Ibid.*, p. 62.
25. Ionesco, *Present Past, Past Present, op. cit.* p. 131.
26. Ionesco, *Fragments of a Journal, op. cit.*, pp. 129-30.
27. Ionesco, *Present Past, Past Present, op. cit.*, pp. 150-51.
28. *Ibid.*
29. *Ibid.*, pp. 171-72.
30. *Ibid.*, p. 154.
31. *Ibid.*, p. 157.
32. Ionesco, *Conversations with Eugene Ionesco, op. cit.*, pp. 123-24.
33. Ionesco, *Fragments of a Journal, op. cit.*, p. 40.
34. *Ibid.*, p. 20.
35. *Ibid.*, p. 40.
36. *bid*

37. Ionesco, "The Point of Departure," *op. cit.*, p. 18.
38. Ionesco, *Fragments of a Journal, op. cit.*, p. 18.
39. Ionesco, *Conversations with Eugene Ionesco, op. cit.*, p. 128.
40. *Ibid.*
41. *Ibid.*
42. *Ibid.*, p. 73.
43. Ionesco, letter to Sylvain Dhomme, in Martin Esslin, *The Theatre of the Absurd* (Harmondsworth, England Penguin Books, 1968).
44. *Ibid.*
45. *Ibid.*
46. *Ibid.*
47. *Ibid.*
48. *Ibid.*
49. *Ibid.*
50. *Ibid.*
51. *Ibid.*
52. *Ibid.*
53. *Ibid.*
54. *Ibid.*
55. Ionesco, "The Point of Departure," *op. cit.*
56. *Ibid.*
57. *Ibid.*
58. *Ibid.*
59. *Ibid.*
60. *Ibid.*
61. Ionesco, *Fragments of a Journal, op. cit.*, p. 44.
62. *Ibid.*
63. Ionesco, *Conversations with Eugene Ionesco, op. cit.*, p. 42.
64. Ionesco, *Fragments of a Journal, op. cit*
65. *Ibid.*
66. *Ibid.*
67. *Ibid,*
68. Huang-Po, *The Teaching of Huang-Po*, John Blofeld, trans. (New York: Grove Press, 1959).
69. Ionesco, *The Hermit*, Richard Seaver, trans. (New York: Viking Press, 1974).
70. *Ibid.*
71. *Ibid.*
72. *Ibid.*
73. *Ibid.*

CHAPTER FIVE: BECKETT

Among the writers considered in this book, Beckett is the most single-minded and consistent in his determination to overcome the tragic heaviness of absurdity. Unlike the other Absurdists, this is the only theme we find in all of his writing from his earliest publication in 1930 to his most recent work. He is also, surprisingly perhaps, the most optimistic about the possibility of finally breaking through to the euphoric light side of absurdity. Because this requires, as we saw in Ionesco, transcending all forms of conventional understanding, including linguistic conventions, Beckett is without doubt the most difficult of all the Absurdists to understand. Even more than Ionesco, Beckett's message is conveyed through the peculiarities of his linguistic medium; content is revealed through form. Since that message is, above all, the desirability of dismantling all habitual, familiar patterns of thought, Beckett's writing style is anything but ordinary.

Those unfamiliar with Beckett's prose works will be surprised, I think, by his long-term, persistent interest in what may be called the philosophy of resignation—a philosophical position articulated by those writers of the past with whom Beckett has expressed the strongest affinity, *viz.*, Schopenhauer, the ancient Stoics, and Eastern, especially Hindu and Buddhist philosophers. This philosophical bent appears as early as 1931 when Beckett's remarkable study of Proust first appeared in print.

In this book, which predates Beckett's stylistic experiments with language, Beckett offers an interpretation of Proust from the standpoint of Schopenhauer in a way which reveals much about Beckett's own intellectual orientation. What Beckett has done in *Proust* is to interpret Proust's concern with the effects of time upon the individual's consciousness of the world in terms of Schopenhauer's theory of Will. According to Schopenhauer, our customary patterns of thought and perception, which are rooted in our biological, instinctual nature, structure the world as we know it and demarcate ourselves from it. Nonetheless, Schopenhauer argues, this is an illusion which can be overcome only by an enormous rejection of all our deepest instincts, replacing our very will to survive by a detached, disinterested aesthetic perception of an ideal reality transcending all linguistic and conceptual distinctions.

Although the terminology varies, the idea, rooted in Kant's transcendental idealism, is basically the same as we found in Camus, Sartre, and Ionesco. The ordinary world of our awareness is a world structured by human consciousness and rooted in a sense of time and purposeful activity. Because of the success of this mutual accommodation of thought and object, we are not normally aware of our projection of interests and desires upon the world, and so, through habit and memory, we take this anthropomorphized version of the world for reality itself, confusing word and object, essence and existence, and this contributes to our sense of comfortable familiarity with the world—which eventually leads to boredom. Nonetheless, we are not always so totally unaware of our creative efforts in the construction of our view of the world. In all those ways in which absurdity enters human experience, we can and do become aware of the projecting nature of human thought, and when this occurs, word and object, thought and reality, become detached from one another. In the brief transition from one acceptable construction to another, the usual comforting sense of familiarity, bordering on boredom, turns to suffering. Time, Habit, Memory, Boredom, and Suffering—these, then, are the technical terms of Beckett's analysis.

> Habit is a compromise effected between the individual and his environment, or between the individual and his own organic eccentricities, the guarantee of a dull inviolability... Habit is the ballast that chains the dog to his vomit...Life is a succession of habits, since the individual is a succession of individuals; the world being a projection of the individual's consciousness (an objectification of the individual's will, Schopenhauer would say), the pact must be continually renewed...The creation of the world did not take place once and for all time, but takes place every day. Habit then is the generic term for the countless treatises concluded between the countless subjects that constitute the individual and their countless correlative objects. The periods of transition that separate consecutive adaptations...represent the perilous zones in the life of the individual,...when for a moment the boredom of living is replaced by the suffering of being.[1]

Here Beckett takes the realist side of Sartre and Camus against the phenomenological idealism of Heidegger and Husserl. Despite our customary forgetfulness of projection ("Habit") which tends to equate reality with *humanly interpreted* reality, we occasionally become aware that thought and reality are distinct and thus cognizant of the fact that existence is not coincident with essence, but transcends all human categories.

The above passage is also reminiscent of Ionesco's analysis of the delicate balance in meaningful discourse between the complete transparency of naive projection and the disturbing opacity of original insight. If we speak entirely our own language, no one can understand us; if we speak entirely the language of others, we are untrue to our own unique insights.

Either we speak and act for ourselves—in which case speech and action are distorted and emptied of their meaning by an intelligence that is not ours, or else we speak and act for others—in which case we speak and act a lie.[2]

Despite the effect of Habit, we are not totally absorbed in conventional clichés and can and do, therefore, originate fresh, individual perspectives which open up new dimensions of the world more adequately reflecting our own individual points of view. But this new perspective, which appears so exciting and creative at first, quickly degenerates, as Ionesco saw, into a familiar, publicly accepted convention. So, the "treaty" or "adaptation" of self to world moves in a series of transitions between opaque awareness of itself (which is Suffering) and a naively transparent forgetfulness of self (which is Habit).

> The fundamental duty of Habit...consists in a perpetual adjustment and readjustment of our organic sensibility to the conditions of its worlds. Suffering represents the omission of that duty..., and boredom its adequate performance. The pendulum oscillates between these two terms: Suffering—that opens a window on the real and is the main condition of the artistic experience, and Boredom...[3]

Most of the time we are victims of Habit, interpreting every object in our experience, including ourselves, as falling neatly within a familiar human category. The object before us, to recall Sartre's examples from *Nausea*, is simply a glass of beer, a tree root, a streetcar seat. Since these categories are our own inventions, it is comforting to see the world conform to these familiar classifications, as Camus points out in *The Myth of Sisyphus*. But since we only see things thereby in terms of their general essence, as examples of certain *kinds* or *types* of thing, we never experience, in ordinary circumstances, the existing reality of the object we so blithely classify. We see its "essence" but not its "existence," its generality, but not its individuality. But when, occasionally, for one reason or another, we are confronted with an object which refuses to be classified, we see the "naked Reality" of this unique individual transcending all conceptual classifications and, in Sartre's technical language, begin painfully to "exist."

Beckett offers several interesting illustrations from Proust of the alternating wonder of reality once the customary conceptual mask of Habit has fallen from it, and the opposite state in which the marvelous slips into the mundane. The first, reminiscent of Sartrean nausea, occurs when the child in Proust's story enters an unfamiliar hotel room.

> There is no room for his body in this vast and hideous apartment, because his attention has peopled it with gigantic furniture, a storm of sound and an agony of colour. Habit has not had time to silence the explosions of the clock, reduce the hostility of the violet curtains,...Alone in this room that is not yet a room but cavern of wild beasts, invested on all sides by the implacable strangers whose privacy he has disturbed, he desires to die.[4]

But when he enters the same room a second time, the reverse experience takes place.

> He arrives tired and ill, as on the former occasion...Now, however, the dragon has been reduced to docility, and the cavern is a room...Already will, the will not to suffer, Habit, having recovered from its momentary paralysis, has laid the foundations of its evil and necessary structure, and the vision...begins to fade and to lose that miraculous relief and clarity that no effort of deliberate rememoration can impart or restore.[5]

In Beckett's view the loss of Habit is not totally without reward, however, and indeed, is the ultimate key to freedom from Suffering.

> The old ego dies hard. Such as it was, a minister of dullness, it was also an agent of security. When it ceases to perform that second function, when it is opposed by a phenomenon that it cannot reduce to the condition of a comfortable and familiar concept, when, in a word, it betrays its trust as a screen to spare its victim the spectacle of reality, it disappears, and the victim, now an ex-victim, for a moment free, is exposed to that reality—exposure that has its advantages and disadvantages.[6]

Here we notice a crucial ambiguity in Beckett's account very much like the ambiguity we saw in Sartre's notion of a "naked Reality." Do we, in the absurd experience, actually see reality as it is in itself, or do we simply realize *that* reality transcends our conceptualizations? The first position is, as we have seen, untenable on the absurdist's own argument for the separation of word and object, essence and existence. Unfortunately it is easy to confuse the two positions, as Beckett appears to have done in this early formulation. This is closely tied, as we will see shortly, with Beckett's use of the idealist language of Schopenhauer which holds out the promise of a veridical alternative to the illusion of ordinary projection.

As Sartre and Ionesco also perceived, stripped of its familiar conceptual garb, the object appears fresh and new, as though seen for the very first time, and absolutely unique and individual. Borrowing Schopenhauer's unusual and somewhat confusing language, borrowed in turn from Kant, Beckett contrasts the general *conceptual* classification of sense impressions in everyday cognition with the direct intuition of the unique essence or "Idea" of the concrete individual itself. In the *Critique of Pure Reason* Kant distinguished the Concepts of the Understanding by which we classify things as they appear to us in sense experience from the Ideas of Reason which include such things as the soul, God and the world as a whole, of which there is no sense experience.

For Kant the Ideas were merely "regulative;" that is, they did not designate real entities which we could understand or know existed. They were simply notions which we needed in order to understand the world as we do. Since conceptual understanding was limited by Kant to things as they *appear* to us in sense experience and Ideas were merely regulative, Kant's philosophy was left with the unhappy consequence that there is no knowledge or even understanding of reality itself. It made sense to talk about a reality transcending human thought, but just because it did transcend human ways of thinking, it could not be thought or described.

This proved to be too much for Kant's Idealist successors, Fichte, Hegel, Schelling, and Schopenhauer, who abandoned Kant's critical attitude toward Ideas in favor of a new conception of Ideas as a non-classificatory way of apprehending reality directly. In German philosophy throughout the 19th century, therefore, classification was limited to mere appearances, while Reality was apprehended in a totally different, if somewhat mysterious way. For Hegel Ideal Reality is the integration of everything into a gigantic contextual whole purposefully evolving through time; for Schopenhauer, on the other hand, the Ideas stand for timeless, eternal, distinct individuals in the Platonic tradition. Like many literary figures of the time, such as Croce and Bergson, Beckett uses Schopenhauer's notion of Idea to represent that direct intuition of individual existence detached from all selfish, practical purposes and desires and in direct contrast to the ordinary, purposeful, practical classification of the individual object into its generic kind or concept.

> But when the object is perceived as particular and unique and not merely the member of a family, when it appears independent of any general notion and detached from the sanity of a cause, isolated and inexplicable in the light of ignorance, then and then only may it be a source of enchantment. Unfortunately Habit has laid its veto on this form of perception, its action being precisely to hide the essence—the Idea—of the object in the haze of conception.[7]

As we saw in our investigation of Sartre's *Nausea*, the conceptual boundaries we cognitively impose on objects includes not only the classification of objects into nameable kinds, but the classification of sense impressions into *objects*. As Kant pointed out, "object" is itself a humanly imposed concept. Thus in *Nausea* objects not only become detached from their names, but eventually dissolve into an indiscriminate mist or fog. Somewhat like Hume, Beckett carries this line of reasoning one step further to include the disintegration of the concept of the *mental* object, the knowing subject or immutable self. This too is a convenient myth no less than the myth of a permanent, stable *physical* object. Subject and object are both in a constant state of flux, and each is constantly altering and being altered by the other.

For Sartre "nausea" and "existence" *heighten* the awareness of ego; for Beckett such experiences *diminish* that awareness. Subject and object arise together in the act of projecting the ordinary world of human concerns. As Beckett remarks in an earlier passage above, when that projection ceases the "ego... disappears." For convenience we can consider the object as a permanent entity for a changing subject or, as Beckett prefers in the later fiction, we can consider a permanent self before a changing object. But both are convenient fictions; in reality there is no such thing as a discrete, distinct subject or object.

> So far we have considered a mobile subject before an ideal object, immutable and incorruptible...Exemption from intrinsic flux in a given object does not change the fact that it is the correlative of a subject that does not enjoy such immunity. The observer infects the observed with his own mobility.[8]

Since subject and object arise in opposition to one another in a practical, active context of a subject wanting and moving to acquire an object, the key to the projection of a humanly interpreted world is purpose and desire. If the projected world is an illusion, then so is purpose and desire. As such diverse philosophers as Schopenhauer, Heidegger and John Dewey attest, we are basically purposeful creatures, doing one thing for the sake of another. Consequently we perceive things in terms of their ability to meet or thwart our needs and desires. Thus we base our classification of things on their reference to our purposes, and our attitude toward things is consequently interested, selfish and practical.

The concept of an object independent of the self appears as the goal of our wants and desires, and the concept of an independent self appears as the source of those desires and of their satisfaction or disappointment. The underlying structure of our view of the world, then, is the notion of an object for the sake of an independent subject. If that is an illusion, then so is the world constructed thereon. Therefore, echoing Schopenhauer and the Hindu and Buddhist philosophers he endorsed, as well as the Stoics, Beckett argues that our desire to possess things is based on an illusion. Either the object changes by the time we get it or we ourselves have changed.

> No object prolonged in this temporal dimension tolerates possession...All that is active, all that is time and space, is endowed with what might be described as an abstract, ideal and absolute impermeability.[9]

It is not that our particular view of things is mistaken, but that every human perception imposes its own distortions, even as it reveals new aspects of reality. There simply is no way of knowing reality as it is in itself. Thought and reality, essence and existence, are ultimately distinct and not to be confused with one another. As such, we must take all conceptualizations, including the concept of a subject and an object, with a certain "grain of salt." So far as our understanding is concerned we are locked within our own minds, imprisoned in a "sealed jar," as Beckett describes it in the novel, *Molloy*, internalizing everything within the self, as Rilke also tried to do.

> The good or evil disposition of the object has neither reality nor significance... Such as it was, it has been assimilated to the only world that has reality and significance, the world of our own latent consciousness, and its cosmography has suffered a dislocation.[10]

Since the problem springs from the illusion of accomplishing goals, achieving ends and satisfying desires, the solution consists in rejecting desire, that is, in overcoming, or at least seeing through, our ordinary biological impulse as purposeful, willing creatures, without which, as we have seen, the construction of our view of the world cannot take place. As Beckett says, Proust's treatment of Memory and Habit are those

> flying buttresses of the temple raised to commemorate the wisdom of the architect that is also the wisdom of all the sages, from Brahma to Leopardi, the wisdom that consists not in the satisfaction but in the ablation of desire.[11]

> We eliminate suffering, not by reducing those things which cause us suffering, but by dismantling the willing ego which makes suffering possible. Wisdom consists in obliterating the faculty of suffering rather than in a vain attempt to reduce the stimuli that exasperate that faculty.[12]

In following so strictly the Romantic, Idealist thought of the 19th century Beckett falls one step short in this early work of the bliss of emptiness he achieves in the later works. Assuming that ordinary forms of thought fail to capture reality as it is in itself, do we conclude that reality absolutely transcends *all* forms of thought, or do we hold out the hope that some other, *extraordinary* form of thought does gain direct access to the thing-in-itself? This is that crucial ambiguity in Beckett's early view we noticed before, an ambiguity which also infects Sartre's notion of our perception of a "naked World" in the experience of absurdity. The Romantic Idealists opt for the second, as a kind of intermediary step to the more radical position of the first. Some forms of thought are illusory, but others may *not* be so. This is a comforting assurance, but in principle the same argument would seem to work for *all* forms of thought. Word and object, essence and existence, are never identical; confusing the two is always an illusion. It is a subtle but crucial move, as we saw earlier, from the notion that we see a "naked World" to the realization *that* reality transcends all forms of human thought. It is one thing to see someone naked; it is quite another to know *that* they are wearing clothing.

Later Beckett himself makes that move, but in this early period he follows Schopenhauer's theory that by renouncing will and the whole classificatory mechanism of the understanding, we achieve an aesthetic and mystical oneness with the essential will-less Idea of the unique individual. Since desire, the ego-object distinction and the ordinary projected world form an inseparable package, rejecting any one of these is tantamount to rejecting the lot; thus, by renouncing the naive desire to possess the object, the projected world dissolves and the ego-object distinction collapses. Thus we recover, as the Romantics hoped, our lost synthesis of word and object, thought and reality, essence and existence, which philosophers have been trying to reunite since Aristotle's first attempt.

This essentially idealist and romantic notion had an extraordinary effect on intellectuals in the early part of the last century, including Bergson, Pater, Croce, and Baudelaire. The ordinary purposeful cognition of the world creates an ego-object split which alienates us from the world; while detached, disinterested mystical and aesthetic perception heals the ego-object split and reunites us with the object. This is a well-known concern of early 19th century Romantics, like Coleridge

> A poet's heart and intellect should be combined, intimately combined and unified with the great appearances of nature.[13]

> [Art is the] reconciler of nature and men. It is, therefore, the power of humanizing nature, of infusing the thoughts and possessions of man into everything which is the object of his contemplations,... [and whose object is to] make external, internal, the internal external, to make nature, thought, and thought nature.[14]

What is not so readily recognized is the impact of this way of thinking on such "moderns" as Nietzsche, D.H. Lawrence, and Baudelaire.

> The most characteristic quality of modern man; the strange contrast between an inner life to which nothing outward corresponds and an outward existence unrelated to what is within.[15]

> There is nothing of me that is alone and absolute except in my mind, and we shall find that the mind has no existence by itself; it is only the glitter of the sun on the surface of the water. So that my individualism is really an illusion. I am part of the great whole, and I can never escape. But I *can* deny my connections, break them and become a fragment. Then I am wretched.[16]

> The eye fixes itself on a tree, harmoniously swayed by the wind; in a few seconds that which in the brain of the poet would be only a completely natural simile becomes a fact. In the tree one's passions, longing, or melancholy come to life.[17]

This Romantic view continues to be of great importance in Gestalt and developmental psychology, *e.g.*, in Werner, Koffka, Arnheim and Kohler who hold that the ego-object distinction rises and falls with goal-directed, purposeful, practical activity. Because it is disinterested and detached from practical considerations, aesthetic experience transcends the ego-object distinction.

No doubt the experience referred to is a genuine one. In aesthetic experience the object does not appear as something for the sake of some further end which I need or want; and so I forget myself as a wanting, desiring ego for a moment and am simply absorbed in the perception of the object for its own sake. What is questionable in this analysis is whether this experience should be interpreted as a direct experience of absolute reality in which ego and object collapse into One, or whether, as I would prefer to say, putting it negatively, the realization that there is no longer any conceptual classification at work, no longer any purposeful opposition of subject and object. We are *released* from cognition without thereby acquiring a *new* cognition. We are *freed* of theories of reality, rather than achieving a *new* theory of reality.

Chapter Five: Beckett

In *Proust* Beckett describes this synthesis of subject and object and the collapse of past, present, and future, as

> the Paradise that has been lost. The identification of immediate with past experience, the recurrence of past action or reaction in the present, amounts to a participation between ideal and the real, imagination and direct apprehension, symbol and substance.[18]

Beckett also agrees with Schopenhauer that by overcoming will or purpose, we transcend our sense of time, and thus of death. As we saw earlier, our sense of time springs from our sense of purpose. By acting now, on the basis of remembered past experience, for some imagined future gain, I structure my world temporally. Our sense of time, in other words, is tied to our practical, purposive posture toward the world—and rises and falls with it. In the mystical, aesthetic vision

> the experience is at once imaginative and empirical, at once an evocation and direct perception, real without being merely actual, ideal without being merely abstract, the ideal real, the essential, the extra-temporal. But if this mystical experience communicates an extra-temporal essence, it follows that the communicant is for the moment an extra-temporal being. Consequently the Proustian solution consists...in the negation of Death because negation of Time. Death is dead because Time is dead.[19]

This is reminiscent of Roquentin's escape in *Nausea* from existence to the timeless, ideal realm of pure essence as exemplified in mathematical figures, songs, and stories. So, too, for Beckett, as for Schopenhauer, as for the Romantics generally, the chief avenue to this new freedom is art.

> So now in the exaltation of his brief eternity, having emerged from the darkness of time and habit and passion and intelligence, he understands the necessity of art. For in the brightness of art alone can be deciphered the baffled ecstasy that he had known before in the inscrutable superficies of a cloud, a triangle, a spire, a flower, a pebble, when the mystery, the essence, the Idea, imprisoned in matter [appears]...And he understands the meaning of Baudelaire's definition of reality as "the adequate union of subject and object."[20]

He even accepts Schopenhauer's elevation of music to the highest place among the arts. According to Schopenhauer, the other arts must approach reality indirectly through the intermediary of materials taken from the ordinary spatio-temporal realm of appearances, that is, through sensory images. Only music can bypass this, penetrating directly to the heart of reality. Because of the ego-object split, it becomes more and more difficult, within this Romantic framework, to find an adequate symbol or image from external phenomena to express the thought within. This is what T.S, Eliot called the problem of finding the "objective correlative," the problem which, according to Hegel, is the main motivation behind the shift from Classical to Romantic Art. The solution to this problem, Hegel said, was to internalize the image.[21] "External phenomena are no longer able to express this inward life," as Hegel said, and this leads to the desire for the kind of art voiced in Rilke's *Duino Elegies*, namely, in Hegel's words, "that mode of expression which is without externality, invisibly declaring itself, in other words a form of music simply, which is neither an object nor possesses form."[22]

The idea of music as the ideal art form towards which all the other arts tend has been closely associated with Romantic thought from its beginnings. Wackenroder, for example, wrote in 1799 that music "shows us all the movement of our spirit, disembodied," and Heine described music as that

> which perhaps aims at nothing less than the dissolution of the whole material world... Music is perhaps the last word of art... To me it is of great significance that Beethoven became deaf in the end so that even the invisible world of tones ceased to have any resonant reality for him,[23]

a view reminiscent of Keat's poetic statement that unheard melodies are sweeter than heard ones. Thus the Romantic, Idealist movement was torn between the desire to reunite external with internal by internalizing the external (subjective idealism) or reuniting them by externalizing the internal (objective idealism). Ultimately, neither works for the simple reason that there remains an external reality which transcends and can therefore never be completely reconciled with thought. This is the old problem of reconciling idealism with dualistic realism.

If we accept the conclusion that linguistic, conceptual thought fails to capture reality as it is in itself, how do we articulate what that reality *is*? As Robbe-Grillet found, it is obviously going to be very difficult to describe linguistically a reality which we assert to transcend all linguistic description. Here meaningful conceptual thought and language simply reach their outer limits. Do we say that since reality is without linguistic distinctions and demarcations it is therefore One and Indivisible, or do we simply say, negatively, that reality is not exhausted in but transcends all linguistic distinctions and demarcations? The first, chosen by Idealists and Spiritualists, affirms the existence of a monistic, transcendent Spiritual Reality behind all appearances, the second, which the Absurdists opt for, asserts that there is nothing describable or even thinkable behind the humanly projected world—often symbolized by the concept of Nothingness, or The Void.

At its outer limits, where ordinary words and concepts have exhausted their customary meanings, apparently contradictory formulations, like these, are used to express the same position, and what seem divergent paths arrive at a single destination. Paradoxically both "the One Reality" and "the Void" become symbols for the same failure of words to capture reality. What is at stake is ironically, not a theory of reality at all, but a theory of language, of how words do and do not relate to reality. In this early period Beckett uses the Idealist symbol of a transcendent, monistic reality; later he expresses himself in the symbols of nothingness.

Although Beckett later abandoned the Idealist belief in a transcendent Ideal Reality to be grasped in some non-cognitive form of intuition, he clings throughout to the notion that the solution consists in overcoming the illusion of the ordinary world of projected purpose. Whether there is a positive alternative or not, this must be rejected.

Beckett's later rejection of Schopenhauer is like the Buddhist rejection of a single Brahmanic Spiritual Reality in favor of the Void, or Nothingness. The ordinary view of the world is an illusion because it confuses concepts with objects, but no advance is made by interpreting this insight to mean that we have gained new knowledge of a new reality where concept and object finally do coincide. This is simply the same confusion all over again. It is better to say, with the Buddhists, that we now know there is *no* knowledge of any absolute Reality in this sense. And the best symbol for this position, assuming we must use *some* symbol, is "the Void." Hence instead of gaining knowledge, we simply give up all attempts to identify word and object.

This is not a metaphysical theory of reality, but a statement about the possibility of having a metaphysical theory of reality. It is not a theory about reality but a theory about theories. As the great 9th century Buddhist scholar Nagarjuna put it,

> The Great Sage preached the law of Emptiness
> In order to free men from all views.
> If one still holds the view that Emptiness exists,
> Such a person the Buddhas will not transform.[24]

> It cannot be called void or not void,
> Or both or neither;
> But in order to point it out,
> It is called, "the Void."[25]

"Reality" and "Void" are therefore mere symbols of the mutually transcending relation of word and object, thought and reality (as are all symbols once we refuse to identify or confuse them), symbols, in short, of the euphoric side of absurdity.

Instead of acquiring a new view of *reality* we gain a new insight into the relationship of word and thought to reality, *viz.*, that the two are distinct, each transcending the other, which is precisely what the Buddhists mean by Nothingness, that reality is, as Beckett says some 20 years later, *The Unnamable*.

In this novel (*The Unnamable*, 1958) Beckett explores in a stream-of-consciousness monologue the theoretical considerations which underlie the best of his late fiction. The problem which these works address is what alternative we have to the illusion of projection. Can we, for example, reject this in favor of some other, non-illusory approach to reality, as the Idealists urge? But this is impossible, as we have seen; there *is* no human way to understand reality as it is in itself. Kant was therefore right after all. The illusion of ordinary thought is not that it is mistaken, but that it falsely identifies word and object, essence and existence. But if reality transcends thought, it transcends all human thought, even the most spiritually refined and metaphysically sophisticated. So that won't work.

Perhaps we could simply stop thinking and talking altogether. But this, as Beckett has already said in *Proust*, flies in the face of our entire biological nature and is enormously difficult if not absolutely impossible. Nor can we literally call a halt to all our desires, needs and purposes, like we might shut off a water tap.

What else is there, then? We can't avoid projection, but we can become aware of it. What we can avoid, therefore, is the naive attachment of word to object. The position developed in *The Unnamable* is not to reject ordinary thought or try to replace it with some other, more sophisticated metaphysics, but simply to see it for what it is, a form of human projection; neither to encourage nor discourage but passively to allow it to take place without attaching to it any real importance. Similarly, in the Stoic "ablation of desire." We can't stop desire, but we can see through it to a source transcending the individual ego. I experience desires which I act on, but I am not aware of and do not control the ultimate springs of that desire, and this realization alienates the desire from me, blocking the ordinary identification of myself with this desiring ego. In Buddhist thought, from which Beckett borrows heavily, I then begin to identify myself with this underlying source of desire of which the ordinary ego we are aware of is but a manifestation.

By becoming aware of projection I continue to have desires and to act on them purposively, but I no longer identify my conscious ego as the ultimate source of the desire. Thus I go through the motions of thought, speech, and action aloof, detached, like the remote onlooker Ionesco speaks of, as in a playful, pointless game. Gradually words and thoughts are thereby detached from their ordinary projective significance, becoming pointless. Thus we still the desire to know, to describe, not by stopping it, but by allowing it to wear itself out, gradually running down like a wound up clock. As talk is exhausted we move toward silence; as the illuminating light of human understanding burns itself out, we anticipate darkness. Thus the goal Beckett holds out to us as a real possibility is symbolized by the weightless, evanescent, silent emptiness of absurdity.

What, for example, are we to say about the existence of individual objects? We realize they arise only through the projection of human concerns and interests. But there they are, nonetheless. How should we respond to them? Let them appear, *knowing* they are human projections.

> And things, what is the correct attitude to adopt toward things? And, to begin with, are they necessary? What a question. But I have few illusions, things are to be expected. The best is not to decide anything... in advance. If a thing turns up, for some reason or another, take it into consideration. Where there are

people, it is said, there are things,...The thing to avoid...is the spirit of system. People with things, people without things, things without people, what does it matter, I flatter myself it will not take me long to scatter them, whenever I choose to the winds.[26]

As Marie says in several of Ionesco's plays, the important thing is not to take any of this too seriously, tracing out all its connections, pursuing explanations, formulating theories, as though we could finally get to the bottom of things, exhausting reality in the net of our thought. The corollary of this, of course, is that in a detached manner there is no harm in desiring, thinking, speaking, and acting—or even explaining.

Beckett's attitude in this passage is also very like the Zen Buddhist attempt to reconcile the proclaimed emptiness of reality with the cluttered world of ordinary sense perception. We are not to pretend the latter doesn't exist, but simply to realize that it is a form of human projection. As the San-lun scholar, Seng-chao wrote in the 5th century,

> When we say that there is neither existence nor non-existence, does it mean to wipe out all the myriad things, blot out our seeing and hearing, and be in a state without sound, form or substance before we can call it truth? Truly, truth is in accord with things as they are and therefore is opposed to none... Not being existent and not being nonexistent do not mean that there are no things, but that all things are not things in the absolute metaphysical sense... Therefore the scripture [of Nagarjuna] says, "Matter is empty by virtue of its own nature; it is not empty because it has been destroyed."[27]

Similarly, in the famous Zen exchange between Wo-luan and Hui-neng, Wo-luan had written,

> I, Wo-luan, know a device
> Whereby to blot out all my thoughts;
> The objective world no more stirs the mind,
> And daily matures my Enlightenment!

To which Hui-neng, Zen's Fifth Patriarch, responded,

> I, Hui-neng, know no device,
> My thoughts are not suppressed.
> The objective world ever stirs the mind,
> And what's the use of maturing Enlightenment?[28]

Similarly, the attempt in the *Bhagavad Gita* to reconcile the active life with the illusion of goal-directed activity—simply act without attachment to the object of desire.

As we saw in *Proust*, despite the extreme relativity of concepts such as the permanent ego or the unchanging object, in order to communicate we must select *some* of these necessary fictions. In *The Unnameable*, as in all his important fiction, Beckett selects the point of view of the unchanging subject in a fixed location, looking out upon a world in which objects have completely dissolved and broken down.

> But the best is to think of myself as fixed and at the centre of this place, whatever its shape and extent may be. This is also probably the most pleasing to me. In a word, no change apparently since I have been here, disorder of the lights perhaps an illusion, all change to be feared, incomprehensible uneasiness.[29]

This is the standpoint of Beckett's central characters in *Endgame*, tied to one spot looking out upon a bleak, empty world.

As Berenger says in Ionesco's A *Stroll in the Air*, the point is to get away from the *need* to explain, to justify, the intellectual's compulsion to go beyond the given trivia of daily life toward the construction of a theory which will tie it all together, making more sense of it than it really has.

> If I could be a forest, caught in a thicket, or wandering around in circles, it would be the end of this blither, I'd describe the leaves, one by one... Those are good moments, for one who has not to say, but it's not I, it's not I, where am I, what am I doing, all this time, as if that mattered, but there it is, that takes the heart out of you, your heart isn't in it any more...it's not love, not curiosity, it's because you're tired, you want to stop... lie no more, speak no more, close your eyes,... after that you'll make short work of it.[30]

The main thing to avoid is the "desire to know," the pretension, that is, of trying to reduce reality to the form of human thought.

> From the unexceptionable order which has prevailed here up to date may I infer that such will always be the case? I may of course. But the mere fact of asking myself such a question gives me to reflect... Can it be I am prey of a genuine preoccupation, of a need to know as one might say?[31]

> Deplorable mania, when something happens, to inquire what. If only I were not obliged to manifest. And why speak of a cry? Perhaps it is something breaking, some two things colliding. There are sounds here, from time to time, let that suffice.[32]

> Madness, the mad wish to know, to remember... I won't be caught at that again... And now let us think no more about it, think no more about anything, think no more.[33]

At the same time, the goal proposed is a difficult one, as Becket recognizes. We are caught in the middle, as Camus also recognized, in the dilemma of being unable to really understand coupled with an inability to ignore the bits of partial understanding we do have. We haven't anything to say, yet we can't be quiet either.

> Yes, in my life, since we must call it so, there were three things, the inability to speak, the inability to be silent and solitude.[34]

The proposed solution, admittedly difficult, is to accept the world as it appears to us without attaching to it any absolute importance, to engage in practical action, as the *Bhagavad Gita* suggests, without attachment to the goal of action, to speak without imagining our words attached to any independent reality. This, of course, is difficult. Our very nature is to project a world of human interests. Even when we realize the absolute correspondence of word and object is an illusion, the projected world does not go away. Yet as Berenger affirms in *A Stroll in the Air*, behind our ordinary biological nature there may lie an even deeper instinct to escape projection, to embrace emptiness, in Berenger's words, "to fly." As the Buddhists say, perhaps our true nature is *not* the ordinary one we are most aware of.

> Impossible to stop them, impossible to stop, I'm in words, made of words, others' words,...the air, the walls, the floor, the ceiling, all words, the whole world is here with me, I'm in the air, the walls,...everything yields, opens, ebbs, flows, like flakes, I'm all these flakes, meeting, mingling, falling asunder...I'm all these words, all these strangers, this dust of words, with no ground for their settling...and nothing else, yes, something else, that I'm something quite different, a quite different thing, a wordless thing in an empty place, a hard shut dry cold black place, where nothing stirs, nothing speaks.[35]

This, then, is the goal of emptiness, however difficult to attain.

> If I could speak and yet say nothing, really nothing...But it seems impossible to speak and yet say nothing, you think you have succeeded, but you always overlook something, a little yes, a little... And yet I do not despair, this time...of not going from here, of ending here. What prevents the miracle is the spirit of method to which I have perhaps been a little too addicted.[36]

> I don't mind failing, it's a pleasure, but I want to go silent. Not as just now, the better to listen, but peacefully, victorious, without ulterior object. Then it would be a life worth having, a life at last.[37]

As we saw in the second chapter (Camus), so long as absurdity is perceived privately as the absence of something which ought to be present, whether reason, meaning, knowledge, or whatever, the perception of absurdity is tragic and heavy. The light side of absurdity consists in removing the hope, or expectation that the world *ought* to be reasonable, meaningful, knowable. If Beckett is silently listening, he is still expecting, hoping, waiting for an answer, like the characters in *Waiting for Godot*, and thus still locked in the illusion of some final and complete answer. In addition to the dilemma of having an answer and not having an answer, there is also the lack of interest in asking the question—and this is what Beckett seeks.

> Silence, yes, but what silence! For it is all very fine to keep silent, but one has also to consider the kind of silence one keeps. I listened. One might as well speak and be done with it.[38]

If, like God, our understanding penetrated to the heart of reality, there would be no problem. If, like a stone, we had absolutely no sense of the world, there would equally be no problem. The problem is that we are stuck in a hopeless compromise between the two, illuminating partial glimpses of the world from interested human points of view, but unable to know things as they really are in themselves. This is what prevents complete acceptance of the empty side of absurdity.

> This meaningless voice which prevents you from being nothing, just barely prevents you from being nothing and nowhere, just enough to keep alight this yellow flame feebly darting from side to side, panting, as if straining to tear itself from its wick, it should never have been lit, or it should never have been fed, or it should have been put out.[39]

What he wants is to be beyond the desire to know, neither knowing nor realizing he doesn't know, and not wanting to know. But this highly desirable goal cannot be achieved at once, but only after the desire to speak and to know is thoroughly exhausted, having worn itself out, as in a Zen koan. As a watch, left to itself, continues to run, but not indefinitely. Sheer inertia carries it along for a while, but hourly slowing down, it eventually comes to a stop. So habit carries thought, speech and action along past the recognition of their illusory goal for a time, eventually wears down, and stops. As Wittgenstein said at the end of the *Tractatus*, we philosophize in order to get rid of philosophizing. So Becket proposes in *The Unnamable* to talk his way into silence.

> My speech-parched voice at rest would fill with spittle, I'd let it flow over and over, happy at last, dribbling with life, my pensum ended, in the silence... Squeeze, squeeze, not too hard, but squeeze a little longer, this is perhaps about you, and your goal at hand. After ten thousand words?[40]

As Berenger realized in *A Stroll in the Air*, the last illusion for the intellectual is the attempt to explain the profound limitations of all explanation, to theorize about the fallibility of theorizing—this, in short, is the last goal-directed activity we take seriously. Thus the image in Beckett's plays of the immobile subject, not going anywhere, not wanting to go anywhere, which also calls to mind the Buddha's refusal to leave his fixed place beneath the Bo tree until he had made an end of his attachments to the ordinary world.

> All this business of a labour to be accomplished, before I can end, of words to say, a truth to recover, in order to say it, before I can end, of an imposed task, once known, long neglected, finally forgotten, to perform, before I can be done with speaking, done with listening, I invented it all, in the hope it would console me, help me to go on, allow me to think of myself as somewhere on a

road, moving, between a beginning and an end, gaining ground, losing ground,... but somehow making headway. All lies. I have nothing to do, that is to say—nothing in particular. I have to speak, whatever that means. Having nothing to say, no words but the words of others, I have to speak.[41]

It's of me now I must speak, even if I have to do it with their language it will be a start, a step toward silence and the end of madness, the madness of having to speak and not being able to, except of things that don't concern me...that they have crammed me full to prevent me from saying who I am...Dear incomprehension, it's thanks to you I'll be myself, in the end. Nothing will remain of all the lies they have glutted me with. And I'll be myself at last, as a starveling belches his odorless wind, before the bliss of a coma.[42]

Other images of this blissful emptiness he hopes to achieve are the Worm, who is truly beyond knowing, and, unlike Ionesco's recurrent theme of luminosity, the absolute blackness when the flickering light of conscious inquiry and projection finally ceases.

Worm, to say he does not know what he is, where he is, what is happening, is to underestimate him. What he does not know is that there is anything to know. His senses tell him nothing, nothing about himself, nothing about the rest, and this distinction is beyond him. Feeling nothing, knowing nothing, he exists nevertheless, but not for himself, for others, others conceive him and say, Worm is, since we conceive him...The one ignorant of himself and silent, ignorant of his silence and silent, who could not be and gave up trying.[43]

As we saw in our discussion of Aristotle in the first chapter, although things exist in the world without the aid of human consciousness, it is only with human thought and the formulation of "essence" that existence becomes an issue or concern. Without essence there is no awareness of existence. Beyond the orbit of this concern for and awareness of existence is the ultimate silence Beckett refers to in an earlier passage above, a silence which is beyond listening, not even knowing it *is* silence, a silence which has transcended the tragic distance between the desire to speak and the impossibility of saying nothing.

The other symbol of euphoric emptiness in *The Unnamable* is total, pitch-black darkness, a recurring image in Beckett's plays, particularly *Endgame*. In this set of images, light symbolizes ideal, absolute knowledge, the complete correspondence of word and object, thought and reality, the kind of knowledge God has (and which, in Beckett's earlier view, the Idealists have). Darkness is the complete absence of that knowledge which we find in Worm. Both are ideal states, however; as human beings, we are caught in between these two extremes capable of neither completely, yet equally incapable of renouncing either completely.

Thus we ordinarily live neither in light nor in darkness, but in "the grey," not knowing but still desiring to know, not saying anything, but unable to keep silent, capable of partial understanding but incapable of total understanding. Just as Beckett's goal is to move from talk we do not take seriously to silence, so we begin in the grey and move toward blackness. And just as silence will finally be achieved by talking ourselves out, so darkness will come when the dim grey light of projecting understanding finally burns itself out.

The lead characters of Beckett's plays are always located in the very last stage of the move from grey to darkness, like Ionesco's characters, though in a different set of images, on the verge of flight, but not able to remain aloft for long.

> Air, the air, is there anything to be squeezed from that old chestnut? Close to me it is grey, dimly transparent, and beyond that charmed circle deepens and spreads its fine impenetrable veils...This grey, first murky, then frankly opaque, is luminous nonetheless.[44]

> Whether all grow black, or all grow bright, or all remain grey, it is grey we need, to begin with, because of what it is, and of what it can do, made of bright and black, unable to shed the former, or the latter, and be the latter or the former alone.[45]

> The grey means nothing, the grey silence is not necessarily a mere lull, to be got through somehow, it may be final, or it may not. But the lamps unattended will not burn on forever, on the contrary, they will go out, little by little, without attendants to charge them anew, and go silent, in the end. Then it will be black. But it is with the black as with the grey, the black proves nothing either, as to the nature of the silence which it inspissates (as it were).[46]

In the grey, looking forward to the black, but not there yet and perhaps incapable of ever getting there—this is the posture of most of Beckett's fictional characters, as we will see. Beckett's final image of the blissful emptiness, unlike Ionesco's image of bright, luminous light, is of the immobile, unchanging will-less self-confronting a darkened, empty space.

> There, now there is no one here but me,...these creatures have never been, only I and this black void have ever been. And the sound? No, all is silent. And the lights, on which I had set such store, must they too go out? Yes, out with them, there is no light here. No grey either, black is what I should have said. Nothing then but me, of which I know nothing, except that I have never uttered, and this black, of which I know nothing either, except that it is black, and empty.[47]

These themes are very carefully worked out in all of Beckett's fiction, most successfully in the plays, but also in his novels, which we will examine first, though very briefly. These novels are written in a Joycean third-person stream-of-consciousness style, though, unlike *The Unnamable*, they do have a thin action plot, dealing with the rather insignificant adventures of a single socially outcast man, whether Watt, Murphy or Molloy, from whom the novels take their titles. These commonplace adventures fairly transparently symbolize the movement of an individual toward the goal of blissful emptiness, the down-and-out characters representing someone almost but not quite having succeeded in transcending the ordinary conventional world of mundane middle-class concerns. Unlike Ionesco's characters who are generally middle-class, educated and professional, Beckett's characters are out of the mainstream of ordinary life. Beckett makes much of the irony that these normally despised creatures are to be envied, not pitied. Their only problem is that they are not far enough out of the conventional rut.

Watt (1953), for example, discovers, like Roquentin in *Nausea*, the painful absurd detachment of word and object, the failure of words to attach meaningfully to their objects.

> For Watt now found himself in the midst of things which, if they consented to be named, did so as it were with reluctance...Looking at a pot, for example,...it was in vain that Watt said, Pot, pot. Well, perhaps not quite in vain, but nearly. For it was not a pot, the more he looked,...reflected...It resembled a pot, it was almost a pot, but it was not a pot of which one could say, Pot, pot, and be comforted. It was in vain that it answered, with unexceptionable adequacy, all the purposes, and performed all the offices of a pot, it was not a pot...[it was] painful to Watt...having to do with things of which the known name...was not the name, any more for him...For the pot remained a pot...for everyone but Watt.[48]

In an earlier novel, *Murphy* (1938), the central character attempts to work his way out of this painful dislocation of word and object, essence and existence. In this early work Beckett is still thinking his way through the Idealist program of retreating from the illusory objective world to a subjective world within. In the novel this is symbolized by Murphy's positive attitude toward insanity, envying the schizophrenic's rejection of the world in favor of a private inner world.

> Murphy's mind pictured itself as a large hollow sphere, hermetically closed to the universe without...[but] not an impoverishment...Nothing ever had been, was or would be in the universe outside it but was already present...in the universe inside it.[49]

> There was the mental fact and there was the physical fact equally real if not equally pleasant...Thus Murphy felt himself split in two, a body and a mind.[50]

Murphy moves from outer to inner in terms of the light-dark images of *The Unnamable*, where light is the projective tendency of mind to illuminate and thereby construct a comprehensible interpreted external reality, while dark is our latent ("virtual") capacity to see through this illusion, turning it off.

> The mind felt its actual part to be above and bright, its virtual beneath and fading into dark...There were three zones, light, half-light, dark, each with its speciality.[51]

The light zone is the ordinary, successful projection of an existing reality external to us and therefore outside the control of our will, somewhat like Coleridge's notion of "primary Imagination."

> In the first were the forms, with parallel, radiant abstract of the day's life, with elements of physical experience available for a new arrangement...Here the whole physical fiasco became a howling success.

The second is the world of imagination, in which we freely reconstitute from elements of ordinary experience pure essences, released from existence, like the song Roquentin admires in *Nausea* and something like Coleridge's "secondary Imagination." This is essentially the Schopenhauerian "aesthetic" stage which Beckett now sees as only intermediary to the more important and final third stage of darkness. Since these pure objects of thought are no longer perceived as being contrary to our individual wills, the attitude toward them is, as we saw in Schopenhauer, one of peaceful contemplation, as Roquentin also found. "In the second were the forms without parallel. Here the pleasure was contemplative."[52]

In the third zone, the dark, we neither naively project a world nor deliberately construct an imaginary one, we simply become *aware* of projection. Part of this awareness is the realization of the limits of the self-contained power and freedom of the conscious ego. We are free, of course, to act upon our desires and concerns as they present themselves to us, but we do not control these desires themselves. They are deeply rooted in our biological nature. An important part of the awareness of projection, therefore, is the recognition that the self-subsistent ego freely acting to possess or avoid self-subsistent objective entities is itself a part, indeed the core of projection, and hence, an illusion. Reality must not, therefore, be equated or confused with it, since reality transcends this human way of thinking. Thus in the dark zone, as Schopenhauer suggests, objective distinctions and subjective distinctions both collapse, including the primary subject-object distinction, into a mystical will-less identification with a transcendent reality.

To compound the comparison, the final release of will acts as a new kind of freedom, an ironic freedom *from* the individual freedom of the will.

> The third, the dark, was a flux of forms, a perpetual coming together and a falling asunder of forms...[a] sensation of being a missile without phenomena or target, caught up in a tumult of non-Newtonian motion...as his body set him free more and more in his absolute mind...in the will-lessness, a mote in its absolute freedom.[53]

For Murphy, who works in a mental institution, the dark zone, to which he aspires, is exemplified in the schizophrenic rejection of reality in favor of the cultivation of some private fantasy. Like the Shakespearean fool, Murphy reverses our usual assessment of madness. The insane are less mad than the madness of normal existence which Beckett describes in *The Unnamable*. Murphy begins to realize that psychiatric treatment merely translates the sufferer from his own pernicious little private dung heap to the glorious world of discrete particulars...to wonder, love, hate, desire, rejoice and howl in a reasonable balanced manner...with the society of others in the same predicament...All this was duly revolting to Murphy, whose experience as a physical and rational being obliged him to call sanctuary what the psychiatrists called exile and to think of the patients not as banished from a system of benefits but as escaped from a colossal fiasco.[54]

It is now this dark zone of blissful emptiness which Murphy seeks, "I am not of the big world, I am of the little world," and which he achieves just as he is dying.

Murphy began to see nothing, that colorlessness which is such a rare post-natal treat, being the absence...not of *percipere* but of *percipi*. His other senses also found themselves at peace, an unexpected pleasure. Not the numb peace of their own suspension, but the positive peace that comes when the somethings give way, or perhaps simply add up, to the Nothing, than which in the guffaw of the Abderite naught is more real. Time did not cease, that would be asking too much, but the wheels of rounds and pauses did, as Murphy... continued to suck in, through all the posterns of his withered soul, the accidentless One-and-Only, conveniently called Nothing.[55]

The Abderite referred to is the Greek stoic, Democritus of the Abdera, who said, as Beckett is fond of quoting, "Nothing is more real than nothing." There are also obvious references to Buddhist thought, not only in the notion of reality as "the Nothing" (rather than the all-encompassing monistic reality whether of the Brahmins or of the Idealists), but also in the reference to time as "the wheels of rounds and pauses." It is not clear which of the Buddhist authors Beckett consulted, though it is clear that he did read some translations of Buddhist texts, as did Ionesco. Nonetheless, it might be interesting to compare Murphy's final statement above with the Zen patriarch, Huang-po's explanation of "the Void" as a symbol of the transcendence of reality from all human categories.

[Reality] is not green nor yellow and has neither form nor appearance. It does not belong to the categories of things which exist or do not exist... It is neither long nor short, for it transcends all limits, measures, names, traces and comparisons. It is that which you see before you—begin to reason about it and you at once fall into error. It is like the boundless void which cannot be fathomed or measured.[56]

Molloy (1966) also describes the attempt to escape the projected world in which we have imprisoned ourselves into a blissful emptiness beyond names, explanations, structures of thought.

For to know is nothing, not to want to know anything likewise, but to be beyond knowing anything, that is when peace enters in, to the soul of the incurious seeker.[57]

> Not to want to say, not to know what you want to say, not to be able to say what you think you want to say, and never to stop saying, or hardly ever, that is the thing to keep in mind, even in the heat of composition.[58]

> And even my sense of identity was wrapped in a namelessness often hard to penetrate, as we have seen I think. And so on for all the other things which made merry with my senses...There could be no things but nameless things, no names but thingless names...What do I know now...when the icy words hail down upon me, the icy meanings, and the world dies too, foully named. All I know is what the words know, and the dead things, and that makes a handsome little sum, with a beginning, a middle and an end as in the well-built phrase...it little matters what I say...Saying is inventing. Wrong...You invent nothing, you think you are inventing.[59]

> There were times when I forgot not only who I was, but that I was, forgot to be, then I was no longer that sealed jar to which I owed my being so well preserved, but a wall gave way and I filled with roots and tame stems...But that did not happen to me often, mostly I stayed in my jar...But in there you have to be careful, ask yourself questions. For my part I willingly asked myself questions, one after the other...And yet it meant nothing to me to be still there.[60]

In the novels Beckett's characters *describe* their plight in terms of such images as darkness, silence, sealed enclosures, and a journey. In the plays Beckett *displays* these images concretely, and as in Ionesco's plays, the characters do the things Watt, Murphy and Molloy *talk about*. Therefore the plays provide Beckett's most successful exploration of such themes, especially *Waiting for Godot* and *Endgame*, which we will examine in some detail.

Waiting for Godot deals with the problem of cutting the last links that bind us to the projected world of human purposes and interests. The central characters in this play, Vladimir and Estragon, find themselves in the difficult intermediary position Beckett defines in *The Unnamable*, unable to say anything and yet also unable to keep silent. They find themselves already on the outer fringes of the conventionally constructed world, past their prime of life, socially outcast or at least insignificant, but not quite able to take that final step. They don't take it seriously any more, but they can't quite give up the game entirely. They have succeeded in penetrating the naive illusion of projection, and no longer attach any real significance to their speech or action. Yet they cling half-heartedly to one final illusion, the hope that Godot will come.

The central dramatic problem of the play is not, then, whether Godot will *come* or not, but whether to continue *waiting* for Godot. The problem is, as we have seen, Beckett's problem whether we *can* give it up entirely.

As with most absurdist fiction, the plot is very thin; Vladimir and Estragon wait each day for Godot with whom they believe they have an appointment to discuss some possible employment. But by nightfall Godot has not arrived, and Vladimir and Estragon debate whether to return the next day to continue their vigil, which, reluctantly, they finally decide to do. But Godot does not arrive the following day, and so it goes day after day. There is never much hope of Godot's arriving. They are not sure there is a Godot, whether he knows them, or even intended to meet with them, and if he did, it is still not clear what time of day or even on what day the appointment was supposed to take place. Still, they are held to their expectation by the thinnest possible diminishing thread. Not really expecting him to come, they can't quite give up the pretense or habit of hoping he will.

Like most great art Beckett's images are rich in multiple, overlapping nuances. The tree, for example, where Vladimir and Estragon wait. Is this the "tree of life" which is dying, the Bo tree where the Buddha waited for enlightenment, or the tree of Golgotha? It is not identical with any of these, of course, but all three meanings are probably meant to enrich this image. Certainly Beckett does not discourage any of them. Vladimir and Estragon, for example, talk about hanging themselves from the tree, they discuss the happenstance that one of the two criminals hung with Christ was saved while the other was not. The name Godot has often been interpreted as a misspelling of God, all of which supports and reinforces this religious interpretation. Godot appears to represent man's thirst for absolute knowledge: in so far as God is a symbol for the absolute, 'Godot' carries this religious connotation. The tree also symbolizes life, the tree of life, as when the characters discuss whether it is losing its leaves. But these nuances of meaning do not support the overall structure of the play. As with Ionesco, the dominant thrust of the play is metaphysical; other layers of meaning, and there are many, are subsidiary and supportive.

The two characters, Vladimir and Estragon, represent the two sides of the problem, the two poles within an individual which makes final release into blissful emptiness difficult. Estragon wants to give up waiting, Vladimir prefers to wait. Each time Estragon proposes they leave ("I'm going") Vladimir talks him into staying a little longer. Thus the two characters represent opposed, but complementary character traits, neither of which can exist without the other. Vladimir is practical, persistent, a man of fixed habits and little humor, a literalist who hates dreams and relies on past regularities. Estragon, on the other hand, is a volatile, humorous dreamer, a poet who has little faith in theories or regularities of any sort. Together they represent the theme of wanting to leave but being unable to do so.

Equally complementary are the other two characters in the play, Pozzo and Lucky, who appear briefly from time to time. Pozzo and Lucky represent the folly of ordinary naive absorption in the world which brings them nothing but suffering, infirmity, old age and death, as in traditional Buddhism. Like Ionesco, Beckett supports his image of absurd heaviness with themes of human brutality, vanity, blind rage and stupidity, with Pozzo and Lucky standing to one another not only in the mind-body relation but also in the master-slave relationship. While Vladimir and Estragon are already on the outer periphery of naive absorption in the projected world, Pozzo and Lucky are caught in the center of that illusion. While Vladimir and Estragon represent an advanced but not final stage toward complete release, Pozzo and Lucky are still at an elementary, primitive stage of human awareness.

Involved in the idea of waiting is Beckett's notion, borrowed from Schopenhauer, of the illusion of purposeful action through time which we saw earlier in his analysis of Proust. The ordinary meaningful structure of the world, as we saw, is based largely on our purposeful posture toward things, doing something today for the sake of something else in the future. Thus we connect objects in the past, present and future into a coherent unity which ordinarily gives our lives meaning. Thus we manage to stretch out our lives in pursuing and accomplishing our life goals. This gives each person's life a structural development or "story-line," and gives each of us a sense of meaningfully filled time. But if that is an illusion, as Beckett believes, the entire facade of that projected world collapses. Past, present, future are no longer connected and time becomes something merely to be spent, filled, gotten through somehow. Nothing is "accomplished" in time but old age and death, toward which we have nothing to do but wait.

This is vividly conveyed in *Waiting for Godot* where the ordinary span of time bridging past and future collapses, leveling and shortening everything in its path. We ordinarily "stretch" out our lives with the accomplishment of our purposes. Without purpose, time "snaps back" to something short in significance, though paradoxically long in boredom. We can see this in everyday life. When we are bored, with "nothing to do," time drags by endlessly, but when someone asks us later what we've been doing, we say, "oh, nothing," which is precisely all we will remember of it later. On the other hand, when we are deeply engrossed in some meaningful pursuit, the hours fly by and we remember it as a full day packed with accomplishment, and this stretches a day which in another sense was so short. The most common experience in daily life of time hanging heavily is waiting for someone, which makes this such a powerful image in the play.

Thus Estragon and Vladimir aimlessly wait, passing time, idling away the hours under a fragile illusion, which they are barely able to maintain, of meaningful expectation. This is no reason for living, but only an excuse. Since nothing significant ever happens, meaningful change is an illusion. As Borges points out in his article on time, without the possibility of purposeful action the sense of time contracts and there is no more significance (*i.e.*, "essence") to the span of 80 years than there is to 80 seconds. Just as objects can be existentially heavy and essentially light, so time can be physically long and experientially short. Indeed it is so short it is reduced to nothing, "shortness" being a metaphor for the unreality of time. Hence the sense of a person stretching out his life with activity and accomplishment is an illusion; he is dead, or as good as dead, as soon as he is born. As Pozzo says,

> Have you not done tormenting me with your accursed time?...One day, is that not enough for you, one day like any other day he went dumb, one day I went

blind, one day we'll die, the same day, same second...They gave birth astride of a grave. The light gleams an instant, then it's night once more.[61]

In this absurdist vision of time, the only thing we can expect time to bring is death, symbolized in the play by nightfall. Each time Pozzo and Lucky appear they have become progressively infirm, decrepit, nearer and nearer to death, although from the standpoint of the absurd unreality of time, Estragon denies that they have changed. But aside from death, time brings nothing, nothing really ever happens. The opening lines of the play tell the whole story.

Estragon: Nothing to be done.
Vladimir: I'm beginning to come round to that opinion.[62]

Since the time must be got through somehow they engage in idle chatter, word games to while away the hours. There is nothing to do but wait. Or at least this is the *most* they can do; the question remains whether they can stop waiting. Vladimir would like to quit wasting time with idle talk and get on with some meaningful activity.

Vladimir: Let's not waste our time in idle discourse! Let us do something, while we have the chance.[63]

This is like Marguerite's position in *Exit the King*, to cling to the world of civic duty and significant action. Estragon, on the other hand, following Marie's advice as it were, would like to stop talking altogether, to go silent, as Beckett proposes in *The Unnamable*.

Estragon: Let's stop talking for a minute...Why will you never let me sleep.[64]

In the meantime, they agree to pass the hours in mindless conversation, in a playful parody of meaningful discourse. The point of talk is gone; all that remains is the habit of talking, going through the motions, as we idly go through a routine game to pass the time. Here Beckett returns to the image in *The Unnamable* of achieving silence by talking ourselves out.

Estragon: In the meantime let us try and converse calmly, since we are incapable of keeping silent.
Vladimir: You're right, we're inexhaustible.
Estragon: It's so we won't think.[65]

After Pozzo and Lucky leave Vladimir says,

Vladimir: That passed the time.
Estragon: It would have passed in any case.
Vladimir: Yes, but not so rapidly.[66]

They play a variety of such games, usually at Vladimir's invitation.

> Estragon: I'm going.
> Vladimir: Will you not play?[67]

This momentarily helps to pass the time and support the fragile illusion of a normal life in a naively meaningful world. In the farcical exchange over the boots, Estragon says to Vladimir, whose nickname is Didi,

> Estragon: We always find something, eh Didi, to give us the impression we exist?[68]

But not for long. In another similar exchange over the turnips and carrots,

> Vladimir: This is becoming really insignificant.
> Estragon: Not enough.[69]

Talk, even the most aimless chatter can exhaust the need to talk, but it can also restore the habitual link to the ordinary world of conventional concerns, keeping alive, though faintly, what Beckett calls Habit. Thus by talking we continue the ordinary madness which prevents our escape.

> Vladimir: All I know is that the hours are long, under these conditions, and constrains us to beguile them with proceedings which—how shall I say—which may at first sight seem reasonable, until they become a habit. You may say it is to prevent our reason from foundering. No doubt. But has it not long been straying in the night without end of the abyssal depths?...
> Estragon: We are born mad. Some remain so.[70]

This is the theme of reverse madness we have seen in *The Unnamable* and in *Murphy*.

Thus, waiting for Godot represents the last remaining link to the comforting ordinary world of conventional expectations.

> Estragon (his mouth full of carrot): We're not tied?
> Vladimir: I don't hear a word you're saying.
> Estragon (chews, swallows): I'm asking you if we're tied.
> Vladimir: Tied?
> Estragon: ti-ed.
> Vladimir: How do you mean tied?
> Estragon: Down.
> Vladimir: But to whom? By whom?
> Estragon: To your man.
> Vladimir: To Godot? Tied to Godot! What an idea! No question of it. (Pause) For the moment.
> Estragon: His name is Godot?
> Vladimir: I think so.

Estragon: Fancy that.[71]

At times it seems best to cling to this thinnest of hopes, despite Estragon's skepticism and reluctance, and so they continue to "squeeze" out more "dead words," clichés, as in Ionesco's *The Bald Soprano*.

> Estragon: So long as one knows.
> Vladimir: One can bide one's time.
> Estragon: One knows what to expect.
> Vladimir: No further need to worry.
> Estragon: Simply wait.
> Vladimir: We're used to it.[72]

On the other hand, the expectation is a transparent sham which Estragon especially detests.

> Estragon: In the meantime nothing happens...
> Nothing happens, nobody comes, nobody goes, it's awful![73]

Vladimir and Estragon are like two sides of a single person. The dilemma they face requires both these points of view: stubbornly hoping and giving up all hope. Since the presence of the other is a constant reminder of that dilemma, each would be happier without the other, yet they can't exist apart from one another.

> Vladimir (who has been alone): All day I've felt in great form... I missed you... and at the same time I was happy.
> Estragon: You feel worse when I'm with you, I feel better alone too.
> Vladimir: Then why do you always come crawling back?
> Estragon: I don't know.[74]

Thus the two exist in a delicate tension. Each prevents the other from his own resolution, Estragon preventing Vladimir from slipping mindlessly back into Habit and Vladimir preventing Estragon from slipping quietly off into oblivion.

Sometimes, as in an earlier passage, Vladimir seems momentarily to convince Estragon that they are right to wait. At other times Estragon gains the upper hand and Vladimir seems on the verge of giving up the futile waiting. At one point Vladimir continues Pozzo's reflection on the absurd shortness, or rather unreality, of temporal extension, arriving finally almost at Estragon's total rejection of habit and purposeful expectation.

> Vladimir: Astride of a grave and a difficult birth. Down in the hole, lingeringly, the grave-digger puts on the forceps. We have time to grow old. The air is full of our cries. But habit is a great deadener...I can't go on.[75]

But at that very moment a young boy appears with a message from Godot, and Vladimir, his hopes again revived, agrees to return the following day to wait for Godot. Estragon, who would rather stop hoping than to have Godot come, is obviously upset over the boy's appearance.

Estragon: I'm unhappy.[76]

For it looks like Estragon's inseparable partner, Vladimir, will never stop waiting till he dies, that is, until nightfall when they can leave. As Vladimir says earlier to Pozzo,

Vladimir: Will night ever come?
Pozzo: You don't feel like going until it does?[77]

From Estragon's point of view the more they wait the more they are drawn into the illusion of Habit, which Vladimir, however, finds a comfort. About the carrot, Estragon says,

Estragon: The more you eat the worse it gets.
Vladimir: With me it's the opposite.[78]

Thus the central dilemma is unresolved in *Waiting for Godot*. Godot will never come; they would like to but are unable to stop wanting him to come. They are unable to take that last step to the wisdom of Worm which Murphy and Molloy do seem to achieve, if only momentarily. The play remains, however, a powerful statement of this basic human dilemma.

The same dilemma motivates another of Beckett's plays, *Endgame*. The central issue in this play is contained in the title, the game of bringing our attachment to the world to a complete and final end, which in the play is symbolized by Clov's desire to leave his tyrannical master, Hamm. Like Vladimir and Estragon, Clov and Hamm represent the duality of human nature. Hamm, like Vladimir, clings to the dwindling world he knows and is familiar with, though more selfishly, possessively than Vladimir (incorporating, in other words, more of the element of Pozzo). Clov, on the other hand, resembles Estragon in trying to abandon this world completely. But, like Vladimir and Estragon, each needs the other and so, as in *Waiting for Godot*, the dilemma of *Endgame* remains unresolved.

If Clov leaves, both he and Hamm will die, Clov since Hamm has selfishly hoarded the entire world's supply of food and Hamm because he depends so heavily on Clov. But so long as Clove remains he will be stifled by Hamm, eventually becoming another Hamm. The other pair in the play, Nagg and Nell, Hamm's ancient and decrepit parents, resemble Lucky and Pozzo's ridiculous attachment to the ordinary humanly projected world. Unlike Ionesco's correlative authority figures, policemen, firemen, etc., the characters in Beckett's plays who represent the drag of conventionality do not have such great power over the central characters trying to escape. The difficulty of ending comes from within the central characters themselves, and the statement of the problem is more internal than social.

Like Ionesco's *Exit the King*, the play is about ending, finishing. Will Clov leave or will he remain, eventually to take Hamm's place? As in *Exit the King*, some vague disaster has occurred; everything has been destroyed except the four characters who live inside a remote walled fortress or lighthouse. As in Ionesco's *The Chairs*, this seems to represent our self-imprisonment within our own minds—the "large hollow sphere" in Murphy, the "sealed jar" Molloy tried to break out of, and finally succeeds ("a wall... gave way"). Hamm can't leave; he is blind and paralyzed (again like Pozzo) and has to be waited on hand and foot by Clov. In this respect Clov resembles the slavish attachment of Lucky to Pozzo in the first act of *Waiting for Godot*. Clov moves Hamm around in his chair, brings him what he needs and takes periodic looks at what is left of the world outside.

Hamm represents all the ugly, selfish, egotistical, possessive attachments which tie us to the world. The problem is how to end this nagging, unpleasant attachment. The tone of the play is established in the opening lines.

Clov: Finished, it's finished, nearly finished, it must be nearly finished.[79]

The most irritating feature of Hamm is his endless stream of repetitious, trivial questions, symbolizing here, as in *The Unnamable*, and *Murphy*, the illusion that by constant inquiry we can achieve absolute knowledge.

Clove: All lifelong the same question, the same answers.[80]

Hamm is of another opinion.

Hamm: I love the old questions. Ah, the old questions, the old answers.[81]

Inside the fortress, then, is human consciousness, distinguishing, questioning, constructing. Outside is nothing, a "grey light" fading into darkness, as in *The Unnamable*. For Hamm, as for Vladimir, the nothingness outside is simply his death, those forces that will eventually annihilate his conscious ego, destroying his carefully constructed fortress. For Clov, it is a means of escape which can be consciously chosen.

Hamm: Outside of here it's death.
Clov: There's no more nature...in the vicinity... Zero.
Hamm: Nothing stirs.
Clov: The light is sunk... All gone... Gray. Gray! Gray![82]

Hamm, too, realizes it is "finished" but unlike Clov he resists it, retreating from it, closing himself off from it within this own mind, and like Camus and

Sartre, opposing his actively questioning consciousness to the nothingness of the world, which Clov would willingly embrace. Eventually Hamm will join the nothing outside when, against his will, he finally dies, but in the meantime he revels in the opposition of his projecting mind to an alien reality, his "essence" against the world's "existence."

> Hamm: It's finished, we're finished. Nearly finished. There'll be no more speech.
> Clov: I love order. It's my dream. A world where all would be silent and still and each thing it its last place, under the last dust.
> Hamm: It will be the end and there I'll be in the old shelter, alone against the silence and the stillness. I can hold my peace, and sit quiet, it will be all over with sound, and motion, all over and done with.[83]

There is no question but that the world is absurd. Reality transcends completely all the meaning, structure and essence human beings try to impose on it. The only question is what attitude to take toward it—heroically defying it like Camus or embracing it like Berenger in Ionesco's later plays.

Hamm and Clov both see it ending, though in different ways. One is simply to know it is an illusion, defying it and waiting for death to end it for us. This is Hamm's position, "Outside of here it's death." Thus Hamm screams at his parents for their desperate clinging to life from their filthy trash cans despite the loss of arms, legs and various senses.

> Hamm: Have you not finished? Will you never finish? Will this never finish?[84]

Like Pozzo, Hamm waits for death, just as Vladimir waits for night to end it for him by ending his life.

> Hamm: One day you'll be blind, like me. You'll be sitting there, a speck in the void, in the dark, forever, like me... Infinite emptiness will be all around you... and there you'll be like a little bit of grit in the middle of the steppe.[85]

The other possibility which Clov, and presumably Beckett himself, seeks is willingly to embrace nothingness, releasing the ego from its distinction from and opposition to the world. At one point it looks as though Clov will leave, but then he sees a young boy outside. Like the young boy sent by Godot, this raises the faint possibility that all is not dead and empty, which depresses Clov, as the appearance of the boy depresses Estragon, with the thought that once again Habit's old illusions have received fresh blood and could continue indefinitely.

> Clov (looking at earth for last time): Nothing..., nothing...good...good... nothing...good. Bad luck to it...(dismayed) Looks like a small boy.[86]

Later Clov again voices his goal of willingly embracing the empty silence beyond his selfish ego.

> Clov: Then one day, suddenly, it ends,..,I ask the words that remain...They have nothing to say. I open the door of my cell and go...I say to myself that the earth is extinguished though I never saw it lit. It's easy going. When I fall I'll weep for happiness.[87]

But as the curtain falls Clov stand with one hand on the door looking back at Hamm and the audience is left wondering whether he finally leaves or whether this is simply one more among many futile attempts to leave, part of a "game" they play, over and over again, of "ending."

The one play in which the attachment to the projected world is finally achieved is the mime, *Act without Words*, which Beckett wrote to follow *Endgame*. In the mime a lone man is flung out onto a "dazzling light," a "desert." He is drawn by whistles in various directions; objects tempt him, including water, but as he reaches for them they retreat just beyond his grasp. Finally, the character overcomes any desire for the objects and makes no attempt to reach out for them even when they are dangled immediately in front of him. In the end he remains immobile, like the Buddha under the Bo tree, refusing to move—Beckett's goal of joyous, empty silence finally achieved.

Notes

1. Samuel Beckett, *Proust* (New York: Grove Press, 1931), pp. 7-8.
2. *Ibid.* p. 47.
3. *Ibid.*, p. 16.
4. *Ibid.*, pp. 12-13.
5. *Ibid.*, pp.26-27.
6. *Ibid.*, p. 10.
7. *Ibid.*, p. 11.
8. *Ibid.*, pp. 6-7.
9. *Ibid.*, 9. 41.
10. *Ibid.*, p. 3.
11. *Ibid.*, p. 7.
12. *Ibid.*, p. 46.
13. Samuel T. Coleridge, letter to Sotheby, 1802, in *Biographia Literaria*, in J. Shawcross, ed., v. 1 (London: Oxford University Press, 1962), p. xxxiv.
14. Coleridge, *Miscellaneous Criticism.*
15. Nietzsche, in Erich Heller, *The Artist's Journey into the Interior* (London: Seeker and Warburg, 1966), p. 103.
16. D.H. Lawrence, *Apocalypse.*
17. Baudelaire, in Heinz Werner, *Comparative Psychology of Mental Development* (Chicago: Follet, 1948), p. 82.
18. Beckett, *op. cit.*, pp. 55-56.
19. *Ibid.*, p. 56.
20. *Ibid.*, p. 57.
21. G. W. F. Hegel, *The Philosophy of Fine Art*, F.P.B. Osmaston, trans., v. 2 (London: G. Bell and Sons, 1920), p. 295.
22. *Ibid.*
23. Heinrich Heine, in Heller, *op. cit.*
24. Nagarjuna, *Madhyamika Shastra*, quoted by Chi-tsang from the Chinese translation, *The Chung Lun*, in *A Source Book in Chinese Philosophy*, Wing-tsit, trans, and ed. (Princeton: Princeton University Press, 1963), p. 367.
25. *Ibid.*, in Heinrich Zimmer, *Philosophies of India* (New York: Meridian Books, 1957), p. 521.
26. Beckett, *The Unnamable*, author, trans. (New York: Grove Press, 1958), pp. 4-5.
27. Seng-chao, "The Emptiness of the Unreal," in *A Source Book in Chinese Philosophy, op. cit.,* p. 353.
28. Hui-neng, in *ibid.*
29. Beckett, *op. cit.*, p. 9.
30. *Ibid.*, p. 158.
31. *Ibid.*, p. 8.
32. *Ibid.*, p. 10.
33. *Ibid.*, p. 68.

34. *Ibid.*, p. 139.
35. *Ibid.*, p. 20.
36. *Ibid.*, p. 30.
37. *Ibid.*, p. 28.
38. *Ibid.*, pp. 116-117.
39. *Ibid.*, p. 30.
40. *Ibid.* , pp. 35-36; cf. Huang-po, *op. cit.*, "'Studying the Way' is just a figure of speech...You must not allow this name ('Way') to lead you into forming a mental concept of a road," a statement that might well have been uttered by Wittgenstein.
41. Beckett, *op. cit.*, p, 51.
42. *Ibid.*, pp. 82-83.
43. *Ibid.*, p. 16.
44. *Ibid.*, p. 17.
45. *Ibid.*, p. 109.
46. *Ibid.*, p. 21.
47. *Ibid.*
48. Beckett, *Watt* (London: John Calder (Juniper Books), 1963 (Olympia, 1953)), pp. 78-79.
49. Beckett, *Murphy* (New York: Grove Press, 1957 (1938)), pp. 107-108.
50. *Ibid.*, pp. 108-109.
51. *Ibid.*, pp. 109-111.
52. *Ibid.*, p. 111.
53. *Ibid.*
54. *Ibid.*, pp. 112-113.
55. *Ibid.*, pp. 177-178.
56. Huang-po, *The Teaching of Huang-Po*, John Blofeld, trans. (New York: Grove Press, 1959), p. 29.
57. Beckett, *Molloy* (London: Calder and Boyars (Juniper Books)), 1966, p. 68.
58. *Ibid.*, p. 29.
59. *Ibid.*, p. 33.
60. *Ibid.*, pp. 51-52; cf. the "sealed jar" with the "large hollow sphere" in *Murphy*.
61. *Ibid.*
62. *Ibid.*
63. Samuel Beckett, *Waiting for Godot,* Grove Press, 1954.
64. *Ibid.*
65. *Ibid.*
66. *Ibid.*
67. *Ibid.*
68. *Ibid.*
69. *Ibid.*
70. *Ibid.*
71. *Ibid.*
72. *Ibid.*

73. *Ibid.*
74. *Ibid.*
75. *Ibid.*
76. *Ibid.*
77. *Ibid.*
78. *Ibid.*
79. Samuel, Beckett, *End Game,* Grove Press, 1957.
80. *Ibid.*
81. *Ibid.*
82. *Ibid.*
83. *Ibid.*
84. *Ibid.*
85. *Ibid.*
86. *Ibid.*
87. *Ibid.*

AFTERWORD

As stated in the Foreword, this Afterword is an abbreviated version of a new book, *Metaphysics and the Middle Way,* the third book of a trilogy, following my two earlier books, *The Meaning of Meaninglessness*[1] and *The Metaphysics of Absurdity*[2]. In *The Meaning of Meaninglessness* I analyzed the meaning of existential absurdity as the unrequited but undeserved expectation that the world correspond to the human projection and construction of meaning. The world is meaningful, I argued, because we project meaning upon it, and that without human projection the world is without meaning. In that book I also contrasted what was to me the unjustified pessimistic existentialist interpretation of this basic fact of humanly projected meaning with the, to me, far more sensible, joyous Buddhist reading of the same basic set of facts. In the second book, *The Metaphysics of Absurdity*, now the main part of this book, I utilized this analysis of meaning and meaninglessness to compare the philosophical (or at least prose) texts of four existentialist, absurdist writers (Camus, Sartre, Ionesco, and Beckett) with their fiction writing, contrasting what Ionesco described as the "heavy" and the "light" aspects of absurdity, parallel to the contrast in the first book between the negative reading of Western writers and the positive view of Eastern, especially Buddhist authors.

In these books the most fundamental concept of projected (constructed) meaning was that of "a real object." In both eastern and western philosophy we find reality defined as something that is completely independent and unchanging. As such it is clear that no ordinary object of everyday experience can be real in this sense. Perhaps atoms, or Platonic Forms, or the Parmenidean One, or God, or the Hindu Brahman could be real in this sense, but nothing else. The Buddhist philosopher, Nagarjuna, goes one step further, arguing that since nothing meets that definition of reality, nothing exists, nothing is real. Or to put it another way, that what we call reality is a human interpretation from a human perspective. For human purposes we call *relatively* permanent, *relatively* independent entities real and treat them as real entities. When we further classify these objects into kinds or classes that we are interested in, we can specify more precisely the relatively permanent, relatively independent status of objects falling within these categories. However much a tree changes from day to day, year to year, so long as it conforms to the concept we have constructed of a tree, it remains (semi-permanently) a tree. Again, only things belonging to conceptual categories exist. Without humanly constructed categories, there are no thing (and alternatively, if there are real things in the world, then at least some categories are natural, essential, and not humanly constructed).

All this leads to the rather stark and, to most of us, unacceptable contrast between a naïve view that objects ought to or do conform to our humanly constructed concepts, and, on the other hand, the nihilistic view that nothing exists, is real, or meaningful apart from such humanly constructed concepts. In recent years I have tried to negotiate a compromise between these two extremes. Obviously, there are objects in the world existing independently of our thoughts, needs and desires. Quite apart from human conceptual construction, there are forces in nature which tend to hold the components of atoms together for millions of years, or in less extreme cases, forces which help maintain the relatively stable identity over time of trees, people, and other entities. So long as we insist on the ancient definition of reality as that which is *completely* independent and unchanging, we can only conclude that these things are not real. What is needed, therefore, is a new conception of reality, and that is what I have tried to outline in this Afterword, *Metaphysics and the Middle Way*—through an examination of some unlikely partners, Jain philosophers and American pragmatists.

For all their differences, Eastern and Western philosophy are in agreement on one very central point. For both a real entity is by definition one which is completely independent, unchanging, and therefore eternal. Parmenides and his followers argued that anything less than this absolutely real object, *i.e.*, completely independent and unchanging, simply did not exist at all. Since that included virtually all objects of our everyday experience (tables, chairs, trees, etc.), an unacceptable sense of paradox was created. Plato and the ancient atomists began a long attempt to find a "middle way" between being and non-being for such everyday entities.

The ordinary objects of everyday experience, they argued, enjoyed a kind of secondary reality insofar as they were *made of* or *based on* genuinely real entities, whether Platonic Forms or atoms. In the absence of such genuinely real entities, the implication was that therefore nothing exists at all—and that is precisely the conclusion drawn by the Buddhists—sunyata, or emptiness, though they too, especially Nagarjuna, argued for a "middle way" between absolutely real entities and complete non-being. What none of these philosophers argued for was a concept of a genuinely real entity that was dependent on other entities and constantly changing.

Here we will make a case for such a definition of reality that is dependent and changing. What do we need as a bare minimum concept of reality? Do we need "real" entities in the strict, Parmenidean sense of things absolutely unchanging and independent? No, but we do need things capable of functioning more or less as the same thing over a period of time and groups of things having fairly stable sets of similarities to one another—without which we could not identify individuals as belonging to recognizable kinds of things with identifiable properties. Can we achieve that without "real" entities in the strict realist sense? Yes, but there must be some "realistic basis" for successfully classifying things in a workable fashion that is not entirely subjective or conventional.

There are obviously many ways of describing a real world of things and kinds of things without falling into the dilemma of either assuming some of these are real in the sense of being absolutely unchanging and independent, or, failing that, of concluding complete nihilism, relativism, subjectivism, or conventionalism.

Neither the facts of our experience nor what we know about the physical world from science support or require the strict, absolute sense of realism attacked by Eastern and Western philosophers. Rejecting realism in this strict, absolute sense is not, therefore, to reject realism altogether. The defeat of strict, absolute realism is not a victory for subjective, idealist relativism. What is needed is an alternative theory to replace strict, absolute realism and one more in line with the facts of our experience and our scientific knowledge.

What we need is a three-pronged theory: first, a "realist" theory of things and kinds of things (which we just outlined above), one which provides the "realistic basis" for the second prong, a theory of aspects that select from many human perspectives those thinkable aspects most useful to us as human beings, based on pragmatic considerations, which is the third prong of the theory. The first and second prongs combine realist and conventional models—there are many reality-based aspects of objects available to us, but as human beings we need to pick one or a limited number which are most interesting and useful to us. Biologically, we can't think but one thing at a time, in a linear fashion, and we have a limited capacity to remember; so how do we make the selection?—pragmatically, based on need—as human beings living in a particular age, culture, geographical area and so on.

The Argument Against Realism

Interestingly, the same arguments are routinely used in both Eastern and Western philosophy against metaphysical realism (the belief that objects exist as they ordinarily appear to us, independently of consciousness). These arguments may be said to be of roughly two types, those which have a relatively "objective," or metaphysical thrust and those of a relatively more "subjective," or epistemological slant.

The more "objective," metaphysical argument is that supposedly real objects are not real because they are not eternally unchanging, completely independent of other objects, and are not uncaused by other objects (that is, that they are not uncaused or self-caused). This argument is generally supplemented, again in both Eastern and Western philosophy, by the more "subjective," epistemological argument that the supposedly real objects of everyday life (trees, mountains, persons, etc.) are not real because our *knowledge and experience* of them varies from culture to culture, individual to individual and even from moment to moment in the life of the same individual, depending on both external and psychologically internal conditions of perception.

This is not an account of what sorts of things are real (physical objects, minds, abstract entities, and so on), but rather a definition of what is meant by "reality," that is, a statement of the criteria or standards which anything must meet in order to be (and to be called) real. In a similar way, we can distinguish, as G. E. Moore did, the question "what is good?" meaning what does the word "good" mean (what are the standards, criteria for anything's being good) from the question "what is good?" meaning what things or kinds of things (pleasure, knowledge, power, etc.) are good. And in the case of knowledge, we can distinguish what is meant by the word "knowledge" and what sorts of things do we actually know.

In each case we first define the term (establish the criteria or standards) and then go on to see what things meet that definition (criteria, standards)—having defined "knowledge" as absolute certainty, for example, as Descartes does, we then go on to see what, if anything, meets that rather strict definition (mathematics, analytic truisms, *cogito ergo sum*, perhaps, but not empirical claims). Or, in the case of "good," having defined "good," for example, as whatever people actually want, we then turn to the question what sorts of things people do want (money, love, security, and so on).

The "objective," metaphysical side of the argument claims that ordinary objects of everyday life cannot be real because they change and are dependent on other objects; the "subjective," epistemological argument claims that these same objects cannot be real since our *experience* of them changes and is causally dependent on other factors. What is similar to the two versions of the argument, then, is that such objects cannot be real because they change and are causally dependent.

This argument is extremely odd; in whichever version it is formulated. First, because it is so widespread, common to both Eastern (especially Indian philosophy and Chinese Buddhism) and Western philosophy. And more so, because the conclusion is so sweeping and devastating, despite the fact that the evidence adduced are simply very well-known, common-sense facts of everyday life that no one would presumably want to deny. The universally held, deep-seated assumption that we live in a world of real objects which we can experience and come to know is denied simply on the grounds, known to everyone, that things change and appear differently to different people at different times and places and under different cultural influences. How could such ordinary, everyday facts lead to such a shocking and sweeping conclusion?

The form of the argument seems to presuppose some presumed standard of reality, namely that in order to be real an object must be unchanging, independent, uncaused (or self-caused), and perceived just as it is in itself. All the anti-realist argument does is to point out the obvious fact that ordinary physical objects are not real in that sense. We are first simply reminded of the standard of reality we all presumably adhere to, in terms of which it is then pointed out that none of the things we ordinarily think are real are real by that standard.

As noted above, we need to distinguish two distinct claims about "reality"—what is the definition (criteria, standard) of "reality"? and what sorts of thing meet that definition (criteria, standard) of reality? That is, what do we *mean* by "reality"? and what *is* real according to that definition? The realist position which the anti-realists attack contains *both* sorts of claims (at least according to the anti-realists)—one concerning the definition of "reality," and the second about what satisfies that definition.

The realist position which is being challenged can be analyzed, then, as two separate claims—the first is a definition or criterion of reality (that in order for something to be real it must be unchanging, uncaused, etc.); the second is the claim that ordinary physical objects meet that definition or criterion. Together we could call the two the "realist thesis."

But stated so baldly, the "realist thesis" is wildly counter-intuitive (or else unbelievably naïve). Indeed, it is so completely contrary to our most common everyday experience that we have to ask whether anyone holds such a preposterous view. Does anyone hold, or did any ever hold such an outrageous position? Whoever claimed that objects in the world of ordinary experience are real in the sense that they don't ever change, are completely independent of other things in order to exist and to continue to exist, and which exist just as we experience them? When it is pointed out against the reality of ordinary objects that they change and are dependent on other objects, one would expect the response, "Of course, whoever said they weren't?!" Perhaps this is simply a Straw Man argument.

Certainly no philosopher ever held such a view (that physical objects were real in the sense that they are eternally unchanging). More likely, the anti-realist argument is directed against the "plain man's" common-sense view, or assumptions of naive realism. But is this what the "plain person" believes? Does the ordinary person (*i.e.*, the non-philosopher) really believe that ordinary physical objects are real in the extreme sense proposed in the anti-realist argument? Well, yes and no—yes, we may say, people ordinarily suppose physical objects are real, but no, they do not suppose that they are unchanging, completely independent of other objects and conditions, and exist just as we ordinarily perceive them. That is, the "plain person" holds that physical objects are real but does not seem to endorse the claim that such objects conform to the extreme realist criterion or definition of reality.

What is not at all clear, in other words, is whether the plain person embraces the realist criterion of reality. How can the plain person simultaneously hold that in order for something to be real it must be unchanging, uncaused, etc., and that physical objects obviously change, and also hold that physical objects are real? Put in this blatant fashion, it is hard to see how this could describe the beliefs of the ordinary person, or indeed of any sane person. Only an idiot could hold all three views at the same time. If reality is defined as unchanging and physical objects obviously change, then clearly physical objects are not real. Or if physical objects are real and they are changing, then reality cannot be defined as what is unchanging. Of the three, the two beliefs most congenial to the ordinary person are surely that physical objects are real and that they change. But then where does this realist criterion come from?

Perhaps the philosophers are to blame. Perhaps if we search through the history of philosophy, East and West, we could turn up some culprits, that is, some philosophers who first concocted this strangely counter-intuitive standard of reality and then wrongly and unfairly attributed that bizarre notion to the poor, unsuspecting "plain person" (who doesn't read philosophy books and so never realized how he was being caricatured). In other words, have there been philosophers who argued that this is the criterion of reality which the plan person is somehow committed to and therefore ought in all honesty to accept and, charitably interpreted, does in a sense accept? Nagarjuna is a likely candidate, along with his San Lun Chinese followers (including, Seng Zhao), and so is Plato.

It is certainly true that Plato is one of those philosophers who urge the argument against the reality of ordinary physical objects, arguing that such objects are not real because they cannot meet the strict realist criterion. Plato certainly endorsed and made use of the realist criterion or definition of reality, and in light of that criterion quite rightly (and rather easily) pointed out that ordinary objects which we encounter in sense experience, existing in space and time, cannot meet this standard and so are not real.

But if we ask *why* Plato proposes the strong realist criterion, that is, what arguments he adduces to persuade us to accept this strict standard, we strangely find no argument whatsoever. Similarly, in the *Seventy Stanzas Explaining How Phenomena are Empty of Inherent Existence*, Nagarjuna simply says again and again that "all phenomena are devoid of inherent existence and are therefore empty." The only reason he offers is that ordinary objects of daily life (which we normally take to be real) are dependent on other objects and conditions and so cannot be absolutely unchanging, self-caused and permanent. As he says, "because things arise in dependence on one another they do not exist inherently as permanent phenomena." If they are permanent, then they wouldn't have ever changed or evolved into their present form. "Whatsoever has already arisen will not be able to arise. Whatsoever has not arisen will not arise. Either a phenomenon has already arisen or else it will arise; there is no other possibility beyond these two."[3]

The main idea (or definition) of reality, namely, that for a thing to be real it must be uncaused, unchanging, and therefore completely independent and permanent, just seems to be taken for granted. All Nagarjuna does is work out the logical implications of that definition of reality for ordinary physical objects. If that is your definition of reality, he seems to be saying, then obviously everyone will have to acknowledge that ordinary physical objects cannot be real in this sense since they are obviously changing and dependent on other objects. As he says, "If a phenomenon were to exist inherently it should be permanent. If a phenomenon were to exist inherently it would either exist permanently or else undergo complete disintegration: it cannot occur in a way which is different from these two."

The idea that an object might be constantly changing and dependent on other objects and yet be real is never even considered. Even Nagarjuna's critic,

Vaibhasika, actually assumes Nagrjuna's reality definition in his objection: "If you assert that phenomena don't exist inherently then you are asserting that they don't exist at all." Nagarjuna easily turns this argument on his opponent: "When you assert that phenomena exist inherently you are asserting that they do not originate in dependence on causes and conditions and thus that phenomena do not exist. For if phenomena do not depend on causes and conditions, then they should have independent existence throughout the three times (past, present, and future)."

This exchange is particularly telling. Vaibhasika seems to be saying that existing inherently is a necessary or defining condition for anything existing at all. If it doesn't exist inherently, he seems to be saying, then it doesn't exist at all. Vaibhasika clearly intends this statement as a kind of *argument ad absurdum*, that since Nargarjuna claims that nothing exists inherently, it follows that nothing exists, and that is patently absurd. What Vaibhasika doesn't allow (any more than Nagarjuna) is that something could exist and yet exist dependently on other things.

Nargarjuna's response is also interesting. By claiming that existing objects must exist inherently, Nargarjuna says (in effect) to Vaibhasika, "it is you who are saying that ordinary things don't exist since you agree with me that they certainly don't exist inherently—that is, completely independent and unchanging. If you define real existence as independent and unchanging, then it is you who will have to admit that no ordinary object meets that standard." It just doesn't seem to occur to anyone, even Nagarjuna's opponents, that something could exist and be real and yet be dependent, changing and impermanent.

As Parmenides said, this just doesn't even make sense. Despite what our five senses seem to tell us, reason tells us that any talk of change involves talk about nonbeing and any talk about nonbeing, of things not existing, is just plain nonsense—it makes no sense to talk about something which is not ("what are you talking about? there is no such thing!"); and if something is, then it can never not be—which means it can never change and that means it can never affect or be affected by another entity—change is simply an illusion.

So, at least from Naganjuna's standpoint, and from Plato's standpoint, the definition of reality as something unchanging and independent is not a claim put forward and defended by Nagarjuna or Plato, but is merely presented as the ordinary, common sense criterion or definition of reality whose disastrous implications for ordinary phenomenal objects Nagarjuna and Plato carefully and mercilessly analyze. Indeed, for them this is the only logically possible position and so the only one which common sense can accept upon reflection. No alternative definition or conception of reality is ever put forward.[3]

The structure of the argument offered by Plato, Nagarjuna, and other anti-realist philosophers suggests that they regard this standard of reality as the commonly accepted one. It is simply assumed, or taken for granted, without argument, as though no one is expected to challenge or disagree with it. The philosophers see themselves as simply analyzing a widely held common-sense assumption (or one which common-sense would be forced to accept upon reflection). We have already seen how it makes no sense whatever to imagine that the ordinary person consciously holds such a theory, or would be able to state, much less defend it—indeed, were such a view explicitly presented for endorsement, the ordinary person would most certainly reject it. Nonetheless, Plato, Nagarjuna, and other anti-realist philosophers seem to imply that this is the commonly accepted, unchallenged, standard criterion of reality implicitly or tacitly held by everyone.

None of the early Greek philosophers challenge Parmenides's definition of reality as that which is unchanging, independent of any outside forces, etc. They all simply take it for granted that Parmenides has articulated correctly the standard definition, or criterion for reality which everyone who stops to think about it already embraces. All they do to combat Parmenides is to work out ways of reconciling Parmenides's definition of reality, which they all accept, with a limited reality for the ordinary world of empirical experience (what Plato called "saving the appearances"), which Parmenides simply dismisses as false.

They all regard Parmenides as correctly analyzing the logical implications of our common sense, everyday sense of reality. Where they differ with Parmenides is in their unwillingness to accept, as Parmenides was apparently willing to do, those absurd implications for everyday life (that there is only one reality, that it is eternally unchanging, unmoving, etc., which is a totally useless guide for everyday life and hence an embarrassment for reason and philosophy). Since similar arguments appear at all times and places in the history of philosophy, both Eastern and Western, it begins to appear that the realist criterion is a very widespread, perhaps universal human assumption, "hardwired" cross-culturally into the homo sapien brain. It certainly could not be an inductive generalization from ordinary sense experience (of constantly changing objects!).

It is presented, rather, as an *a priori* assumption—that is, prior to all sense experience. Ordinary people don't "believe" this realist criterion as an actual, or "active" belief. That is, they would not readily assent to it as one of their firmly held convictions. Nonetheless, they (and we) do seem to assume it and rely on it as a general and largely unnoticed background assumption, organizing and guiding much of our thought and experience.

The question is, is the realist criterion a background assumption of ordinary people or is this only the philosopher's supposition? One reason for affirming that this is indeed what most of us ordinarily assume is the extreme ease with which ordinary people fall into the philosopher's trap. That is, when shown that the object under consideration changes and may not exist just as we perceive it, most people tend to agree that it is therefore not real, or not fully real. Now, unless we attribute an extreme gullibility to ordinary people, doesn't this indicate that the ordinary person does in fact embrace, however unconsciously, the realist criterion?

It is just because this assumption has not been consciously considered or reflected on that the mere reminder that ordinary physical objects are, after all, subject to change, are dependent on all sorts of other objects and conditions, that they are seldom, if ever, perceived just as they are in themselves, and so on, is all that is required to completely overthrow the universally held and seemingly stubborn belief of common sense that ordinary physical objects are real. The philosophers have not discovered a new standard of reality, nor have they uncovered a hitherto undetected flaw in common sense beliefs, nor have they made some earth-shaking discovery, for example, that physical objects change—they have simply analyzed and consciously reflected on these common sense beliefs and then pointed out the obvious fact that these standards are never fulfilled in ordinary human experience.

Even today most people will tend to think that if their mind is completely dependent on their body (that is, that it cannot exist apart from their body), or that there is nothing within the mind which remains the same from birth to old age (that is, no single strand of memory or feeling or thought), then in that case, most people will conclude that the soul or mind does not exist as a real, independent entity. If the mind/soul only exists as a by-product of the body, then most people are prepared to conclude that therefore the mind/soul does not exist, meaning that it does not exist as an independent, unchanging entity. Similarly, most people today tend to think that if everything in the world is made of atoms, and that atoms remain the same while the physical objects made up of atoms come and go, then atoms are therefore "more real" than ordinary physical objects—simply because they are "more" permanent, unchanging, independent, and so on.

How then can we account for the apparent extreme stupidity of the ordinary person who seems to simultaneously believe that physical objects are real and change and that reality cannot change? For one thing the plain person may never have considered these three statements together—juxtaposed at the same time. For another, the ordinary person may tend to think in relative terms of more or less—so a tree is more real than a shadow, the lake than a ripple, and so on—a thing is *relatively* real if it is *relatively* unchanging. It is in this sense that many people tend to think that if an atom is more permanent than the objects it is made of, it is therefore more real, or if the objects in a dream depend on the mind then the dream objects are less real than the dreamer's mind, and by the same token if the mind itself is dependent on the body, then the mind is less real than the body. It is only by carefully reflecting on one's everyday beliefs that one can be brought to see that in the strict sense, carried to an absolute extreme, our ordinary beliefs about the reality of physical objects are inconsistent and incoherent.

In much the same way, Descartes's definition of knowledge as complete certainty obviously derives from ordinary common sense. In everyday life we certainly hold that a person cannot be said to know something unless they are sure of it. But how sure does one have to be? 85% certain? 90%? 95%? Here common sense avoids the absolute extremes of the philosopher. Without really thinking it through most people are happy to say they know something if they are relatively certain it is true. But if you press them—"are you absolutely,

100% certain? is there no conceivable way, however remote, you could be proved wrong?" virtually everyone is prepared to admit that they are not completely, 100% certain. And if you press them further—"then do you really know it?" most people do in fact hesitate, seeing that, by their own standards, anything less that complete certainty is less than complete knowledge.

The main difference between the plain person's criterion and the philosopher's is just the difference between what is relatively so and what is absolutely, completely so. So, in the case of reality. For all practical purposes, large trees, mountains, even people are sufficiently stable and unchanging— enough so that we can identify them and re-identify them over time—and over a long period of time relative to our own life-times. But at least in the case of trees and people everyone realizes that they do change and indeed finally die and cease altogether to exist. What is lacking in daily life is the pressing question of reason (and philosophy), "so, by your own standard, these things which are only relatively permanent are only relatively real—wouldn't anything really (absolutely) real therefore have to be absolutely permanent?" And in all fairness, one has to expect the plain person to grudgingly admit that this is so. At least in the history of philosophy, both East and West, this is the response of the ordinary person (at least as recorded by philosophers—in the absence of any contrary claims ever recorded).

So it seems true that we all embrace (in some sense and to some degree) the strict realist definition of reality. But to the extent that the realist criterion is "hard wired" into our human brains, necessary, as Kant would say, to any human experience, the argument against the reality of ordinary physical objects seems to go against human nature itself and would therefore seem extremely hard for anyone to accept (or feel comfortable with)—although many philosophers, both East and West, over many centuries have apparently accepted this anti-realist position. The idea that we directly perceive real objects in the physical world is a view so deep-seated, so stubbornly held that if it is mistaken, it is a fundamental "illusion," as Freud used that term to mean a false belief which nonetheless continues to appear to be true even when we know it is false.

How have philosophers responded to this attack on the reality of everyday objects? Well, in many different ways. Some philosophers have, of course, *led the attack*, delighted to confound and bewilder common sense with their brilliant and paradoxical logical dialectic, but the majority of philosophers have sought to defend at least a modified form of realism. Parmenides argued, quite simply, that reality can only be a single unchanging, eternal One, and that anything else (any multiplicity, any change) must therefore be an illusion. Zhuangzi's friend, Hui Shih, is an example of an Eastern philosopher who developed the other side of this argument, that since everyday physical objects are constantly changing, none of them can exist as separate entities, and therefore everything merges into one.

But this position so radically contradicts our ordinary experience of the world that it is unacceptable to most philosophers. The whole point of doing philosophy is to analyze and make sense of our ordinary experience of the world, the world as it ordinarily appears to us. To simply deny that this world exists therefore defeats the unspoken but very real agenda of human reason and the whole enterprise of philosophy. Most philosophers East and West have therefore tried to "recover" a limited sense in which we may speak of the existence of ordinary objects.

In fact, the only philosopher who steadfastly refused to develop such a "middle way" was Parmenides, and, apart from his student, Zeno, no one seems to have followed in his footsteps. Parmenides simply *defines* reality in such a way that change cannot occur; what appears in everyday life to be a great diversity of many different objects constantly changing Parmenides says is simply an illusion, that is, is simply false. This is an interesting case because it brings out quite forcefully why such a position must in the end be utterly unacceptable. We turn to philosophers to make sense of the complex and often confusing world in which we live. We need to understand how things work and how they are causally related to one another. This is not only from a sense of epistemic curiosity about the world we live in, but pragmatically as something absolutely necessary to successful living, and indeed for our very survival.

Parmenides is clearly of no help to us. It is logically impossible for anything to change, he says, nothing can grow, move, affect or be affected by other things. But this dismisses just the sort of information we desperately need—what causes deadly diseases, famine, childlessness, and so on. The closest Parmenides comes to a "middle way" compromise with common sense is in his second book, *The Way of Appearance*, in which he discusses the causes of seasonal changes, why it rains at certain times of the year, and so on. But what he stubbornly refuses to do is show how the "way of appearances" is *related to* "the way of truth and reality," that is, to develop a "middle way" theory of reconciliation by showing how reality appears to us as it does, however falsely. In Plato's famous phrase, Parmenides refuses to "save the appearances."

The only other philosopher who even approximates Parmenides' complete rejection of the "middle way" between appearance and reality is Shankara, the 9th century Indian Vedanta philosopher who interprets classical Hindu texts (especially the Upanishads) in a similarly uncompromising way—in reality there is only one eternal and unchanging thing in the world, known as Brahman or Atman; everything else, including the apparent diversity of constantly changing objects is simply an illusion. But, unlike Parmenides, Shankara at least tries to explain how Reality produces such an illusion on the analogy with the way in which illusory objects appear to us in a dream, or as the optical illusions produced by the magician whereby, for example, a rope appears to us to be a snake. Shankara, in other words, uses metaphysical Idealism to explain the relation of appearance to reality, in short, to "save the appearances."

At first Spinoza might seem another philosopher who comes close to rejecting the "middle way" reconciliation with common sense—refusing to "save the appearances." It is true that for Spinoza there is, strictly speaking, only one real thing (or substance) in the world, and that is God, because (a la Parmenides) only God is really unchanging, completely independent of other things, and absolutely permanent and eternal. Certainly, if God creates everything else in the world, these other things cannot be completely independent and eternal. Nonetheless, unlike Parmenides, Spinoza does not simply dismiss the vast array of physical and mental phenomena as illusory, but makes a concerted effort to "save the appearances" by his account of these other things as "modes" (or "modifications") of the one real substance.

In general, then, any philosophical position worth its salt must at least attempt to "save the appearances." You don't have to admit the absolute, ultimate reality of things as they appear to us in daily life, but you do have to give some account of how what is real can appear in false and illusory ways. You cannot just dismiss the whole of our everyday experience as a false illusion; you must somehow *account for it on the basis* of what you claim to be Reality.

Of course, ultimately, Parmenides is right—nothing can be real in the strict, absolute sense but the unchanging and eternal One, but what about all the other things we find in the world around us? Surely, they exist in some sense or other. If they are not fully real, as Parmenides has shown us, how are these other things *related to* the true reality? How do they, as they must, share at least a pale reflection of that reality which they cannot claim absolutely for themselves?

Most philosophers have therefore not been content merely to show that the objects of everyday life cannot be real in the strict sense, but have wanted to go on to discover some way in which these objects which are admittedly not fully real nonetheless have a limited, or relative existence by being *connected* somehow with something else which *is* truly real in the strict, absolute sense. This is what is meant in this context by "the middle way," that is, the middle way between saying ordinary physical objects are real in the strict sense of being permanent, unchanging, and so on, and saying that they are sheer illusions and don't exist at all. Thus, from the beginning, in both Eastern and Western philosophy, the "middle way" has been sought as the main task of metaphysics.

How, then, have those philosophers who tried to "recover" some limited reality for the ordinary objects of common sense responded to the attack on the reality of such objects? One response has been to look for some *other* kind of object which *could* fulfill the realist criterion—and to which ordinary physical objects were somehow *related*. Without abandoning the realist standard of reality, they reasoned that if ordinary physical objects are not real in this sense, then perhaps some other sort of object is—through which ordinary physical objects could share some sort of limited, reflected reality. The Pre-Socratics, along with the Hindu philosophers of the Upanishadic period, assumed there must be some "ageless and deathless" ground of being underlying the changing, ephemeral, and hence unreal, world of everyday experience. For Plato the Forms (Ideas) met the realist definition of reality; for the early Greek Atomists, it was the atoms.

Plato argued that only the Forms were real in the sense that only they were eternally unchanging, independent of any other objects, not caused by anything else, and existed just as they were cognized in pure intellectual intuition. Insofar as ordinary physical objects "participated in," "imitated" and "approximated to" the Forms, they, too, shared a limited and relative being, "rolling about between being and nonbeing," as Plato said, parasitic on the firm reality of the Forms.

The Atomists argued similarly that although ordinary physical objects could not be real because they were subject to change and so on, the smallest constituent *parts* of these physical objects *were* absolutely unchanging, independent of other objects, uncaused, and existed just as they were apprehended by logical insight. Of course, today we know that those things which modern European scientists *called* "atoms" (the smallest units of oxygen, hydrogen, etc.) are *not* unchanging, eternal, etc., but for the ancient Greek Atomists this would only show that these entities were not really "atoms," after all.

Atoms are *defined* metaphysically as the smallest units which cannot be further divided. If one imagines breaking up bits of matter, say a drop of water, into smaller and smaller pieces, then logically we can deduce that either this splitting can go on indefinitely (infinitely), in which case there would be no unchanging smallest part, *i.e.*, no "atom," or else there is a terminus to this splitting and we arrive finally at what cannot be further divided, in which case there *are* atoms. The ancient Greek Atomists argued that the former hypothesis was impossible, since in that case ordinary physical objects would be made of infinitely small stuff, that is, nothing, in which case there wouldn't be any ordinary physical objects, which there surely are, and that therefore only the atomic hypothesis ultimately made sense. And, once again, insofar as ordinary physical objects were said to be made up of real atoms, they, too, enjoyed a limited and relative existence parasitic on the reality of the atoms.

In a similar way, but with a more "subjective" and epistemological focus, Empiricists argued that if physical objects did not exist just as we perceive them, there must be something else which did exist just as we perceive them, namely, "sense data," the "immediately given," from which the perception of ordinary physical objects is constructed—*i.e.*, a kind of epistemological atomism. These are all attempts to formulate a metaphysics of the middle way.

Another approach, that of Aristotle, was to find some s*emantic* correlate within ordinary physical objects that satisfied the realist criterion of reality. Although an individual tree changes, is causally dependent, and so on, the "essence" of treeness, or treehood is unchanging, and, like Plato's Forms, causally independent (but unlike Platonic Forms in being incapable of existing apart from particulars). Thus, for Aristotle, we can say that the person we haven't seen for ten years is the same person even though she has changed in many ways, because the "essence" of that person has remained the same, even though various "accidental" properties (weight, hair color, muscle tone), have changed. Once more, because changing entities contain a real core of unchanging essential nature, they, too, have a limited and relative existence based on the reality of essences.

Although the theory of evolution would seem to deny the immutability of essences (the essence of oak has not always existed, for instance), it is possible to patch up the theory by holding that the essences exist eternally awaiting actualization—so, for example, the essence of oak has always existed but was only actualized at that stage of biological evolution when oak trees first began to appear. But since this means that essences can exist apart from individual physical objects which embody them, this approach amounts to Platonism which Aristotle would surely have rejected. All an Aristotelian could maintain today is that essences of biological species are relatively permanent, or long-lasting.

Since some essences seem to be "natural" (like the essence of an oak tree) while other essences appear to be more conventional (like the essence of a novel), philosophers in modern times have tended to treat previously designated "natural" essences more and more as merely conventional, thus psychologizing and anthropologizing all essences, reducing them finally to humanly constructed concepts used to linguistically represent and describe the world. At first, for example with Kant, a kind of subjective universality was retained for certain very basic concepts ("object," "cause")—concepts shared by all human beings and so fundamental to human existence that without them thought and language would be impossible. But eventually these, too, gave way to ordinary conventional human concepts which differed from other concepts only in the degree of their relatively greater stability and importance in maintaining a particular "form of life."

In the Latinizing of Greek philosophy the concept of being, or *ousia*, became substance, which had the sense of the underlying reality supporting and in a sense "having" the properties, qualities, modifications which we are aware of, can experience and describe. Like other notions of reality, substance also had the sense of something which did not change, though its properties could change. The problem with this notion, as Locke discovered, is we don't *know* anything about this underlying substance except what we infer from its properties, modifications, etc., since these are all we can experience, know or describe of the underlying substance.

A very different approach to the "middle way" is that of Kant, that there is nothing we can ever discover, experience or even conceive of which could possibly meet the strict criterion of reality, and we must therefore give up the pretensions of reason to discover such an ultimate reality and reject as unattainable the constant "illusion" and persistent temptation characteristic of human existence to try and find such a "reality." Kant is thus left with the sad conclusion that we can never rid ourselves of the dream of reality, nor can we ever find it. Like the analogy Sartre uses of the carrot dangled before the donkey—the donkey can neither forget about the carrot nor ever eat it! Kant acknowledges this "built-in" standard of reality as an unquenchable desire but insists that it is and must remain unfulfilled.

We can't get rid of the realist standard and we can't find anything which meets that standard, and so we must simply recognize the realist standard as a highly misleading part of our mental equipment as human beings. Kant seeks to recover a limited sense of reality for ordinary physical objects by showing how the perception of the world in terms of semi-permanent physical objects is universal and necessary for all human beings. Thus at least in talking about other people we can always assume that, like us, they will always see the world in terms of reasonably stable physical objects. Relative to a human frame of reference, at least, we can be assured that there will always be enough identifiability, permanence, and causal regularity to make knowledge of the empirical world and communication among people possible. This is how reality will always appear to human beings, according to Kant. But, according to Kant, we also recognize that this is only the way reality *appears* to us; that is, we have a conception of a reality which can never be discovered, experienced or known beyond the limited ways it *appears* to human beings.

Finally, there is the Buddhist "middle way" which is to *overcome* ordinary human nature, that is, to *get beyond, get over* the temptation, or "illusion" to want to constantly discover something real within our experience. With Kant we retain the perpetual longing for reality which we know we can never attain; in some Buddhist schools we get over this perpetual longing for such a reality.

To most of us and to most philosophers, overcoming the longing for something real within our experience (real in the strict sense of the realist criterion) and learning to accept the emptiness (*i.e.*, the lack of reality in this sense) of everything will seem terribly pessimistic, discouraging, and nihilistic. But of course it is only pessimistic in contrast to the deep-seated longing for some underlying reality, that "ageless, deathless ground of being" the ancient Greek and Indian philosophers sought. Without that longing there is no disappointment in our failure to satisfy that longing. But can we overcome that persistent desire? Is it possible? Isn't the Buddhist "middle way" an attempt to radically alter human nature, and is that possible?

So deep-seated within us is this insistence on an unchanging, independent reality that it may seem like a permanent part of our human nature—but this is precisely what the Buddhists think we can overcome, though not easily. And this is another way of saying that, however deep-seated within us and however difficult to change, it is *not*, after all, an absolutely permanent part of human nature—and is therefore changeable. Perhaps like Kant's "Categories" there is nothing which is absolutely unalterable in human nature, but only a matter of degree, with some human attitudes, assumptions, ways of thinking more deep-seated and relatively unalterable than others—but none absolutely so. Certainly we have found during the 20th century that individualistic egoism and racist ethnicity are far more deeply rooted in human experience than we had supposed, but it is too early to say that they are absolutely permanent fixtures of the human psyche.

Freud spoke of "illusions," mistaken views that we *know* are mistaken but can't get rid of. Perhaps there are *degrees* of "illusoriness" of race or gender, even of ego or selfhood. However much we intellectually and rationally "know better," we seem "hard wired" to privilege our own race, gender, and ethnicity. We "know" perfectly well that men and women are equal, but men find it hard to understand why women can't be "more like a man," and vice versa, women would like to see men become more like women (more open to their feelings, placing a greater priority on relationships, commitment, and so on). And where we know and want to believe that the ego or self is a social and biological construction, it is virtually impossible not to see ourselves as permanent and enduring entities.

This is similar to Chi Tsang's doctrine of "double truth," which we will discuss later, that there is an everyday sense in which there is a world of multiple entities of different kinds that we must accept on a day to day basis and an absolute sense that ultimately all is empty.

Notice that the anti-realist argument does not actually remove or destroy ordinary physical objects or our everyday experience of them. All it does is change their characterization (description, classification) from "real" to "not real." When the argument has done its worst, these objects are still there in front of us just as before. What has changed is that we no longer say of these things that they are "real." We simply reclassify them as "appearance" instead of "reality."

But they are still there in some sense or other. If they are not there in the sense of being "real," then in what other sense do they stand before us and interact with us in daily life? This is what is meant by the Buddhist "middle way," that they are there in one way but not in another way. (Actually, this phrase, "middle way," was used at least twice in the history of Buddhism, once by the original Buddha, Sakyamuni, himself, arguing for a middle way between the extremes of physical excess and asceticism, and a second time, some seven hundred years later, by Nagarjuna, founder of the Madhyamika school of Mahayana Buddhism, as the middle way between realism in the strict sense we have been discussing and complete nihilism.)

What difference does it make whether we say that ordinary physical and mental objects (like my self) are to be classified as "real" or "unreal"? In one sense, as A. J. Ayer and other anti-metaphysical positivists have asserted, it makes no difference whatsoever. Because the question of their "reality" or "unreality" is a metaphysical one, the positivists argue, it is empirically unverifiable and therefore cannot make the slightest difference in the actual world of our everyday experience. And in a sense this is perfectly true. Whether I say that the weeds in my vegetable garden are real or unreal, whether I hold them to be material or mental, they are there and I must either weed them out or lose part of my garden.

But from another point of view it does make a difference what metaphysical view one holds. The world may visually *look* much the same to a materialist and a dualist, for example, but they may well feel differently about death, the dualist seeing the possibility of life after death and the materialist seeing none. From the Buddhist point of view, all of our human anxiety about life stems from the mistaken belief that our selves are real and substantially unchanging entities, and that we live in the midst of similarly real and unchanging real objects.

It is because we hold these realist beliefs, the Buddhists say, that we fear death (anxious not to lose this precious, real thing we call our selves), and to worry about the loss of loved ones, as well as the loss of material things and our ability to continue to enjoy them. The solution to this overwhelming human life problem, according to Buddhism, is therefore the realization that these things, including my self, are not real. So in *some* ways it makes a big difference whether we think of such things as "real" or "unreal."

But even though the Buddhists of the "middle way" are careful to distinguish the absolute sense in which these objects are not "real" from an everyday, relative sense in which they do nonetheless form an important part of our everyday existence which cannot be ignored so long as we live in the world, the Buddhists are overwhelmingly concerned only with the first of these senses, connected as it is in their minds with the practical, religious solution to life's major problem, and are not therefore much interested in developing a clear sense of the second sense and how that differs from and is related to the first.

According to the Buddhism of the Middle Way, we are not to deny the empirical existence and everyday importance of physical and mental objects, recognition of which they concede is absolutely necessary to our ordinary perception and communication with fellow human beings in a shared empirical world. To avoid the pain of living, however, we must realize that, nonetheless, these objects are not real in the absolute, ultimate "realist" sense.

But even if we acknowledge that the relative existence of ordinary objects of everyday experience is of secondary importance, from a religious perspective, it is nonetheless an important and interesting philosophical problem. It is also important in clearing away possible stumbling blocks to an acceptance of Buddhism—namely, the need to answer critics (who have raised essentially the same objections for over two thousand years) that Buddhism is idealistic, nihilistic, negative, and unrealistic. Assuming ordinary physical objects, as well as mental objects, like one's self, are not absolutely real, what are they?

One solution, prominent in both Western and Eastern philosophy (including some forms of Buddhism) is Idealism, the view that everyday objects exist only "in the mind," that, like objects in a dream, they appear to us but have no existence apart from our being aware of them—for them, as Berkeley said, to be is to be perceived. Idealism is supported by the fact that, by hypothesis, we have and can have no direct knowledge of a mind-independent entity (how could we be aware of something we're not aware of?). If we can never experience such a thing, Idealists argue, what's the point of talking about it? Do we have any right to even talk about what we have no way of knowing?

Idealism is also strengthened by our knowledge of how much biological, psychological and cultural factors obviously affect perception. It is only because of our sensory apparatus as members of the human species that we see the particular range of the light spectrum and so little of the possible olfactory information available to dogs, for example. We know from history and anthropology that different groups of people tend to see the world in rather different ways. And we know that individual people will see things differently depending on their mood, point of view, bias and so on. We know, in other words, that our perception of the world is to a large extent distorted, that we are at least partially responsible for the way the world appears to us. But *how far* is this true? To how great an extent? Could it be 100%, in which case we are totally responsible for the appearance of physical objects. Not just that we are mislabeling or misconstruing objects which nonetheless exist and which we nonetheless do perceive though in inadequate ways, but that, like the objects in a dream, we completely fabricate such objects which have absolutely no basis outside our own consciousness.

Idealism is a perennially attractive position. But it faces many problems. First, it is hard to overcome the overwhelming impression that perception confronts us with an independently existing world, that there is an important difference between dream and waking experience. Also, the things we perceive often seem to resist our will and desire, and so to exist stubbornly independent of us. Also there always seems to be more to any object we experience than our particular experience of it at any given moment, and in that way objects seem to transcend, or go beyond, and not be exhausted by, our perceptions of them. Finally, different people seem to be able to look at and describe the same objects in roughly similar ways which would seem to be impossible if each is a fabrication in the minds of these different observers.

A kind of compromise between Idealism and realism is Conceptualism, of a Kantian variety for example. Conceptualism acknowledges that there is an independently existing world and that it is "given" to us in sense experience, but also concedes to Idealism that everything we know and can say or think about this sensory given comes from our own conceptual apparatus. The given is merely a formless mass which is given cognitive shape or form by the mind. The problem with this position, however, is that it cannot explain why one concept applies to a certain bit of the sensory given better than another concept (or, to put it the other way round, why a particular bit of sensory experience is more appropriately classified one way rather than some other).

Unless there is some "connection" between the given and the conceptual, that is, something in the given which enables us to establish and apply standards for the correct application of human concepts, then the sensory given contributes nothing to knowledge and is epistemologically useless—and so is not really a "compromise" with Idealism, after all. But if there is some "connection," then it would seem that the sensory given puts some constraints on our conceptual classification of it, a constraint determined presumably by its own character, structure or form.

Another major weakness in the idealist/relativist position is that, carried to its logical conclusion, it would make any communication between people impossible. If two people are describing the same object in different ways, then either there is a real object existing independently of their different interpretations of "it" or there is not. If there is no "it" about which their different versions are descriptions, then there is really no disagreement and no possibility of coming to an agreement—each person would then live in a different, isolated world of their own in which there is no possibility of a relative success or failure of words to correspond to reality.

Only in the first case, where an independent "it" exists, can we meaningfully speak of different opinions about the same thing, each of which may be partially true and partially false, with one view more nearly correct than the other, in which two people can genuinely disagree and, more important, in which two people can agree or come to agree.

Even where we disagree, you seeing it one way, me seeing it another way, we at least share a common world—we have different opinions about the same things in the same world. And this means that we do agree on some basic points—that that is a person, for example, though you think it is Taiwo and I say it is Tanya. We also know how to go about resolving our disagreement, that is, coming to an agreement, about who the person actually is, by turning to a more careful look at the evidence to be gathered from a shared, public world, correcting our perceptions and coming finally to an agreement ("Yes, you're right; it's Taiwo"). This is not to argue for some sort of epistemological infallibilism. Even if it later turns out that it is neither Taiwo nor Tanya but someone else, maybe even impersonating one or the other, that can also be discovered by further investigations of the same, ordinary sort. (Or even if the disputed item of investigation turns out to be a Chad Hanson life-size sculpture, and not a person at all!) The point is that at any stage the two of us confront a common world where disagreements are always partial (never total) and can be resolved, step by step, by quite ordinary means which we both accept and are familiar with from everyday life.

But if we acknowledge that there is something in the sensory given which enables us to apply this concept rather than that, then we are conceding that there are regions of the physical world which can be objectively differentiated from other regions, and, if language is to work at all, that these differences are sufficiently stable and long-lasting and determinate to allow a fixed vocabulary and stable concepts to be used.

Rehabilitation of Metaphysics

The need to steer a "middle way" between the extremes of naïve realism, on the one hand, and idealism and complete relativism on the other, seems clear and would be too obvious to be worth mentioning were it not for the current fashion to reject all "metaphysics" as hopelessly outmoded. But the current wholesale rejection of metaphysics assumes a dichotomy between naive realism and complete relativism, failing to consider the possibility of a "middle way" between these two extremes.

The recent wholesale rejection of metaphysics is based on a number of common misunderstandings of metaphysics. Metaphysics is rejected, for example, because it is essentialist, eternalist, and unverifiable dogmatism. But while all these charges characterize some kinds of metaphysics, they do not describe, or even typify, the whole of metaphysics. Some metaphysicians have stressed that reality is eternal and unchanging, but, as early as Heraclitus and later with Hume, other metaphysicians have stressed the changing and even empty character of reality. And while some metaphysicians have emphasized the essentialist's search for the common denominator in any collection of similar things, some, like Leibniz, have stressed just the opposite, the absolute individuality of each particular thing. And while some metaphysicians have dogmatically pronounced as absolutes what could never be intersubjectively verified or agreed upon, other metaphysicians have been equally insistent on the controversial nature of metaphysics and its tentative, provisional nature.

In other words, the argument against metaphysics is a Straw Man (Person) Argument—all metaphysicians are caricatured as belonging to one weak and indefensible sort (dogmatic, eternalists, simplistic, reductionist, etc.) and the rejection of this caricature is supposed to demolish the lot. But this argument does even touch metaphysicians of a different sort. This caricature may not be viciously intended. It may well be the case that few of us can honestly remember the range of metaphysical possibilities.

An odd thing frequently happens in the history of philosophy. At first philosophy is the criticism of traditional, established thinking—this is the origin of philosophy (around 500 BC in Greece, India and in China). But later philosophy itself becomes part of the established tradition—so when that is criticized, who is criticizing what? At first it seems that non-philosophers are criticizing philosophy. But not necessarily—it could also be read as new philosophers criticizing old philosophers. On the first reading we are tempted to talk about the "end of philosophy," the "end of aesthetics," or the "end of metaphysics." But it can be equally understood as the "beginning of a new philosophy," the "beginning of a new aesthetics," or "the beginning of a new metaphysics."

So in this case, yes, it's true that metaphysics became traditional, established centering on dogmatic assertions about abstract, formal, essentialist, rigid, unchanging, fearful of change, marginalizing darker forces, emotion, etc. And that has been rightly criticized—but that doesn't mean the end of metaphysics, but only the end of one type of old-fashioned metaphysics and the beginning of a new and better (or at least more timely) metaphysics.

Metaphysics is an investigation into the question of the way in which things exist, how they "are" in the broadest sense, what it means to say that something is, by what criteria we can say that *one* thing exists rather than a *collection* of things, how we know when one thing comes into existence and later ceases to exist rather than continuing to exist in an altered form.

But however out of touch with current sensibilities, we have been arguing that it is more and not less metaphysics that is needed, in particular, a more thorough and sophisticated account of the kind of limited or relative reality objects can possess consistent with acknowledging that such objects do not and cannot comply with the "realist criterion" of reality, one, that is, which argues for and tries to make sense of the claim that objects can exist and still change and be dependent and never be perceived just as they are in themselves.

Strangely, all metaphysics since Parmenides has sought the "middle way." The only metaphysician who simply affirmed the eternal and independent nature of reality was Parmenides—everyone after that tried to reconcile Parmenides' definition of reality with the changing, dependent world of everyday life, trying, as we saw above, to recover a limited reality for all those things which can't satisfy Parmenides' criterion of reality. Aristotle, for example, does not say that physical objects aren't real; he tries to find something within them which makes them real in Parmenides' sense. Similarly, the Atomists do not say that tables and chairs are not real; they try to explain how such objects are made out of and can be explained in terms of things (atoms) which *are* real in Parmenides's sense.

Even Nagarjuna and his Chinese followers (San Lun) developed ways of reconciling sunyata (emptiness) with ordinary phenomenal reality. Nagarjuna and later Chi Tsang developed the theory of two truths—in one sense (an absolute sense) it is true to say that no objects exist anywhere, while in another sense (a relative sense) it is false to say that there are no objects. As a San Lun monk I may be asked to walk into town to buy a variety of different vegetables (a combination of rice, radishes, cabbage, etc.)—if, instead of bringing back a mixed bag of rice, radishes, cabbage, etc. I come back with nothing but radishes—I have clearly made a mistake—which I cannot get out of by pleading that "all is one" "nothing exists anyway, so what's the problem?"—no, at this everyday level, there are many different things in the world and they fall into different categories—there is rice, there are cabbages, and radishes, and so on. "We asked you to get a mix of rice, cabbages and radishes which you failed to do—so go back and do it right!"

Later that night, after supper, we discuss how, in the final analysis, from the standpoint of eternity, in reality, no things exist, there are no real things anywhere in the world, all is empty—I glance at the chief cook and we share a smile (this is going to take some time!).

As the Greeks rightly said, the world is not a chaos but a cosmos. Somehow, there is an order to things. Even though there are no eternal, unchanging, uncaused, completely independent entities that we know of, there are nonetheless relatively stable patterns, forms, configurations of forces which we daily confront which hold things together in a semi-permanent pattern which, even if they do not form absolutely water-tight, mutually exclusive classes or kinds, nonetheless do tend to cluster together in groups which have similar features, modes of recognition, and roughly similar causal properties. And even after all the admitted subjective factors in our perception of the world have been taken into account—biological, psychological, personal, cultural, and so on, some of this order and regularity appears cross-culturally part of the objective world over which we human beings have no control, whether individually or collectively.

Consider biological species, for example. Of course, contrary to Aristotle, there are borderline cases, transitional cases, and evolutionary mutations. There is the problem of distinguishing different species from subspecies and geographical varieties (West Coast mule deer and East Coast white tail deer which can interbreed, producing various intermediary mixtures; or, similarly,

Western and Eastern bluebirds). Instead of assuming that all animals designated by the same classificatory name, either in ordinary language or by zoological nomenclature, have an identical "essence," let us represent the similarities and differences among animals by a "cluster map," in which every animal is represented by a single dot and the dots are arranged closer to or farther apart from other dots depending on the degree of similarity and difference of features.

Thus, in a cluster map every single animal is distinct from every other animal, as indicated by the fact that each is represented by a distinct dot. Nonetheless, when we have completed the mapping we can see, especially from a distance, "clusters" representing species and clusters of clusters representing genuses, and so on. From a distance, in other words, we would see a "clump" of an almost solid mass of dots (like a black area in a newspaper photograph made of closely packed black dots on a white background) representing a particular species, say white tail deer, and a larger "greyer" clump representing the genus in which many species (say, of deer) belong.

Of course, if there were no clusters, then we would realize that there was absolutely no basis in reality for our practice of grouping certain animals into species. Suppose we group animals by color, or according to which county they lived in. In that case classifying animals into groups would be as conventionally arbitrary as classifying units of measure (inches, feet, yards, miles, etc.), in which case there would be no clustering whatsoever. But of course there *is* clustering by species, and this explains and makes clear the realistic basis of our zoological system of classification. Naturally, we have rounded off, minimizing the smallest differences between individual members of the same species (and this is what Aristotle did not realize). In daily life we also exaggerate (for simplicity, convenience) the degree of similarity and minimize the differences we could notice if we chose to.

All deer look alike until we really pay attention to a particular group of deer that we see every day, and then we can begin to identify different individual deer just as we easily identify individual people, cats and dogs. Nonetheless, there is a realistic basis for saying that two deer are closer in kind than a deer and an elk and among deer and elk considered together as compared with lions and tigers considered together. By plotting all mammals on a "cluster map," there is no doubt the deer would form a tight cluster, indicating that, though they share no absolute "essence," they are more similar to one another than they are to other mammals.

Similarly, genetic testing would also indicate strong "clustering" of animals within a species (but not genetic identity, except in the case of identical twins). This would be an interesting way to consider racial types, a cluster map which would *not* reveal any clear "clusters" of the kind we would see in the case of species. Even if we selected only skin color, there would be an almost infinite gradation between the very darkest and the very lightest person in the world today. Even among Africans there would be a range of lighter to darker, as there would among Europeans, or among Asian Indians, Chinese, etc. Similarly, if we mapped hair type, head shape, or any other commonly designated "racial" feature. In all such cases we would see quite clearly there simply are no natural kinds within the species homo sapiens.

Only by contrasting Europeans as a group with Africans as a group (say, when Europeans first came into contact with Africans in the 16th century) is there the appearance of something resembling natural kinds. But once we fill out the picture with the Indians, Malays, Chinese, North Africans, and so on, this sharp contrast disappears. We can now see that it is a matter of historical accident that a large group of predominantly white Europeans were until the 16th century more or less isolated (geographically and culturally) from a large group of predominantly dark-skinned Africans (and other physically distinct more or less homogeneous groups) who were themselves also more or less isolated (geographically and culturally) from other groups until modern times—and that this has created the illusion of distinct races as natural, biological kinds.

If we could imagine taking the same human beings existing in the world in 1500 and randomly scattering them around the world so that all ranges of dark to light-skinned people were living in Europe, and in Africa and in China, and so on, the idea of race would obviously never have occurred. Instead there would be only an awareness of many different inheritable and observable features as we find today in our recognition of variations in hair color, eye color, complexion, body type, shape of nose, chin, etc. among Europeans, or among Asians, or among Africans, even within the same family.

Think of Wittgenstein's notion of family resemblance—Susan's eyes are more like her mother's father than either her mother or her father. And so today if we take all the people alive on the planet now and place them on a cluster map, we would find that there simply is no cluster. In that sense, as the Ghanaian philosopher, Anthony Appiah, says, there are no races; race is a myth (though a myth we may have come to love and feel we need—first for whites to feel they are superior to blacks and later for blacks to feel they have some group identity). There are genetically based differences among individual people, of course (without which we could not distinguish one person from another), but no tight clustering and therefore no natural kinds.

Here we can see a kind of "middle way" between the insight of Idealism and our stubborn intuition of realism. Admittedly we construct human representations of the world as it appears to us in sense experience, depending on our biological make-up, as well as our collective "interests" as genetic and as acculturated human beings. But these constructions, if they are to work at all, must have a basis, or "connection" in reality, otherwise it is difficult to see how we would have survived this long had we simply fantasized without any realist constraints of any kind.

Consider as an example, different conventional ways of representing three-dimensional objects by lines drawn on paper. Of course, there are many ways to do this. Each culture develops its own set of conventions, and then by internalizing those conventions each culture finds its own conventions "realistic" and all others "stylized and unrealistic." And so we can conclude that there is no really realistic way to represent reality on a two dimensional plane—

all are conventional, none are absolutely realistic. But this does not mean that within any given style of representation there are no standards of realism. For example, if our convention plots only the spatial configuration of objects, each of which is represented by either circles or straight lines, then two small circles situated to the left and right of the top of a straight line indicating the nose is the correct way to represent a human face, while two small circles one above the other and both to the left of the line indicating the nose is the wrong way to draw a human face. Nor does it mean that all conventions are equally possible. If spatial depth is conventionally represented by vertical height on the two dimensional picture surface, then the correct, that is, realistic way to represent a house behind a tree is to draw the house higher on the picture place than the tree.

Thus, each system of representation has its own "connection" with reality which determines within that system what is realistic and what is not. The system is conventional only in the sense that we have selected one of many possibilities; not that anything is possible. The drawing with the tree lower on the picture plan than the house can easily be read as "tree in front of house" because objects in the distance do indeed appear higher on the retinal projection than those closer to the viewer. Imagine how difficult it would be to introduce the opposite convention, in which the tree lower on the picture plane should be read as "tree behind house." It is difficult to see how we could establish this convention convincingly; there seems to be no possible "connection" with reality.

In other words, we can use this two dimensional space arrangement to represent "tree in front of house" because a tree in front of a house really does look something like this from a certain elevation in front of both the tree and the house. Not that it looks exactly like this; a photograph, for example, would not show the entire front of the house unless the house was at a very great distance behind the tree (since the tree would block part of our view of the house). Nonetheless, the photograph would be sufficiently like the drawing to make it possible to establish the necessary "connection" with reality on which to establish a viable convention. After all, even in the photo, the base of the tree is higher on the picture plane than the base of the house.

So long as there is some "connection" with reality we are willing in our representational conventions to make compromises with reality for the sake of clarity and design. This "connection" with reality is the major difference between artistic and linguistic conventions. Once we see the "connection" with reality, we know how to go on to interpret new pictures. Suppose we are shown a drawing and told that it is a picture of a house.

We notice that the drawing represents the house by the simple convention of outlining the object from a typical viewing perspective with one single line. Once we have seen just this one picture of a house we can immediately go on to interpret thousands of new pictures done in the same "outlining" style—that is a tree, that is a car, that is a mountain, and so on. But as everyone knows who has tried to learn a foreign language, knowing that the word "house" means house doesn't help in the least figuring out what the word "tree" means. If line is conventionally used to trace object boundaries, then the shape of the line must resemble the boundary of the object as typically viewed.

Pictorial conventions tell us very generally how to draw any recognizable object and spatially relate it to others; they do not specify how we are to draw each and every particular object—the rule just states that in each case we are to trace its boundary with a single line. If you know what objects look like then you can draw any object and you can recognize a drawing of any object. Linguistic conventions, on the contrary, must be learned piecemeal for each new object.

The point is that in order to be workable, conventions must be based on reality. Conventions must satisfy human needs and interests and also realistic constraints. Consider, for example, various possibilities for constructing a workable convention for distinguishing "mental" and "physical" aspects of a person. The boundaries between the physical and mental characteristics of a person are obviously very porous, indefinite, indistinct boundaries at best. And clearly the metaphysical division of a person into an immaterial mind and a material body, which begins in the Western tradition with Socrates, is not the only way to construct this distinction.

But there is a natural, as well as a pragmatic, basis for some such distinction. Some things are relatively more private to the individual, hidden from others, felt from the "inside" differently than other features which are more immediately observable by other people. Most people can't tell how angry you are (though you know it very well), but they can easily see how blotchy your face has become (which you don't notice until you look in the mirror). There is also the fact that a person's memory of themselves and constructed self-image is far more enduring and consistent than their aging body.

An eighty year-old woman may still think of herself as she was at eighteen. Consider also certain wide-spread human interests we have in identifying particular physical features of people for sports or modeling or construction work for instance, versus our interest in clear signs of intelligence, humor, sensitivity, and so on, for jobs in book editing, teaching, or counseling. There is a enough realistic base here to draw some sort of distinction between physical and mental if we wish and if we find that useful to satisfy our human interests, but without in any way showing that there are two distinct substances involved—the mind and the body. In other words, we can talk about "mind" and "body" without embracing a dualistic metaphysics of two substances, one material and the other immaterial, though there is a realistic basis for that kind of dualism, as well.

There is a real basis for differentiating mental and physical capacities of human beings; there is also a need in most human societies to mark that difference linguistically and to culturally utilize it—so such a distinction will most likely appear in almost all societies at all times and places. But there is no necessity in pushing this distinction further into a metaphysical dualism of two utterly distinct substances—mind and body (raising then the mind-body problem how the two interact). Similarly, even though individualism only became important as a self-conscious ideal in Europe beginning in the 16th-17th century and is still more prominent in Western countries than elsewhere, it is nonetheless based on the fact that each person really is different and the integration of the individual into the group is in fact always and everywhere a matter of degree and some degree of opposition and resistance.

Here is an example of a "middle way" between rejecting the belief in a permanent, indestructible, unchanging immortal soul without rejecting the need in most languages and in most societies to refer to an individual's mental characteristics. That is, it is an example of steering the middle way between Parmenidean realism, on the hand, and complete relativistic subjectivity, on the other.

Here is another useful thought experiment: in our continuing efforts to create robots, we might decide that the private, mental component was too inefficient, too much trouble, that it would be better to do away with all the problems of hurt feelings, failed communication, ego trips, and so on, and therefore decide not to program into our robots any private feelings. In that case there wouldn't be any realist basis for making the kind of decision most cultures make regarding the mental and physical life of human beings.

On the other hand, if we were interested in modeling our robots on human experience, then we would certainly want to add to their hard-wiring the ability to feel what is happening to them, to respond in personal ways, to be hurt, shocked, disappointed, pleased, saddened, to want things, to plan desired outcomes, much of which would then occur to them (as to us) as something private and hard to communicate, and so on. And in that case there would exist the realist basis (which we had deliberately implanted) for distinguishing the physical from the mental life of our robots.

And of course, in that case they would be harder to handle, to deal with—just like human beings. Would they in that case have rights? Indeed, why do we think it is wrong to kill human beings? Why is this considered far worse than killing (and eating!) chickens or fish? Of course, it is true that it was Europeans in the 18th century who developed the concept of universal human rights, and today many people in non-Western countries challenge this concept of universal human rights as yet another example of Eurocentrism. And if animals could speak, wouldn't they cry "speciesism"? But, after all, human beings *are* different from other animals in ways which would command respect even if these traits appeared in nonhumans (or could be proved to exist in nonhumans)—having long-range goals, autonomous life plans, interests, and so on.

Would we also want to provide our robots a kind of *overview* of these more private episodes, resulting in each a sense of him or her self? And would we want to go a step further and give each of the robots a sense of the *value* of and the need to *protect, nourish, develop* their selves? In that case wouldn't we have to respect them just as we do human beings? In that case, wouldn't killing (or dismantling) such beings amount to murder? Wouldn't they in that case have interests, rights, and so on?

If so, then we can see from our thought experiment the realist basis on which our notions of mind, self, a person, the value of a person, human rights, etc. arise. It is not just convention or conceit which suggests to most human beings that a person is more valuable than a stone or a plant or even than another animal. People are organized in a way which creates structures (those which form the basis) of mind, self, personhood, rights, etc. which other entities don't have—although other creatures have other structural features which are unique to them and which therefore differentiate them from all other kinds of things. Notice, too, that the argument that animals, especially the higher animals, have rights is based on the degree to which they resemble human beings—having interests, a strong desire for self-protection, and so on. It is only because robots don't yet and animals don't so clearly or so much have these traits that we rightly treat human beings as exceptional.

Similarly, what we call a "thing" needn't be an absolutely permanent, unchanging, independent substance, but rather an organized and functioning collection of smaller "things" (which are themselves organized collections of other "things," and so on), bound together by forces powerful enough to withstand for a while, but not forever, some but not all opposing forces threatening to break up that "thing." And so such a "thing" continues more or less the same—at least with more or less the same organization and functioning, if not with all the same physical parts, for a time and then disintegrates. While it exists each thing has its own relatively stable character which the forces which hold it together preserve as long as it lasts—from a rain drop to a person, from an atom to a university, from a cloud to a symphony. Of course, in each case there is a degree of conventionality allowing us to collectively "choose" as human beings how much change and of what kind we will allow before we say the object (a tree) has ceased to exist and another (a log) has taken its place. Nonetheless, there is a basis in reality for our continuing to refer to such a configuration of balanced forces as "the same thing."

Consider what we know about the atom. Of course, what modern scientists have called the atom does not meet the rigid realist criterion of reality of the ancient Greek atomists. These smallest units of oxygen, carbon, and so on, are not eternal, unchanging, and absolutely independent. Under enormous pressures they can and do change, can be split and disappear as "atoms."

Nonetheless, they do form relatively stable configurations of more elemental particles of matter and energy held together by extremely powerful forces. These atoms, although not absolutely unchanging and eternal and independent, have nonetheless—many of them—survived more or less in the same configuration pattern for millions of years, indeed since the beginning of time (on the "Big Bang" theory) minus the first three seconds!

As both Western and Eastern thinkers have pointed out, the water forming a river is constantly changing. You can't step into the same river twice—or even once. But there are forces (gravity and the contours of the land) which give the river a kind of recognizable identity over time. That is not to say that even the contour of the river is absolutely unchanging. Indeed we know that towns, like

Cairo, Illinois, that used to be on the river are now miles from it, and that where there are deserts today, for example the Sahara desert, there used to be lakes and rivers which are now completely gone. Nonetheless, these changes have occurred so slowly and so uniformly and continuously, that the changes themselves form a relatively stable pattern.

From the atom to a river we can see the same principles at work. In either case we find an assemblage of more or less permanent forces which together create a reasonably stable pattern of constituents which, for all practical purposes, can be considered an individual object—though certainly not meeting the strict realist criterion of absolute permanence, independence, and the rest. Indeed, we can imagine a whole range of entities from the most stable and permanent to the least—from a hydrogen atom at one end of the scale to a ring of cigarette smoke someone has just blown at the other end.

Relative to a human frame of reference, some "things" may be too transient or of too little interest to be identifiable or nameable (or to be worth identifying or naming, at least in ordinary circumstances)—ripples in a pond are too transient, whereas a large ocean wave could be identified, by surfers, for example (though even a large wave would seldom be given a name, primarily because it is too transient to be re-identified as the same one we saw a week, a day, or even a few minutes later). Tropical depressions are seldom sufficiently distinct from their surroundings and/or stable enough to be identified and named, whereas tropical storms can and are identified and named. A river is fairly stable and sufficiently important for human interests and needs to be identifiable and nameable as a "thing," but probably not a temporary "whirlpool" formed in one of its eddies, though a group of hikers could certainly point it out and discuss it among themselves. At one time clusters of individual houses form identifiable villages which later form a larger cluster of a larger town or city which is in the process of joining together with other towns and cities into an enormous metroplex—though such communities could choose to retain their separate identity, even though completely surrounded by the larger urban sprawl.

Again, in each case we find a combination of convention based on real forces is at work. It is conventional whether to refer to the disturbances on the surface of the water as a property of one thing (a "disturbance" or a "choppy surface") or as a series of discrete, identifiable entities, such as "waves," "ripples," "undulations," and so on (which then could be individually named if we somehow found it socially useful to do so). But all of these descriptions, if workable at all, are based on real physical forces which do create relatively distinct more or less identifiable lumps or clusters which provide the realistic basis for various workable linguistic conventions ("choppy," "waves," "ripples," and so on).

Suppose we organized a contest to see who could blow the most smoke rings from a single drag on a cigarette. Though it is not customary to do so, we could easily and objectively count the number of rings (perhaps for a contest or an entry in the Guinness Book of Records), though this might involve having to set up objective criteria for what counts as "a ring" (*e.g.*, must be elliptical and have a definite hollow space in the center and last more than one second). And if we also wanted to award an additional prize for the longest lasting smoke ring we could identify particular rings and time them ("Susan Fink's third ring lasted just over six seconds, just behind Josephine Zook's second ring which held together nearly eight seconds.")

The "forces" which shape, organize, and hold together the parts making up a symphony are conventional, man-made, artificial. As Aristotle said, in works of art the form is provided by human beings. Where there are people there is the possibility of agreement to conform to conventional rules (language, laws, mores, and of course, art). And as long as that agreement remains in force these structures bound together by convention will remain in tack. It is these conventional rules which insure that different performances of Brahms Fourth Symphony will sound more or less the same and therefore be more or less the same piece of music, whether played in Shanghai in 1988, Vienna in 1888, or in Dubuque in 1937.

Another useful thought experiment: we can easily imagine a world in which there was no realistic basis for thinking or talking about things or kinds of things—first a world in which change is so sudden, continuous and evenly spread throughout that human beings would simply be incapable of picking out anything, identifying it, re-identifying it, giving it a name, describing it (even describing how it changes)—cinematically we can produce such a world. Secondly we can imagine a world of things stable enough to name, identify, and so on, but a world in which each thing is exactly as similar to and different from every other thing.

Imagine a world consisting of A, B, C, and D. We can identify each one and describe, name, etc. all four. But A is equally similar to B, C and D and equally different from B, C and D; and so for B in relation to A, C and D; C in relation to the other three and so for D in relation to the others. Of course, with just four we might imagine doing away with common nouns and just *naming* the four. "What is that?" "Oh, that's B, and that one over there is C," (without being able to say *what* B is—"yes, I know that's B, but what *is* B?" (what kind of thing is B?)—no answer; in this world B is just B). But now multiply the number from four to four billion—now there's a problem. We can't name them all—can't remember if number 245,167,229 is the same as or different from number 4,587,089.

If these "things" are evenly spread out throughout the environment, we couldn't think or talk about them—we could see them but not in the way we usually see things as belonging to this or that class of things—seeing that as a book, this as a watch, and that one over there as a frog. At first we might imagine that however different from one another, there would still be lots of things which fly in the air, and lots of things which are edible, and lots of things which were red, and so we could construct categories, however arbitrary, saying of these things that there are things that can fly and things that cannot, or things that are red in color and things that are not, or things that are edible and things that are not. But the problem would be whether we could pick out the edible from the inedible without actually eating them; whether we could spot a flying thing unless it was actually flying; a red thing unless we were actually looking at it.

We couldn't say, "Don't eat that, it's not edible." Or "Be careful it may suddenly fly away." Why? Because we can only identify edible things if they belong to *other* categories (an orange mushroom with red spots, for example). So, we might come up with the highly pragmatic category of edible (versus non-edible), but how could we construct criteria for inclusion in "edible"? What are edible things like? Either we do it by enumeration (A, C, D, G, M, etc. are edible), which will be practically impossible with four billion things, or we have to classify the things into groups with real shared properties (the mushrooms all look like this; the edible mushrooms all have this feature)—but this can't happen in our imaginary world because there aren't any regular groupings of similarities and differences—*e.g.*, the ones with wings can fly; the one with scales can swim; the berries on the plant with three-lobed yellow leaves are poisonous, and so on. Organisms could survive in such a world, but they wouldn't be like us (perhaps more like amoeba or plankton); we have evolved to survive in a world of individual objects belonging to recognizable kinds with stable causal properties—properties, most importantly, that benefit or harm us.

So, what do we need as a bare minimum? Do we need "real" entities in the strict, Parmenidean sense of things absolutely unchanging and independent? No, but we do need things capable of functioning more or less as the same thing over a period of time and groups of things having fairly stable sets of similarities to one another—so that we can identify individuals as belonging to recognizable kinds of things with identifiable properties. Can we have that without "real" entities in the strict realist sense? Yes, but there must be some "realist basis" for successfully classifying things in a workable fashion.

So there are obviously many ways of describing a real world of things and kinds of things without falling into the dilemma of either assuming some of these are real in the sense of absolutely unchanging and independent, or, failing that, of concluding complete relativism, subjectivism, and conventionalism.

Thus, neither the facts of our experience nor what we know about the physical world from science support or require the strict, absolute sense of realism attacked by Eastern and Western philosophers. Rejecting realism in this strict, absolute sense is not, therefore, to reject realism altogether. The defeat of strict, absolute realism is not a victory for subjective, idealist relativism. What is needed is an alternative theory to replace strict, absolute realism and one more in line with the facts of our experience and our scientific knowledge.

Aspection

What we need is a three-pronged theory: first, a "realist" theory of things and kinds of things (which we just outlined above), which provides the "realist basis" for the second, a theory of aspects, which select from human perspectives those thinkable aspects most useful to us as human beings, based on pragmatic considerations, which is the third prong of the theory. The first and second is a combination of realist and conventional models. There are many reality-based aspects, but we need to pragmatically pick one or a limited number, keeping in mind our biological limitations—we can't think but one thing at a time, have a limited capacity to remember, and so on. So, how to make the selection? Pragmatically, based on need—as human beings and as human beings living in a particular age, culture, geographical area, and so on.

A theory which initially seems hopeful in that respect is a theory of aspects—the idea that all human perception is the grasp of limited aspects of real objects from limited human perspectives in which it is *known* that each aspect is only an aspect which is only a partial grasp of the object of which more (that is, more aspects) can be known by further investigations and shifts of the human perspective. As we will see, this metaphysical theory of aspects is supported by the epistemological focus of a kind of neo-pragmatism, which we will introduce in the next section.

One of the earliest theories of aspection is the Jainist, especially Hemacandra's (1088-1172), theory of naya. The theory of aspects is useful in showing how the same thing can be correctly perceived and described in different, seemingly opposed ways. Consider the old Jainist story of the five blind men trying to describe an elephant which they can only feel with their hands. One grabs its tail and describes the elephant as a snake; another feels one of the elephant's legs and reports the elephant to be like a tree trunk; still another blind man presses both hands on the elephant's torso and declares the elephant to be like a wall; yet another, grasping the elephant's ear, affirms the elephant to be like a banana leaf, and so on. Each of the blind men thinks he is right and the others are mistaken, but from the vantage point of we, the listeners, who have seen at least pictures of elephants, we know that each of the blind men are partially correct and that all of them are partially incorrect; none of them grasps the elephant as a whole, but each correctly grasps a part of the elephant's features.

Hemacandra works out the implications of this notion of the many-sided nature of reality (anekantavada, literally "not one essential nature") each of which can be perceived by adopting a different human point of view, or standpoint (naya). Hemacandra's theory is best known to us today through Mallisena's 13th century commentary (Syadvadamanjari) of Hemacandra's *Examination in Thirty-two Stanzas of the Doctrines of Other Systems*. According to Hemacandra, although we can *refer* to an object as a whole, as it is in itself, we can never *perceive* it as such or *describe* it as such. Any statement about the object must be from a designated point of view. That is, strictly speaking every statement must begin with the prefatory phrase, "In a certain sense, p," or "From a certain point of view, p." Even where for the sake of simplicity we routinely omit this phrase, it must be understood to be intended.

Although his critics claimed that his view would lead to contradictory statements about the same object, Hemacandra correctly points out that it is precisely the naya qualification which *prevents* contradiction. In Plato, for example, if an apple on the tree is first green and then red, Plato wants to say that it is both green and red, or worse, green and not green, thus contradicting itself in a way which, for Plato, throws the entire phenomenal world known to sense experience into doubt.

But if we add the naya in each case, we avoid any contradiction. Early in the season the apple was green; later in the season the same apple was red. For the young, inexperienced army officer the war was a good thing; for the villagers it was very bad. As a fictional entity, Tom Sawyer exists; as a historical citizen of the United States he does not exist (and never existed). From the standpoint of linguistically exhausting the Tao, it is indescribable (and even unnameable); from the more limited perspective of calling attention to a principle of natural spontaneity which is known to us in many ways, it is describable (and nameable—named "Tao" and described as the principle of spontaneity of all natural phenomena).

So, for Hemacandra, nothing can be known, perceived, or described absolutely; everything can only be known, perceived and described relative to a specific point of view. At the same time, however, Hemacandra avoids subjectivism, nihilism, and skepticism—we can know and truthfully and objectively describe real aspects of real objects from specified points of view.

Part of Hemacandra's theory anticipates what Hegel and others recognized as the relativity of "determinate" being to a particular categorical standpoint. Nothing exists as a bare particular, a bare thing; everything exists as a member of this or that class or category. And that means that to exist it must exist as this or that and not exist as any other kind of things—it is a tree and not a log, or a chair, or a newspaper (though later it may cease to exist as a tree and begin to exist as a log and still later as a chair or as a newspaper). At first this may seem contradictory—saying that the object both exists and does not exist, but, of course, once we supply the point of view, aspect, etc., it is not contradictory—as a tree it exists; as a log it does not exist (later, when the loggers have finished for the day, we can say, "this morning it existed as a tree and did not exist as a log; this afternoon it exists as a log and does not exist as a tree.") Once we have specified the complete context of the assertion, there is no contradiction whatsoever.

Hemacandra also anticipates the problem Locke and others discovered regarding our knowledge of substance. Since we only know the modifications or qualities of a substance, we never seem to know the substance itself. Everything I perceive, know or can describe about any object is just different properties of it. Somehow, as Locke says, we have this belief that all these properties somehow belong to some underlying substrate, or substance. But when we examine the matter closely we see that we have no information about this substrate or substance over and beyond the properties we attribute to it and which we say belong to it or inhere in it. As Hemacandra says, "A 'pot,' when differentiated in regard to parts: round lip, broad bottom, belly, upper and lower parts, etc., is modifications only, but not an entity beyond them called 'pot.'"

Like Kant, Hemacandra recognizes that we can *refer to* the entity as a whole (that is, a synthesis of all its aspects), though we cannot *perceive it or describe it* as such. When we say "from this standpoint, we perceive this aspect of the pot," we recognize that this aspect is one aspect among many, all members of some larger synthesis. That's what we *mean* by an aspect—an aspect is always an aspect of something else. For Kant the thing in itself of which the appearance is an appearance cannot be experienced, but we nonetheless can refer to it as a "regulatory" concept—like the idea of the horizon.

Linguistically, if I want to relate different aspects of the same object (the pot is heavy, it is rough, it is black, is it old and chipped), or if I want to relate aspects which I know of an object to others I would like to find out about, I refer to all these known and unknown, actual and potential aspects as aspects of one and the same object. This is how the notion of a "real object" functions linguistically in my life—not as something I ever come to understand in its totality, but as a useful and even necessary reference point to show the relations and interconnections of aspects to one another.

Without such a heuristic device I would be unable to talk about learning more about some entity, or correcting my mistaken knowledge about it, or discussing with you how my understanding of it differs from yours, and so on. Even though it is merely a heuristic device (like the carrot continually dangled in front of the donkey, in Sartre's example), it is a very useful and indeed necessary "regulative" idea, as Kant would say.

So in Hemacandra—when we describe an object, we *know* this is only one aspect of it as seen from one angle or point of view, and we know there is *more* of the object to be seen from other angles and points of view—and we can know that, without knowing what all these other aspects are. When I see a hill I know there is another side though I have no idea what the other side of the hill is like (which is precisely why I climb over the hill to discover).

Nonetheless, there is an important difference between Hemacandra and Kant. For Kant, because we can never know *everything* about an object, we can never know the real object, and this is where Hemacandra's theory parts company with that of Kant. From the fact that every experience and description of an object is made relative to a point of view, Kant concludes that we can never know reality, the thing in itself. But this doesn't follow at all, as Hemacandra correctly sees. The fact that we cannot know the thing as it is in itself doesn't mean we can't know the thing itself; we know something about the thing itself—though not *all* about it, that is, not as it is in itself.

When I look at the hill I am about to climb, I cannot see the other side of the hill; I don't know how the hill was geologically formed; I don't know how many people have climbed this hill before me; I don't know what commercial uses, if any, have been made of this hill (grazing, mining, etc.). And in that sense I only know the hill from one limited perspective; I only know one aspect of the hill.

Nonetheless, what I see is the hill itself—not some mental apparition, or appearance.

Kant is victim of the Lockian analysis of substance and properties—since we only ever know the properties of a thing it seems to follow that we can't know the thing itself, as though there is a great unbridgeable divide, with appearances, or phenomena on this side of experience and Reality, or Noumena on the other side, a completely different sort of thing altogether which we can never experience. But by knowing a property of the thing we do indeed know that very thing—by knowing what the Norwegian flag looks like I know something about the flag itself—not some subjective phenomena on the other side of which is a ghostly Real Flag. We know truthfully and objectively what it is really like from one point of view (and a point of view which is useful to us).

This is a very good example of language playing games with us. I see and know the properties of X; this logically seems to imply that there is an X in addition to its properties; but then when we ask what we actually know about this X, we have to admit, nothing! M It seems as though I only know how it appears, that is, I only know appearances (mental, subjective things) not the reality which somehow causes those appearances. But then how do I really know that this X actually causes the appearances? Maybe it's all in my mind!

And that leads to skepticism—we simply don't know and can never know reality at all. And so we seemed eternally doomed, trapped in some strange solipsism, knowing only appearances in my own mind—in the end, knowing only my own mind! But that's not what we originally meant at all—when we say we see and know properties of X, we just mean that the object is perceptible in a certain way (visually, auditorily) not that the object caused some mental event in some mysterious way connected with it.

There is also an implied theory of aspects in the Taoist philosopher, Zhuangzi. Zhuangzi constantly calls on the reader to imagine what it would be like to be a fish, a small bird, a huge (mythological) bird, a butterfly, a deer, a sea gull. By asking us to imagine what the world would be like that from these different perspectives, he leads us to see the relativity of the aspect of the world to the perspective adopted (what is a long flight to the small bird is short to the large bird; what is beautiful to human beings is ugly or frightening to the fish or the deer; what is nourishing to a person is deadly to the sea gull, and more generally, what is right and correct according to one perspective is not right and correct according to another perspective.

Also implied is the ability to transcend the limitations of any and all particular perspectives to see things from the standpoint of eternity, which, even if not entirely possible, at least indicates our ability to recognize our limited point of view *as* a limited point of view, one among many, as well as our ability to "stretch out" for larger, more encompassing perspectives from which to view things, and in that sense to transcend a particular point of view and to distinguish that from the object of which it is one among many aspects.

The theory of aspects, in other words, overcomes the temptation to consider differences in descriptions of the same object as subjective creations, or mental projections. Objectively speaking, the elephant really has the features correctly detected by the five blind men. The tail of the elephant really is like a snake, and the torso really does resemble a wall, while the ears are truly similar to banana leaves. These are objective, universally recognizable features of an elephant. The blind men are mistaken only in supposing that each of them has discovered the elephant as a whole.

Of course, all perception and verbal description is relative to a subjective point of view, but not in a way which implies that we are forever locked away in a private world of our own illusions, or that every description is equally correct and equally incorrect, or that we can never grasp or know the real object—or, worse, that there *is* no real object in the first place. The theory of aspects indicates that perception and description are "subjective" only in the sense that at most one particular, partial aspect of the object is revealed at a time relative to the adoption of a particular subjective point of view or perspective.

Looked at from above (an aerial view) a man in a sombrero looks like a fried egg or a dough-nut (that is, as two concentric circles); looked at from the front, back or side, it looks like a person in a large hat (though only the front view will reveal the face, and so on). The relativity of aspect to subjective point of view is not subjective in the way in which a day dream, fantasy or dream objects are subjective—that is, private fantasies existing only "in one's head," but only in the sense that a different part of the object is revealed by adopting a different point of view or vantage point—look at it from the top and it will look like *this*; look at it from the side and it will look like *that*—objectively, publicly, to anyone.

Aspects are "subjective" relative to the perceiver, in the sense, first, that aspects are only revealed by adopting a particular human point of view, and secondly, that each point of view reveals a different aspect. Aspects are "objectively" real in the sense that they are real parts of the real object potentially available for inspection (by adopting the appropriate point of view). Thus there is a one-to-one correlation between aspect and point of view— change the point of view and you thereby change the aspect; if you want to see a different aspect of the object then you must shift your point of view. What is "subjective" in all this is simply how one approaches an object, from what angle or standpoint one chooses to view the object—*not* what the object will look like from that standpoint.

In some cases selection of a point of view is a matter of personal choice; in other cases it is dictated by biological constraints on us as human beings, and in still other cases by the adoption of cultural conventions imposed on us by a particular social group. If you choose to look at a rectangular table from the top, you will see a rectangle (and not a circle), but you will not see the legs of the table. Insofar as that choice is yours, perception is relative to your subjective decision. But once you have selected the point of view from which to view the object it is no longer up to you what the object will look like—if the table top is rectangular, that is how it will look to anyone viewed from the top.

If you are a human being there are parts of the color spectrum you are able to perceive and parts of it you are not, and as a member of the human species, which has evolved a well-defined sense of color, color will be an important focus for you in identifying objects and communicating that information to others. And if the linguistic conventions of your particular culture group has traditionally blocked off a certain portion of the visible color spectrum available to human beings, and moreover has adopted a particular word, "red," to refer to whatever falls within that range, then relative to your biology and culture, you must call anything falling within that range "red" (if you want to communicate with members of that culture group).

But it is objectively and really true that, once these cultural and linguistic conventions have been decided upon, a fire engine is red, and not blue or green. Once your biological constraints and your cultural conventions have been fixed, then "red" is objectively correct and "blue" is objectively incorrect. Relative to your biological limitations, your cultural conventions, and your personal choice of preferred point of view—once these have been assigned, the color (and the shape) of the object will be determined by the object itself and not anything subjectively peculiar to you.

To put the point another way, the theory of aspects makes it clear that "subjective" factors (personal, biological, and cultural) are only part of the causes or explanation of perception—the other part being the objective character of the object being perceived. Perception, we may say, is the product of two factors, one subjective and the other objective; both are necessary and neither is sufficient. An older theory of epistemology makes this point by saying that perception is relational, that is, that perception is always a two-term relation of subjective point of view and objective features.

The theory of aspects is especially useful in overcoming the tendency to try and understand perception in terms of an inevitable dichotomy of subject and object, mind and matter. "On the one hand," according to this dichotomy, "there is a viewing subject; on the other hand, there is an object. If the viewing subject perceives a contradictory object which cannot possibly exist, say one both with legs (when the table is viewed from the side) and without legs (when the same table is viewed from the top), then, assuming a real object cannot be both with and without legs (which is obviously contradictory), these contradictory perceptions must not belong to the object.

But if they don't belong to the object, where do they come from? Since everything is either physical or mental, then, since these perceived features are not physical, they must be mental. So, the view of the table with legs and the view of the table without legs are not parts of the table at all, but rather episodes in the mental life of the viewing subject—like a dream or a fantasy." What the theory of aspects does is to impose a *third* possibility on this simplistic subject-object dichotomy—namely, the aspect, which is neither wholly objective nor wholly subjective, but one which has both objective and subjective features.

The most famous illustration of this third possibility is Wittgenstein's use of Jastrow's "duck-rabbit" drawing. The very same drawing sometimes looks like a rabbit and sometimes like a duck, though never both at the same time. The duck aspect is a way of seeing the same lines which can also reveal a rabbit aspect when seen another way. The same lines can be "seen as" a duck and also "seen as" a rabbit. Either aspect is objective in the sense that it is a way in which those lines printed on that piece of paper are perceived. And they will be perceived in these two ways by almost anyone who is familiar with line drawings and knows what ducks and rabbits look like.

It is not like seeing recognizable shapes in the clouds where ten people may see ten different things. In the duck-rabbit illustration virtually everyone sees either a duck or a rabbit and nothing else. And everyone can point out the same features of the duck and the rabbit in the drawing—"those lines there are the ears (of the rabbit) or the bill (of the duck); that rounded line is the back of the head of the duck or the face of the rabbit." And yet each aspect is also subjective in the sense that it requires an interpretation by a viewer. A viewer unfamiliar with line drawings or one who had never seen a duck or a rabbit could see the lines but would be unable to see those lines as a duck or a rabbit. (Or, in a world without human beings, the line drawing might exist, having survived some catastrophic event which had decimated the human population, but there would be no duck or rabbit aspect.)

At first it may seem strange to think there can be things which are neither mental nor physical, but once we stop to think about it we can see that there are many quite ordinary things which are neither mental nor physical. The laws of the city or state we happen to live in, for example, or a novel, short story, play or poem—these things are neither mental nor physical, neither completely objective nor subjective but somehow a combination of both, occupying the third realm of aspects.

Nor does this hold only for strange or unusual examples, like the duck-rabbit illustration. *All* perception can be analyzed in this way—the duck-rabbit illustration is peculiar only in the way it makes the point so vividly, strikingly, and therefore so persuasively. But *all* perception is a product of these two features—the object as it exists in itself (in the duck-rabbit illustration, that particular configuration of lines on paper) and a human interpretation (as a duck or as a rabbit).

Because of my cultural background, I see the object I am working on as a computer, and the one I am sitting on as a chair. The only difference between these more mundane examples and the duck-rabbit illustration is that we are so *familiar* with these interpretations (of the computer and chair), we do not see them as *interpretations*.

We don't see any alternative, competing interpretations and so don't see our perception as an interpretation at all, but rather as an objective reading off of an objective label. But we can easily *imagine* alternative interpretations, by people living in radically different cultures from our own, for example, who had never seen a computer or even a chair (but in some other way). In the movie, *The Gods Must be Crazy,* a coke bottle falls from an airplane onto the path used by southern African Bushmen, who take it to be some sacred object which has been dropped by the gods above for some mysterious reason. To see a chair as a chair and a coke bottle as a coke bottle are interpretations, just very standard, familiar ones in our particular culture. Everything we experience is an aspect of an object, an object seen as or under a human interpretation—not the thing as it is in itself, but the real thing as it appears from a particular human vantage point—in short, a real aspect of a real object.

The theory of aspects also makes it clear that it is impossible to see *all* aspects of an object at the *same time*. One can never see the entire object just as it is in itself; all we can ever apprehend are individual aspects discriminated one at a time. And finally, the theory of aspects shows that the sense we have of the object as a whole comes from *gathering together* and *connecting* the different aspects and imagining how others we have not experienced but could experience are related to those we have experienced. In Kant's example of our perception of a house (which obviously can't be seen all at once), we see first the front of the house, then the side, then the back, and so on, which we then relate together in imagination to form a sense of the house as a whole.

So far we have considered mainly spatial standpoints—looking at the table from the top or from the side, seeing the house from the front or from the back, and so on, because these are the most obvious. But the theory also applies to attitudinal perspectives—looking at things cynically, optimistically, hopefully, morally, aesthetically, and so on. Each object in the world has an infinite number of different aspects, not all of which we can see and only a few of which we have any interest in observing. A wine taster is trained to focus on certain aspects, and this act of focusing does in fact reveal genuine aspects of the wine unnoticed by others drinking the same wine (although they, too, *could* perceive these aspects if they choose to and if they develop the proper focusing skills). A composer will attend to the thematic development in a piece of music and this act of attention will reveal objective compositional aspects unavailable to most ordinary listeners.

Suppose there are four people looking at the same stand of trees. The first is looking for signs of fluorocarbon pollution and sees it (or its absence); the second is looking for signs of good, bad or indifferent forest management (culling the smaller and older, diseased trees, for example) and will perceive that aspect of the stand of trees; the third is looking for a good place to hunt squirrels and that is what she will see (that is, is good, bad or indifferent for squirrel hunting); and the fourth is interested in the beauty of the spot and will see whatever beauty is there to be seen. The political liberal will perceive evidence of police brutality toward peaceful, lawful demonstrators; the political conservative will see evidence of restraint and professionalism on the part of the police facing an angry, dangerous and unruly mob in the same riot-control situation.

Of course, to *describe* the theory of aspects does not prove that theory *true*. But the force of the theory is that it provides a way out of the subjective, idealist, relativist interpretation of the facts of perception and experience. Our bias is to cling to some version of the realist theory. The strict realist hypothesis clearly won't do, for reasons we have seen and which several thousand years of philosophical argumentation, both Eastern and Western, has clearly demonstrated. And the reasons which lead to its downfall seem to point to its opposite—a relativist and subjective idealism, which contradicts our deepest common sense instincts and beliefs and which seem clearly dictated by the facts of our experience.

This is not a theory we readily embrace but a dilemma we see no way out of. I assume that we would prefer a "way out" of this dilemma and would take any reasonable alternative, that is, any modified realist position which could account for all the facts of our experience which apparently have led to a relativist and subjective idealism—and this is what the theory of aspects does. It doesn't have to prove itself; it only needs to show that it consistently accounts for all the facts but in a way which is consistent with a basic realism (though not the strict absolute realism seemingly assumed in much of our common sense outlook)—and that is precisely the value of metaphysics.

Far more difficult than the task of *proving* itself is the problem of actually *replacing* the deeply embedded assumptions of strict realism. As we saw earlier, these assumptions (which anti-realist philosophers attack) are at worst "hard-wired" components of an unchangeable human nature and at best extremely difficult to overcome. Perhaps, as Kant suggested, the best we can hope for is to realize that we are constantly subject to this pervasive illusion—we can't get rid of the realist assumptions; we can only become aware of them and, at least intellectually, think beyond them. The theory of aspects can help us think beyond strict realism.

Pragmatism

As mentioned earlier, the theory of aspects, which is primarily metaphysical in its thrust, is supported epistemologically by a kind of neo-pragmatism, which argues for the "pragmatic" or practical need in everyday life to be able to distinguish objective from subjective, real from apparent, true from false. While we abandon the *absolute* distinction of true/false, fact/interpretation, objective/subjective, we can continue to use these distinctions in a relative sense as a useful, heuristic device. This is the point of the Chinese Madhyamika (San Lun) doctrine of er ti, double truth, as developed by Chi Tsang—truth in the absolute sense and truth in the relative, mundane, everyday sense.

There is no set of things which are always and only "facts" and another set of things which are always and only "interpretations." What is a "fact" in one context can be an "interpretation" in another context (and a "fact" once more in still another context). Nonetheless, the distinction between facts and interpretations is still important since in any given context they mark an important difference to which we want to call attention. So, we talk in one context about "facts" that are given various "interpretations," and yet we understand that in another context, those same facts might be treated as interpretations.

For example, it may be a "fact" that Jones committed suicide by jumping out of a fifteen-story window, and we look for interpretations of that fact (why did he do it?) Only if the fact is later called into question by new evidence will we begin to treat it as an interpretation. Perhaps new evidence suggests Jones may have been murdered and then thrown from the window. Then the fact is that he fell from a fifteen-story window, and the interpretative question is whether he was murdered or committed suicide.

In this relative use of the distinction, a fact is simply what is not disputed by a particular group of people at a particular time, and an interpretation is what is disputed in that particular context. Understood in this way, it is still a very useful distinction, though not an absolute one, because it enables us to discuss the adequacy of particular interpretations according to how well they account for the facts—again, where "fact" and "interpretation" are understood relative to a particular situation.

Similarly, for the "reality/appearance" distinction. We call things real when we are relatively sure we know what they are; we call them appearances when we are not so sure. Suppose we disagree who that person is standing over there in the corner. I say it is Tanya and you say it is Taiwo. We approach more closely and see that it is Taiwo. I was "wrong" and you were "right." Relative to this situation, we can distinguish reality from appearance (it seemed to be Tanya but was really Taiwo) and truth from falsity (it is true to say that it is Taiwo and false to say it is Tanya), although the distinction is not absolute in the sense that it is immune from error (that is, being "right" in all other situations).

Later it may turn out that it was Taiwo's twin sister, Tabatha, or someone impersonating Taiwo, or a holograph of Taiwo, or an artwork by Duane Hanson. But if we do find out that one of these latter possibilities is the case, it will only be because we have new evidence, and then in the context of that evidence we will again be able to distinguish the reality from the appearance, the true from the false, though again not beyond the possibility of error. So long as long as we do not call the same thing both true and false, real and not real in the same context, it is useful to distinguish truth from falsity and reality from appearance.

Finally, the same sort of point seems to apply to the question of objectivity. It is true that no knowledge is completely free of subjective bias and that all knowledge must be interpreted through a particular conceptual framework that embodies particular interests. But it is still useful to distinguish between objectivity and bias, between history and propaganda. Today we can recognize biases in our recent past—a Eurocentric bias, for example, or a male bias. But this does not mean that we are now completely free of all bias. In any given situation we are aware of certain biases and we try to remove those. At that point we surely have other biases which we aren't aware of. Still later we may become aware of these other biases and seek to remove them, and so on. At any given stage we need to be able to and therefore find it useful to draw a distinction between what at that point in time is seen as biased (*e.g.*, male bias) and the more objective correction of that bias (*e.g.*, recognition of greater gender equality). In the distant future we may even come to see gender equality as itself biased (and therefore in need of correction), though it is difficult now to see how that would be possible.

In the same way we can recognize the truth relative to a particular set of cultural conventions without insisting on the notion of absolute truth (something's being true in any and all sets of cultural conventions). So, for example, within our present set of cultural conventions, we think it is true that the earth travels around the sun and not the other way round. We also think it was wrong to kill the American Indians and drive them from their lands. So, within that cultural context, we can meaningfully speak of finding and knowing the truth, arguing for one position and against another, and so on, although recognizing at the same time that other people in other cultures may not see it our way or agree with us (or that we ourselves may later change our minds and begin arguing on the other side).

But even here, it is possible to consider the other culture's point of view, to sympathetically try to "put ourselves in the other person's shoes." Of course, we are still judging things from our own cultural perspective, but the attempt to consider the perspective of another culture can modify our own perspective. After all, these cultural perspectives are not permanent, genetic features we were born with. We have collectively "chosen" them over many years and they continue to slowly evolve over time. Most people in the distant past thought the sun orbited the earth every twenty-four hours, but after Copernicus that view was gradually rejected in favor of the heliocentric hypothesis (that the earth rotates on its axis every twenty-four hours and orbits the sun once a year).

In the 17th and 18th centuries the European settlers in the New World of North America saw the Indians as cruel and savage barbarians who could be rightfully killed or driven off, but later (beginning around 1830) the white settlers slowly began to see the Indian's side and this affected (modified, altered) their own perspective, until the pendulum has now swung almost completely to the other side (in which the Indians, as in the movie, *Dances with Wolves*, are now perceived as noble creatures, in tune with nature, and the settlers as unjust and cruel invaders, beginning with Christopher Columbus— once a hero and now a villain).

Although we no longer believe in the geocentric hypothesis (the earth centered theory of the solar system), we can easily see the plausibility of that theory and understand how people could have believed it (the sun does appear to rise in the east, visibly move directly overhead at noon, and set finally in the west). Perhaps it is possible for us today—maybe even for contemporary American Indians—to sympathetically imagine what it must have been like as an early European farming family in Western Pennsylvania living in constant dread of Indian attacks and imaginatively come to understand their hostility towards the Indians. (Admittedly, this would be difficult; like the gender equality assumption mentioned above, it is always hard to see our current biases as biases—as the West African proverb puts it, "a skunk has no nose.")

Does this diminish the argument that universal human rights absolutely exist? Not necessarily. The metaphysical existence of human rights has been challenged from the beginning, certainly by Jeremy Bentham, who called the idea "nonsense on stilts." Whether such rights exist eternally and absolutely or not, there is certainly now a universal, cross-cultural consensus that the standard lists of major human rights represents a universally recognized standard of international behavior—and is so treated within the United Nations, for example.

Is it a problem that we publicly recognize that these standards can change and evolve? Not really, since we live here and now, this internationally recognized standard is all we need to fight the human rights battles around the world which seem important to us today. Indeed, it is questionable how far we should saddle, even if we could, future generations with our moral standards. They may not value what we value; they may not want to preserve what we cherish or to prevent what we despise. Our right to impose on our offspring probably extends no further than "the foreseeable future"—our children and their children, let us say, whose moral outlook we can reasonably expect to more or less resemble our own (and who will have the power to alter our best efforts where they disagree).

Conclusion

And so, in conclusion, we have to ask whether I have adequately addressed the problems laid out at the beginning. There, you will recall, I pointed out how my two previous books, *The Meaning of Meaninglessness* and *The Metaphysics of Absurdity*, had left us with an unacceptable contrast between a naïve view that objects ought to conform to our humanly constructed concepts and the nihilistic view that nothing exists, is real, or meaningful apart from such humanly constructed concepts.

In this essay I have tried to negotiate a compromise between these two extremes. Obviously, there are objects in the world existing independently of our thoughts, needs and desires. Quite apart from human conceptual construction, there are forces in nature which tend to hold the components of atoms together for millions of years, or in less extreme cases, forces which help maintain the relatively stable identity over time of trees, people, and other entities. So long as we insist on the ancient definition of reality as that which is completely independent and unchanging, we can only conclude that these things are not real. What is needed, therefore, is a new conception of reality, and that is what I have tried to outline in the present work through an examination of Hemacandra's theory of perspectival aspection and a kind of neo-pragmatism.

One problem I can imagine my critics asking: does the theory of aspects really avoid the problem of subjectivity? Can we really say that aspects are partly objective and partly subjective? Aren't they really just a fancy kind of subjective, mental entity? Are aspects really a different kind of metaphysical entity—neither mental nor physical? Here my only argument is an appeal to everyone's intuition—don't you think city and state laws exist? Don't you think there are poems, short stories, novels in the world? If so, do you think these things are physical objects? And if not, do you think they are mental entities? And if you simply reject out of hand anything that is not mental or physical, aren't you guilty of metaphysicophobia?

Another problem my imaginary critic poses: does my so-called "neo-pragmatism" really overcome relativism, or isn't it just a restatement of relativism? In a way I accept this criticism. Like Kant, I am arguing for a way of seeing the world relative to human beings—but universally and necessarily for all human beings. In this sense my position is a kind of non-technical "phenomenology." We human beings construct the world according to our human needs and biological equipment. This is how the world looks to a human being—not necessarily (or probably) what the world is really like. In reality, from a "god's eye" perspective, there may not be any objects or kinds of objects causally connected. We already have a sense from science that the world is not as we perceive things in everyday life. But the interesting thing about this is that although we believe these anti-intuitive theories about the world, we can't see the world like that—these scientific theories remain intuitively obscure. Whether in reality there are four or more spatial dimensions, we will always see semi-permanent physical objects spread out in three and only three dimensions. The same argument could be made in regard to time.

Another problem, my hypothetical critic concludes: have I really overcome the Existentialists' fear of the loss of inherent meaning? As human beings don't we naturally expect the world to conform to our way of looking at things? We act purposively, doing one thing for the sake of another, seeing one thing as leading to another, and so we naturally expect the world as a whole to be similarly purposeful. One could even argue that the only "sufficient explanation" of anything is a teleological explanation. And if I have argued that it is possible, though very difficult, to see through this persistent illusion—to know that our innate teleological sense is a human construction, aren't I contradicting what I said earlier about being unable to see the world as the scientist describes it? Not really. In both cases I am saying that we can know that we have a human bias without being able to see the world in any other way. Mystics claim not only to know that our human way of seeing things is but one of many possibilities, but to actually be able to see things as they are in themselves—to achieve that god's eye view of things. I haven't gone as far as that. My position is much closer to that of Kant—we know our view of the world is limited but we don't know what the world is like beyond our limited understanding of it.

Notes

1. H. Gene Blocker, *The Meaning of Meaninglessness,* (Martinus Nijhoff, 1974).
2. H. Gene Blocker, *The Metaphysics of Absurdity,* (University Press of America, 1979).
3. Nagarjuna, *Nagarjuna's Seventy Stanzas: A Buddhist Psychology of Emptiness,* Geshe Sonam Rinchen, David Ross Komito, editors; Tenzin Dorjee and David Ross Komito, translators (Ithaca, NY: Snow Lion Publications, 1987).

BIBLIOGRAPHY

Ando, Takatura, *Metaphysics,* (The Hague: Martinus Nijhoff, 1963).
Aristotle, "Metaphysics, 1034a5," from *The Basic Works of Aristotle,* Richard McKeon, ed. (New York: Random House, 1941).
Beckett, Samuel, *Molloy; Malone dies; The unnamable,* (London: Calder, 1959).
——, *Murphy* (New York: Grove Press, 1957(1938)), pp. 107-108.
——, *Proust* (New York: Grove Press, 1931), pp. 7-8.
——, *The unnamable,* Limited ed. (New York,: Grove Press, 1958).
——, *Watt* (London: John Calder (Juniper Books), 1963 (Olympia, 1953)), pp. 78-79.
Bergson, Henri, *An Introduction to Metaphysics,* T.E. Hulme, trans. (New York: The Liberal Arts Press 1949).
Blocker, H. G., *The Metaphysics of Absurdity,* (University Press of America, 1979).
——, *The Meaning of Meaninglessness,* (Martinus Nijhoff, 1974).
——, "The Meaning of a Poem," *The British Journal of Aesthetics,* v. 10, 1970.
Boehm, Rudolf, "Husserl und der Klassische Idealismus," in *Vom Gesichtspunkt der Phenomenologie,* (Martinus Nijhoff, 1968).
Camus, Albert, *The Myth of Sisyphus,* Justin O'Brien, trans. (New York: Vintage Books, 1955).
——, *Notebooks, 1935-42,* Philip Thody, trans. (New York: Alfred A. Knopf, 1969), p. 10.
——, "On Jean-Paul Sartre's *La Nausee,*" from a review in Alger-Republicain, October 20, 1938, in *Lyrical and Critical Essays,* ed. Philip Thody, Ellen Conroy Kennedy, trans. (New York: Alfred A. Knopf, 1969), p. 199.
——, "Three Interviews," in *Lyrical and Critical Essays,* Philip Thody, ed., Ellen Conroy Kennedy, trans. (New York: Alfred A. Knopf, 1969), p. 346.
Carnap, Rudolf, "The Elimination of Metaphysics Through Logical Analysis," Arthur Pap, trans., in *Logical Positivism,* A. J. Ayer, ed. (New York: The Free Press, 1959), p. 69.
Celms, Theodor, *Der Phaenomenologische Idealism Husserls* (Riga, 1928).
Chao Sêng and Walter Liebenthal, *The Book of Chao.* Monumenta serica Journal of Oriental studies of the Catholic University of Peking Monograph XIII (Peking: Catholic University of Peking, 1948).
Coleridge, Samuel T., *Miscellaneous Criticism* (Cambridge: Harvard University Press, 1936).
Danto, Arthur, "The Transfiguration of the Common-place," *The Journal of Aesthetics and Art Criticism,* v. 33, 1974.

Ding-hwa, E.H., "The Transmission of the Lamp: Early Masters. Sohaku Ogata, trans. Foreword by Paul F. Schmidt. Wolfeboro," *Philosophy East and West*, v. 44.
Esslin, Martin, *The Theatre of the Absurd*, (Harmondsworth, England: Penguin Books, 1968).
Gilson, Etienne, *Being and Some Philosophers* (Toronto: Pontifical Institute of Medieval Studies, 1952).
Hare, R. M., Freedom and Reason (Oxford: Oxford University Press, 1963).
Hartman, Klaus, *Sartre's Ontology* (Evanston: Northwestern University Press, 1966).
Hegel, G.W.F., *The philosophy of fine art*. 1975, New York: Hacker Art Books.
Heidegger, Martin, *Being and Time*, John McQuarrie and Edward Robinson, trans. (London: S.C.M. Press, 1962).
Huang Po, *The Teaching of Huang-Po*, John Blofeld, trans. (New York: Grove Press, 1959).
Husserl, Paul Ricoeur, *An Analysis of his Phenomenology* (Northwestern University Press, 1967).
Ingarden, Roman, *Der Streit um die Existenz der Welt* (Max Niemeyer Verlag, 1964-1966).
Ionesco, Eugene, *Conversations with Eugene Ionesco*, transcribed by Claude Bonnefoy, Jan Dawson, trans. (New York: Holt, Rinehart, and Winston, 1971).
——, "Dialogues avec Ionesco," transcribed by Lerminier, in Richard N. Coe, *Ionesco* (London: Oliver and Boyd, 1961).
——, *Fragments of a Journal*, Jean Stewart, trans. (London: Faber and Faber, 1976), pp. 41-42.
——, *The Hermit*, Richard Seaver, trans. (New York: Viking Press, 1974).
——, letter to Sylvain Dhomme, in Martin Esslin, *The Theatre of the Absurd* (Harmondsworth, England Penguin Books, 1968).
——, "Point of Departure," Leonard C. Pronko, trans., in *Theatre Arts*, June 1958.
——, *Present Past, Past Present*, Helen Lane, trans. (New York: Grove Press, 1971).
Jaeger, Werner, *Aristotle*, Richard Robinson, trans. (London: Oxford University Press, 1948).
Kockelmans, Joseph, Edmund Husserl's *Phenomenological Psychology* (Duquensne University Press, 1967).
Landgrebe, Ludwig, *Major Problems in Contemporary European Philosophy* (Ungar, 1966).
Lawrence, D. H., *Apocalypse*. Lungarno series no 6 (Florence: G. Orioli, 1931).
Lerminier, G., "Dialogue avec Ionesco," *Pensée française*, v. 1959.
Merleau-Ponty, Maurice, *Phenomenology of Perception* (Humanities Press, 1962).
Milne, A. A., Ernest H. Shepard, and E.P. Dutton (Firm), *Winnie-the-Pooh*, (New York: E.P. Dutton & Company, 1926).
Nagarjuna and Kenneth K. Inada, *Nagarjuna, a translation of his Mulamadhyamakakarika with an introductory essay*, 1st Indian ed. Bibliotheca Indo-Buddhica series (Delhi, India: Sri Satguru Publications, 1993).
——, *Nagarjuna's Seventy Stanzas: A Buddhist Psychology of Emptiness*. 1987, Ithaca, NY: Snow Lion Publications.
Randall, John Herman, *Aristotle*, (New York: Columbia University Press, 1960).
Robbe-Grillet, Alain, "From Realism to Reality in *For A New Novel*, Richard Howard, trans. (New York: Grove Press, 1965).
Ross, W.D., *Aristotle's Metaphysics*, vol. 1 (Oxford Clarendon Press, 1958).

Russell, Bertrand, "A Free Man's Worship," from "Mysticism and Logic," reprinted in *Selected Papers of Bertrand Russell* (New York: Random House (Modern Library), 1927).
Sartre, Jean-Paul, *Being and Nothingness*, Hazel Barnes, trans. (New York: Philosophical Library, 1956).
——, "Existentialism and Humanism," Philip Mairet, trans., in Morton White, ed., *The Age of Analysis* (New York: Mentor Books, 1955), p. 122Jean-Paul Sartre, "Existentialism and Humanism," Philip Mairet, trans., in Morton White, ed., *The Age of Analysis* (New York: Mentor Books, 1955).
——, *Nausea*, Lloyd Alexander, trans. (New York: New Directions, 1964).
Tymieniecka, Anna-Teresa, *Why is There Something Rather the Nothing* (Van Gorcum, 1966).
Tsang from the Chinese translation, *The Chung Lun*, in *A Source Book in Chinese Philosophy*, Wing-tsit, trans, and ed. (Princeton: Princeton University Press, 1963).
Warnock, Mary, *Existentialism* (London: Oxford University Press, 1970).
Werner, H., E.B. Garside, and G. Murphy, *Comparative psychology of mental development*. (New York: Harper & Brothers, 1940).
Wild, John, *The New Empiricism* (Englewood Cliffs: Prentice-Hall, 1962).
Yulan, Fung, *A History of Chinese Philosophy, vol 2.* , Derk Bodde, trans. (Princeton University Press, 1952).

www.ingramcontent.com/pod-product-compliance
Lightning Source LLC
Chambersburg PA
CBHW052114300426
44116CB00010B/1659